D0604160

CustomerCentric Selling

CustomerCentric Selling

Michael T. Bosworth

John R. Holland

McGraw-Hill

New York   Chicago   San Francisco
Lisbon   London   Madrid   Mexico City   Milan
New Delhi   San Juan   Seoul   Singapore
Sydney   Toronto

1 2 3 4 5 6 7 8 9 0   DOC/DOC   0 9 8 7 6 5 4 3

ISBN 0-07-142545-4

First Edition

This publication is designed to provide accurate and authoritative information in regard to the subject matter covered. It is sold with the understanding that neither the authors nor the publisher is engaged in rendering legal, accounting, or other professional service. If legal advice or other expert assistance is required, the services of a competent professional person should be sought.

—From a Declaration of Principles jointly adopted
by a Committee of the American Bar
Association and a Committee of Publishers

McGraw-Hill books are available at special quantity discounts to use as premiums and sales promotions, or for use in corporate training programs. For more information, please write to the Director of Special Sales, Professional Publishing, McGraw-Hill, Two Penn Plaza, New York, NY 10121-2298. Or contact your local bookstore.

CustomerCentric Selling is a registered trademark and Sales Ready Messaging and Solution Development Prompter are trademarks of CustomerCentric Systems, LLC.

Library of Congress Cataloging-in-Publication Data

Bosworth, Michael T.
   CustomerCentric selling / by Michael T. Bosworth and John R. Holland.
     p. cm.
   ISBN 0-07-142545-4 (alk. paper)
   1. Selling. 2. Sales Management. 3. Marketing. I. Holland, John. II. Title.

HF5438.25 .B669 2003

658.85—dc22   2003016375

To my wife, Linda, who tolerates my passion for work and keeps things running smoothly during my frequent travels. To my children, Lauren, Johnny, and Katie, who are a constant source of pride and joy. With special thanks to my parents, John and Mary.

John R. Holland

To my inner circle—Alicia, Brendan, Brian, Steve, Sam, Dick, Dave, Susan, Rosy, Ricki, Patti, and Suzanne—who keep me grounded, validated, and appreciated. To my uncle, Jack Lester, who is my model for living life with a positive mental attitude.

Michael T. Bosworth

Contents

Acknowledgments

THIS BOOK IS THE CULMINATION OF A 10-year professional and a 19-year personal relationship between the authors. Many of the ideas in the book were hashed out over meetings, lunches, and conversations spanning several years. We have come to value the power of clear communication. We have come to value the difference between sales training and process. We hope this book will help our readers realize and appreciate the difference. With regard to sales process and selling, it is hard to imagine two people who were more consistently on the same page, always ready to brainstorm new approaches.

We want to thank and recognize the other Cofounders and Coauthors of the CustomerCentric Selling intellectual property, Frank Visgatis and Gary Walker. As business associates, thought leaders, and close friends, their contributions to CustomerCentric Systems have been and continue to be essential to our growth and success. We feel fortunate, given the effort involved in launching the business, that we had four heads. May we never have to take a vote on any issue.

Over the years, we have enjoyed the tremendous advantage of working with many different types of companies and learning something from each one along the way. The most significant impact, however, has been that of colleagues and clients. We would like to recognize them now in no particular order:

- Alicia Weeks and Margie Offereins, for their contribution to the growth of our business. They were both able to sell and manage large-scale implementations of CustomerCentric Selling in the very early stages of our development.
- Gerhard Gschwandtner, for his support, encouragement, and collaboration. Having CustomerCentric Selling and Mike Bosworth as a cover story of *Selling Power Magazine* was validation that our launch had been successful. Gerhard is a wonderful sounding board for our new concepts and ideas.
- Tim Riesterer, for his thought leadership as relates to Marketing's role in creating Sales-Ready Messaging and the necessity for content to make technology valuable.
- Larry Cleve, for having the wisdom to make an early commitment to CustomerCentric Selling and the courage to resist being pressured into a default that nobody would have questioned. We also owe a debt of gratitude for the numerous "Larryisms" added to our vocabularies.
- Wendy Komac, for committing to and doing an outstanding job of driving the implementation of a sales process within her organization. Her relentless energy and commitment to the process have yielded tremendous results.
- Peter Fisher and George Kenney, who helped us understand the potential impact our methodology can have on the venture capital community.
- John Hawes, for being willing to allow us to influence his vast knowledge of sales process, programs, and training. We hope to continue to deepen our relationship.
- Jeffrey Krames, our publisher extraordinaire, for his quiet countenance and encouragement, even on school nights. It has been a pleasure to work with him.

What Is Customer-Centric Selling?

WHAT IS THIS BOOK ABOUT, and how can you use it to your benefit?

The main focus of this book is on helping individuals and organizations involved in sales to migrate from one kind of selling to another. Specifically, we seek to help people move from traditional sales techniques to "customer-centric" selling behavior. We believe that our methodology—CustomerCentric Selling—can help you become more customer-centric, and therefore more successful.

We are in the sales process, messaging, and training business. The ideas in this book are the result of many years of field testing—first as salespeople ourselves, then at multiple levels of sales management, and subsequently as principals in a firm that teaches our methodology to our clients.

As teachers, we work with all levels within our client organizations. We teach chief executive officers (CEOs) how to own and shape their customers' experience. We teach sales executives how to define and manage their revenue engines. We teach marketing executives how to own and manage their content and Sales-Ready Messaging. We teach first-line sales managers how to assess and develop the talent of their salespeople, manage to a sales process, and build a quality pipeline. Last—but certainly not least—we teach salespeople customer-centric behavior. In doing so, we focus on how to influence the words sellers use when developing buyer needs for their offerings.

What Is Customer-Centric Behavior?

What is this customer-centric behavior? It has seven basic tenets. These are summarized in Figure 1-1, and are explained in sequence in the balance of this first chapter. As you read these descriptions, we invite you to imagine a spectrum of selling behavior ranging from traditional on one end to customer-centric on the other, and to locate yourself on that spectrum. Are you where you want to be, to be as successful as you can be?

If not, what needs to change?

1. Having Situational Conversations versus Making Presentations

Traditional salespeople rely on making presentations, often using applications like PowerPoint. Why? Because they believe that this approach gives them the opportunity to add excitement, in the form of highly polished graphics, animation, and so on. It gives them the opportunity to turn down the lights and increase the dramatic effect of their presentation.

In selling, we find that conversations are far more powerful than presentations. And yes, it is possible to converse with audiences using Power Point—as opposed to presenting to them—but it is far more difficult. Have you ever had a conversation with a friend or a colleague that was based on a prescripted slide show? Of course not. So it shouldn't come

Traditional	Customer-Centric
Make presentations	Converse situationally
Offer opinions	Ask relevant questions
Focus on relationship	Focus on solution
Gravitate toward users	Target business people
Rely on product	Relate product usage
Need to be managed	Manage their managers
Attempt to sell by	Empower buyers to
• Convincing/persuading	• Achieve goals
• Handling objections	• Solve problems
• Overcoming resistance	• Satisfy needs

Figure 1-1 Selling Behavior

as a surprise that when senior executives see salespeople enter their offices with a laptop under their arm, many roll their eyes and sneak a peek at their watches.

Here is the issue: *In order to be effective, a salesperson must be able to relate his or her offering to the buyer in a way that will allow the buyer to visualize using it to achieve a goal, solve a problem, or satisfy a need.* This, in turn, requires a conversation. For a variety of reasons, though, only a small percentage of salespeople are able to converse effectively with decision makers. And presentation software—slick and eye-catching as it can be—can undermine even those talented few.

CustomerCentric Selling has been designed to help you engage in relevant, situation-specific conversations with decision makers, without having to depend on canned slide presentations. In short, we can help you become more effective.

2. Asking Relevant Questions versus Offering Opinions

Traditional salespeople tend to offer their opinions to their buyers, while customer-centric salespeople tend to ask relevant questions.

What's the basic issue here? Most sellers come to a vision of a solution to their buyer's problem before their prospective buyer does. When a traditional seller sees the solution, he or she tends to project that vision onto the buyer. He or she says things like, "In order to deal with that problem, you will need our seamlessly integrated software solution."

But meanwhile, what's happening on the other side of the table? Very often, the prospective buyer is thinking something along the lines of, "Oh, yeah? Do we now? Says who?"

This is simply human nature at work. Most people don't even like their loved ones telling them what they need, much less a salesperson. Most people, when in the role of a buyer, resent having a seller try to control or pressure them.

People love to buy, but hate feeling sold. We have found that top-performing salespeople use their expertise to frame interesting and helpful questions, rather than to deliver opinions. Asking questions shows respect for the buyer. When buyers come to grips with a series of intelligent questions—questions that are on point, which can be answered, and the answers to which build toward a useful solution—they do not feel that they are being sold.

3. Solution-Focused versus Relationship-Focused

Traditional sellers are relationship-focused, and customer-centric sellers are solution-focused.

If the seller does not understand how the buyer will use his or her offering to achieve a goal, solve a problem, or satisfy a need, he or she really has no choice but to fall back on relationships. Why does this happen? In many cases, the answer lies in the training that the salesperson receives. Most sales organizations commission their product marketing department to teach salespeople about their products.

Not surprisingly, the result is a sales force that can tell you all about the esoteric features of their products, but can't tell you how the products are used. And the rare product marketers who do understand the uses of the products tend to have that understanding at the day-to-day user level, not the decision-maker level.

Salespeople who are not trained to converse with decision makers about product usage gravitate toward focusing on their relationship with their buyers. Many traditional salespeople have convinced themselves, over the years, that the seller with the strongest relationship will win. And in situations where the seller is selling a commodity product to a repeat buyer—where there are no differentiators other than relationships—we agree. But in situations where the buyer is attempting to achieve a goal, solve a problem, or satisfy a need, we disagree. Under those circumstances, the successful seller has to do far more than simply cultivate relationships. Given a choice of having a buyer like us or respect us, we'd opt for the latter. Certainly the two are not mutually exclusive, and after you earn a buyer's respect, there is a high probability that a strong relationship can be established.

4. Targeting Business People versus Gravitating toward Users

Traditional salespeople gravitate toward the users of their products, while customer-centric salespeople target business decision makers.

The strength of traditional salespeople lies in talking about their offerings, and users are the group most likely to be interested in or tolerate this approach. Note that talking to the users is not the same as talking to a decision maker in a way that will allow that individual to visualize the usage of the product to achieve a goal, solve a problem, or satisfy a need. In order for salespeople to have the confidence to engage in a conversation with business people, they must be prepared to engage in business conversations. A business conversation should be usage- and results-oriented, rather than feature-oriented. It focuses on why the product is needed; how it can be used to achieve a goal, solve a problem or satisfy a need; and how much it costs to use versus the benefits it presents.

Most selling organizations give their salespeople "noun-oriented" product training—that is, a great deal about the product's features but very little about how it is used in day-to-day applications. Not surprisingly, when these organizations hire salespeople, they tend to gravitate toward people who are able to understand the product on that level—that is, as trained users—and then reinforce that perspective. In other words, it's a vicious cycle: a suboptimal selling structure perpetuating itself.

This cycle can be broken. As you will see throughout this book, CustomerCentric Selling maps out how marketing departments can make the transition from product training to product-usage training by creating Sales-Ready Messaging for targeted conversations. This training enables and empowers traditional sellers to target business people and engage in customer-centric conversations.

5. Relating Product Usage versus Relying on Product

Customer-centric conversations take place when sellers are able to relate conversationally with their buyers about product usage. Traditional salespeople—working for traditional organizations and using traditional product marketing approaches—have no choice but to rely on their product to create interest. They educate their buyers about the product, assuming that the buyers can figure out for themselves how they would use the product.

In some special circumstances, this strategy works—but only for a while. Here's a scenario you may recognize: A technology company introduces a hot new product. It finds a guru to endorse the technology, writes a "white paper" full of snap and sizzle, hires a good PR firm, and wows a couple of technology trade shows. Sales take off.

But how much actual selling took place, in this scenario? Were the salespeople helping potential customers visualize how they could achieve a goal, solve a problem, or satisfy a need by using the new technology? Or was this a case where the early-market buyers were sufficiently smart and innovative to figure out their own product usage, through (or even despite) having a traditional product presentation?

So sales take off, and the people at the technology company come to believe that they are superior sellers and marketers. Then, mysteriously, sales plummet. What's happening here? Geoffrey Moore's insightful book *Crossing the Chasm* (2002) highlighted the difficulty technology companies face when they run out of Innovators and Early Adopters. The self-sufficient buyers—those who didn't need effective selling—have come and gone, and there is no one in line behind them.

We frequently are hired by companies that have fallen into this chasm. They have exhausted the supply of Innovators and Early Adopters, and now they have to figure out how to find a new kind of prospect—that is, targeted buyers who don't know that they need the offering and don't have a vision of how they would use it.

This is where sellers who are customer-centric succeed. This book will help you and your organization become customer-centric. It will give you a framework for creating Sales-Ready Messaging (that is, product-usage messaging) that will enable your traditional salespeople to evolve to CustomerCentric Selling.

6. Managing Their Managers versus Needing to Be Managed

We believe that most traditional salespeople need to be managed mainly because they work for traditional sales managers. What do we mean by this? Traditional sales managers monitor activity rather than progress. Most of them don't have *progress* defined in their sales process. Most don't have a way to assess and grade opportunities across multiple people and offices—in other words, to compare apples to apples. Most don't even have a defined sales process.

Why is this? Most sales managers are promoted to that position not because of their superior management ability or potential, but because they have sold the most. And, statistically speaking, the chances are very good that they have sold the most because they are intuitive, naturally talented salespeople. If they did have a selling process, the odds are they are unable to articulate it.

When they find themselves in their new management position, they attempt to manage the only things they believe they can control. They manage activity. They track and assess things like the volume of cold calls, letters, demonstrations, and proposals. They monitor quantity of activity, which gives them limited ability to influence the quality of activity. They monitor energy level, rather than progress.

When newly promoted managers were salespeople, their quality measurement was intuitive. Their ability to sense when a buyer starts to feel pressured, to establish trust and competence, to help the buyer visualize solving his or her problem, to walk away from situations they didn't think they could win—all were intuitive. And as a new sales manager, how do you transfer your intuitive selling skills to your less talented team? With great difficulty. Thus, new sales managers tend to manage the only thing they believe they can control—activity.

There is a better way. Customer-centric salespeople are able to converse situationally and ask relevant questions to empower business decision makers to understand how they can achieve their goals, solve their problems, and satisfy their needs. Their managers simply need to monitor their progress and help them succeed. Customer-centric salespeople tend to call on their managers when they need company resources to help them make a sale. For example, they might need an executive sales call, a headquarters visit, a presales technical consultant, or extra administrative support. And in our experience, customer-centric salespeople get the support they need when they need it, because they are able to demonstrate to their managers that they have earned the right to command finite company resources. Before they ask for resources, they can document a decision maker's goal, current situation, and vision of using their offering to achieve a goal, solve a problem, or satisfy a need.

7. Empowering Buyers versus Attempting to Sell Them

In our workshops for salespeople, we frequently conduct an interesting exercise. We ask participants to take out a blank sheet of paper and to pretend that they are the authors of their own dictionaries. Then we ask them to define *selling*.

We're always astounded at the perceptions that professional salespeople have of their own profession. They define selling as, for example, convincing, persuading, getting someone else to do what you want, handling or overcoming objections, taking at least five no's before giving up, negotiating to get what you want, and—of course—the big one: closing. ABC—always be closing. Close early! Close often!

Looking at this list and thinking about the mindset that lies behind it, is it any wonder that most people—even salespeople—do not like being approached by salespeople?

We also work with buyers. When asked to describe salespeople, most buyers use terms like aggressive, insincere, pushy, manipulative, overfamiliar, prone to exaggerate, poor listeners, and so on. When asked to net these negatives down to one word, the number one response we get from buyers is *pressure*. When buyers deal with sellers, they feel pushed, manipulated, pressured into doing things that they end up wishing they hadn't done.

These preconceptions are traps. If sellers are going to escape from them, they will have to learn to sell differently. Their concept of selling will have to be reframed so that it becomes customer-centric (again, empowering buyers to achieve their goals, solve their problems, or satisfy their needs). This is not all that difficult to accomplish. Why do we say that? Because we have taught thousands of self-declared "nonsalespeople" how to sell. By nonsalespeople, we mean people who do not want to think of themselves as salespeople in the traditional sense—engineers, accountants, lawyers, consultants, scientists—people whose worst nightmare is calling home and telling their mothers they have decided to become a salesperson!

Think about the engineer nonsalesperson, for example. Engineers love to help people solve problems. By and large, engineers do not want to behave like traditional salespeople, but when the concept of selling is reframed, they are very happy serving as customer-centric salespeople. By no means can all engineers be taught to sell, but there are a number of them who have a positive mindset, have few preconceived notions, and are open to the challenge.

We believe a seller's objective, going into a new relationship with a buyer, should be to help the buyer achieve a goal, solve a problem, or satisfy a need—and then be prepared to leave if the seller doesn't believe the prospect can be empowered to accomplish one of those goals. This may sound like only a small shift away from a traditional sales approach, but in fact, it's fundamentally different. Imagine yourself as a buyer. Wouldn't you rather have a meeting with someone who had that attitude, rather than the mindset of a traditional salesperson?

Even the "Naturals" Can Improve

Over our careers, we have met a number of truly gifted "natural" salespeople. They make it look easy. On a consistent basis, they achieve 200-plus percent of quota, despite the fact that most of them cannot define what makes them successful.

We can. If you look back at the seven comparisons we have just made, these natural salespeople are consistently customer-centric along the first six measures. That's what explains their success.

But in our experience, even these naturals have room for improvement on the seventh and final measure. Most of them believe (like their less skilled peers) that selling is convincing, persuading, and so on. So we believe even the most gifted sellers can become more customer-centric. We believe the key to a natural salesperson succeeding as a sales manager is to first become consciously customer-centric. CustomerCentric Selling, as explained in this book, is designed to help all sellers assess where they are, and give them a specific methodology to help them become more successful.

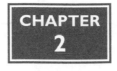

Opinions—The Fuel That Drives Corporations

THIS IS A CHAPTER ABOUT OPINIONS: how they are shaped, and how they could be shaped.

Opinions play an all-important role in our personal and professional lives. When you think about it, we rarely make a significant move without soliciting other people's opinions. At the same time, when we want help in making important decisions, most of us are pretty selective about the people we're going to listen to.

When organizations need to make important decisions, most hire experts to become familiar with their situation and make recommendations. A case can be made that CEOs receive huge compensation packages because of their ability to evaluate situations and formulate opinions—informed guesses that ultimately shape the strategic direction of their company.

Not everyone's opinion is valued equally, of course. As we proceed down an organization chart, the power of individual opinions to shape company policy decisions drops off sharply. In fact, most organizations have structures in place to ensure that decisions will be made based *only* on opinions that have been arrived at (or least blessed) by higher-level people. In a manufacturing company, for example, employees on the shop floor execute procedures—act on opinions—that have been developed by others. Few, if any, policy decisions are made on the shop floor.

But there is a major exception to this rule: the sales function. Yes, in most cases a business plan is finalized, and specific marketing plans are put into place to execute it. And yes, for most companies with a sales organization, the revenue plan is broken down into revenue objectives (quotas) for each territory. And yet, while salespeople may be given very specific targets to achieve, they are also given enormous latitude in arriving at opinions, and making decisions, that not only affect the organization's performance, but also ultimately shape the customer's experience. In how many organizations are salespeople given the latitude to decide

1. How to position their offerings to buyers?
2. Which accounts and titles to call on?
3. Which accounts to include in their pipelines?
4. Which accounts to close and when?
5. How to interpret lost opportunities?
6. Which changes in offerings are needed to improve competitive positioning?

Without necessarily understanding that they're doing so, companies rely on the opinions of traditional salespeople to build a pipeline, create a forecast, and deliver top-line revenue. Depending on the specific circumstances, this may be exactly the right thing to do—or it may be an out-and-out disaster. The most common reason that new companies fail is that Sales does not deliver according to plan (although, of course, the reasons for that failure to deliver may be complex). So let's peel the onion and take a closer look at how salespeople form opinions, and how those opinions come to bear on their company's success or failure.

Who's Responsible for What?

When we ask CEOs a critical question—"Who positions your company's offerings?"—we often hear the same response: "Marketing." This is true whether they are using a direct or an indirect sales organization. In our experience, though, this is a gross oversimplification—to the extent of not being a response at all. So what we tend to do next is ask the CEO to consider the following scenario:

Your company makes a major new product or service announcement and trains the entire sales organization on the offering in regional meetings for 2 days. The following week, your salespeople begin calling on buyers and customers. Let's assume that calls are made by three different salespeople attempting to sell the new offering to the same title and vertical industry, and let's assume that these calls are videotaped. Would someone reviewing those tapes be able to determine if

1. The same offering was being sold?
2. The salespeople worked for the same company?

At this point, most executives—especially those who have come up through the sales ranks—face a sobering reality that they don't like to dwell on: The burden of positioning offerings falls, by default, on the shoulders of individual salespeople. This is true no matter how many hours the Human Resources (HR) department has devoted to carefully creating job descriptions and detailing responsibilities across the entire Marketing apparatus. In the final analysis, many CEOs simply abdicate responsibility for their customers' experience—as well as the attainment of top-line revenue targets—to individual salespeople.

A CEO can safely assume that Tactical Marketing has responsibility and exerts control over literature, brochures, advertising, Web site content, trade shows, seminars, and so on. But marketing support and the control of the selling process are far more tenuous. At the end of the day, the positioning of offerings boils down to the words and phrases salespeople use when they communicate with potential buyers. So how consistent is the message that is being delivered? Most CEOs, when answering truthfully, have to say, "Not very consistent."

Who's to blame? We now hear from many senior sales executives that Marketing has become irrelevant in terms of supporting their selling efforts. According to the American Marketing Association's Customer Message Management Forums held in 2002, between 50 and 90 percent of the material created by Marketing to support Sales is never used by salespeople. Of course, Marketing should not shoulder all the blame for this situation. Part of the problem results from the fact that in many cases, no effective interface between Marketing and Sales has been defined. In addition, it is virtually impossible to provide effective support if an effective sales process has not been established.

We have already discussed how most PowerPoint presentations and glossy brochures are of minimal help to salespeople in structuring conversations with buyers, or in closing business. Much of today's marketing collateral simply is not designed to be used by salespeople while making calls.

Similarly, much of the training provided to salespeople also misses the mark. It is, for the most part, product-centric, not customer-centric. We've already seen how traditional salespeople tend to launch almost immediately into a product pitch, without regard for what the buyer may either want or need. Well, cramming a newly hired salesperson's head full of product information points that salesperson down this same exact path—the *wrong* path if the salesperson is expected to engage in a customer-centric conversation with a buyer. Yes, there is a need for product training, but we believe it should be distinguished from sales training.

Companies that are unable to bridge the gap between Tactical Marketing and Sales have no alternative but to rely on—and be at the mercy of—the opinions of their salespeople. Is that such a bad thing? Well, salespeople are just like doctors, lawyers, electricians, or the members of any other profession in that

- 10 percent are exceptional
- 70 percent are average
- 20 percent are marginal

The small percentage who are naturally customer-centric are capable of overcoming the lack of marketing support. They are able to resist the temptation to recite verbatim what they have learned in product training. On a sales call, they can listen, and respond, and ask smart questions to properly position offerings during conversations with their buyers. The question or challenge then becomes, "What production can be gotten from traditional salespeople?"

Hiring and Training: Where Selling Begins

Let's examine the hiring and training of new salespeople, explore how offerings get positioned, and see how a series of opinions ultimately rolls up into the CEO's revenue forecast.

Some large organizations have established hiring profiles designed to help them to select candidates who possess what they believe are the requisite education, intelligence, and personal characteristics to become successful revenue-producing salespeople. Other large organizations prefer to start with a blank canvas, in the sense that they favor hiring recent college graduates, with the intent of teaching them everything they need to know about the company's offerings, about vertical markets, and about how to sell.

After an orientation period in the branch office where they will be working, these new hires are often sent to a central location for indoctrination. The duration of these indoctrination sessions can range from a few days to several months, depending on the complexity and number of product offerings. Classroom sessions often run all day, with evening assignments or after-hours case-study work also being fairly common. In addition to product training and immersion in their company's sales culture, sales trainees are introduced to corporate policies and procedures, headquarters staff, administrative reporting, and so on.

The primary objective of these sessions, however, is to teach new hires about the company's product and service offerings. Frequently, these corporate training sessions are designed and delivered by Product Marketing staff who have limited direct experience with, or even exposure to, customers and salespeople in the field. The focus is more inward ("These are our offerings") than outward ("Here are some ways your customers and prospects could use our offerings to achieve their goals, solve their problems, or satisfy their needs"). Attendees are asked to memorize specifications of different offerings. They learn to deliver canned presentations, perform demonstrations, handle objections, and recite competitors' strengths and weaknesses.

As suggested above, most such training presents the company's offerings as *nouns*, with a relentless focus on what it is and what it will do. This rarely works. A few years ago, we ran into a salesperson working for a company that sold adhesives. Asking him about his offerings prompted an astounding "core dump" about viscosity, drying properties, resiliency, and so on.

Within the first few seconds of this onslaught, the salesperson had lost our interest. He didn't seem to be aware of that. He droned on for many more minutes, telling us far more than we ever wanted to know. Finally, he paused to take a breath. Leaping through this narrow window of opportunity, we commented that he had described his products as if they were nouns. We then suggested that he try to discuss his adhesives as if they were verbs.

Give him credit: He gave it a shot. He stepped away from his normal presentation mode (inward focus) and came up with applications of his products (outward focus). He described how some of his customers were using his company's adhesives, which was far more interesting and easier to understand than listening to him drone his way through a laundry list of properties, attributes, and features. And something else interesting happened, too: We had a conversation. No, that conversation could not have been described as scintillating, but as a sales approach, it represented an enormous improvement over his feature-dump approach.

Perhaps because they are aware of (and maybe even feel a little guilty about) the intensely inward focus of their new-hire training, some companies attempt to provide their new salespeople with industry knowledge. These studies of industry segments typically represent a small percentage of the total class time. They often appear to be an afterthought, or filler—a kind of cultural time-out.

In this small percentage of the overall sessions, attendees are exposed to the functions and responsibilities associated with the various job titles within vertical markets. They may be introduced to industry buzzwords and potential buyer hot buttons, both of which they are encouraged to work into their sales calls. Hope springs eternal. The hope is that by using these terms, salespeople will appear to possess industry knowledge—perhaps even expertise—which of course should prove useful when the salesperson attempts to relate to the person on the other side of a desk or on the other end of a telephone line.

In our experience, it's a forlorn hope. The new salespeople rarely gain expertise through these truncated, but often intense, industry segments. For them, it's information overload—the equivalent of trying to drink from a fire hose. And even if they're successful at ingesting and regurgitating buzzwords, the potential buyer is rarely impressed. The seller may just be one question away from exposing an underlying lack of understanding of the buyer's business environment. The buyer lives this industry every day. When a salesperson misses by an inch, he or she misses by a mile.

Another difficulty with this overall sales-training approach is that it is not integrated. It presents product, sales, and industry information separately, and leaves all three in separate "silos" of information. Salespeople are thus required to do the integration themselves, and to create a coherent message that they can deliver during sales calls. This is a huge challenge. Even customer-centric salespeople can require months in the field to accomplish this integration and convert product knowledge into product-usage knowledge. Think about how wasteful it is for salespeople to learn to achieve this integration and conversion individually. And how unreasonable it is to expect traditional sellers to ever get there.

Positioning: The Next Challenge

How the product is described to potential buyers is its position in the market. Positioning is all-important in the sales process. Although many people harbor a negative stereotype of salespeople, that may be in part because they don't fully appreciate the skill needed to successfully position a product in the mind of the buyer—or the training that lies behind that success.

In the mid-1970s, one of us—fresh out of college—was hired by IBM's General Systems Division. The assignment: to sell first-time computer users on the benefits of migrating from their manual accounting systems to a computerized setup. Most of us trainees fell into the trap of believing that we were selling hardware and software. It took us a frustrating couple of months to make the leap—to understand that the decision makers we were pitching to had little or no interest in learning about computer hardware and software. In fact, the product approach actually frightened some of them. It reinforced all their worst notions about the complexity and general scariness of computers.

On the other hand, if the business owner could be shown reports generated by our systems, and if these reports could be shown to be useful tools for making real-life business decisions, we were home free. For example, seeing an inventory report with items sorted by date of last usage would enable buyers to visualize reducing inventory. Who cared about CPU processing speeds, disk capacities, and the like? The hardware and software needed to be described only as the means to a desired end. Remember that this was IBM, which at that time was considered to be the gold standard in most aspects of business, the company that all the others were imitating. IBM, with all of its vaunted staff, expertise, and experience, was leading its new hires down the wrong path. It was teaching them to position products as nouns, rather than verbs.

And the positioning problem is not limited to new hires. For companies with multiple offerings selling into multiple vertical industries, the challenge of positioning offerings becomes formidable, even for the most talented and experienced salespeople.

For example, think about the wide range of people with different job functions a salesperson must communicate with in order to get an enterprise productivity-improvement offering sold, funded, and implemented. In the case of some enterprise sales, this cast of characters can range from technical staff within the information technology (IT) department, through middle management and line vice presidents, and all the way up to the chief financial officer and the CEO. Think how different each of these calls should be. Consider, too, how the length of the sell cycle can vary, depending on whether the salesperson's point of entry into the buyer's organization is low, middle, or high.

Let's go back to the less experienced salesperson. Imagine that a new hire has completed his or her company's 6-month training program, and that you have the distinction of being the first buyer (victim?) that he or she is calling on. Picture where this call is likely to head, right after the introductions. Unless the salesperson has rare innate customer-centric sales talent, he or she is likely to jump right into the pitch, regardless of the interests of the buyer sitting across the desk. Most likely, the salesperson is thinking, "Hey—if my company thought it was so important for *me* to understand our offerings, then it must be important for the buyer to understand them as well."

When was the last time a salesperson called on you and took too long before discussing the offerings? Prior to the salesperson's getting into the sales pitch, did you indicate any need for the offerings or any reason that you would be a potential buyer? When the salesperson was reciting features of the offerings, what percentage of them were you actually interested in, or felt could be useful to you?

The answer in most cases, of course, is "a very low percentage." So why do traditional salespeople go this route? Talking about their offerings represents their comfort zone, partly because it was what their company trained them to do. It allows them to feel like experts, and to control the meeting. But leading with features is, in most cases, like driving a car off a cliff. Sure, you're in charge. But do you really want to be in charge of a car crash, or a failed sales effort? Wouldn't it be better to succeed?

Why *Not* Lead with Features?

The irony is that leading with features—operating in the comfort zone, as described above—can also cause a salesperson to lose control.

How? Once a specific offering (it) is mentioned, many buyers ask a very logical question: "How much does it cost?" But this is often too early in the conversation to discuss pricing, because no goals, problems, potential usage, or value have been established in the buyer's mind. A stick of gum costs too much, no matter what it costs, if you haven't decided that you want or need a stick of gum.

The traditional sales technique at this point—when price comes up too early—is to attempt to provide waffling kinds of responses ("Your mileage may vary") in an attempt to dodge the question. This can create a negative impression, and sometimes causes the seller to conform to the pervasive, unflattering stereotype of a "slippery salesperson." But there's an even worse scenario: Particularly among traditional sellers, there is also a powerful desire to hang onto this buyer at all costs, which can prompt the salesperson to quote unrealistically low numbers. If the sale progresses, the buyer will remember the unrealistically low figure quoted in the initial meeting. Eventually, it can become a barrier to moving toward a buying decision.

Yes, price is a qualifier, and it should be shared with buyers relatively early in the sales cycle. But until the buyer begins to understand the potential usefulness of the product, his or her reaction is very likely to be, "Hey, that seems expensive." And once that conclusion is drawn, the seller faces an uphill battle to regain mind share. And while there is no easy way to prevent buyers from requesting pricing information earlier than the salesperson would like to divulge it, discussing the potential usage of the product can defer these discussions until later in the sales cycle. The more valuable the usages that are discussed *before* cost is shared, the more reasonable that price is likely to sound when it finally is disclosed.

So again, this makes a case for discussing uses rather than features. But that's rarely what gets discussed in traditional sales calls. Given their training, their enthusiasm, and their formidable quotas, traditional salespeople feel compelled to present each buyer with every possible feature.

Assume a buyer is exposed to twenty-five product features, but needs only five of them. The buyer is very likely to draw the conclusion that the product must be too complicated and too expensive. In other words, it looks like overkill for the buyer's requirements. Buyers will object to having to pay for features that they believe they won't ever use. (No matter that they may be wrong in this; it's what they believe that counts.) Some traditional salespeople have been trained to believe that selling begins after the buyer says no, but the fact is, it's extremely difficult to turn someone around after he or she has voiced an objection about a feature. The traditional school of selling holds that an objection is a selling opportunity. We strongly disagree. Once a buyer has voiced an objection, the salesperson has to get the buyer to change his or her mind, and this is something that most people are reluctant to do.

The fact is, although traditional salespeople lead with their product to head off potential objections, they are far more likely to generate these kinds of objections when they take this approach. Part of the problem is a control issue. Who is controlling the conversation during a "spray and pray" session? The salesperson? He or she is doing all the talking, and the buyer is in the unenviable position of passively listening. Most human beings like to be in control, and buyers are no exception. In fact, they may be fully accustomed to being in control of most of the conversations they have in the workplace. So they may feel a strong need to seize control of this conversation—and the easiest way to do so is by offering objections. This job is made far easier if a seller generates a tidal wave of features. All the buyer has to do is wait for a bad feature, and then pounce.

Opinions: Right and Wrong

Let's go back to the scenario introduced earlier in this chapter: Let's assume that a new offering is announced, and that traditional salespeople from New York, Chicago, and Los Angeles who have been with the company for an average of 5 years attend 2 days of training. Their first post-training calls are scheduled for Monday. Each will be calling on the CFO of a manufacturing company.

If these calls were videotaped, would an outside observer realize that all three were selling the same product? Would the observer conclude that the salespeople worked for the same company? What might be the range of expectations in the minds of the three CFOs? Which of these three accounts should become part of the company's pipeline? In whose opinion?

Does it look as though all three are selling the same product? In most cases, as noted, the answer is no. Most likely, the presentation of the company's offerings and the shaping of the discussion with the buyer have been left to the salesperson to figure out. The result is a wide variety of sales approaches (although most will tend to be in the traditional vein).

After training, in many cases misdirected and all too brief, newly hired salespeople are asked to begin volunteering opinions. First, they must condense their understanding of the company's offerings into some format with which they can communicate a coherent message to buyers. This is an opinion. Once that task is completed, they have to analyze their territory—to decide what their target markets are and what titles to call on—and then to start filling their pipelines. Again, these steps begin with opinions.

Meanwhile, new hires understand that their honeymoon period is likely to last about 60 days, after which their pipelines must grow. Again, opinions come into play as the salesperson decides what approach to employ: go for quantity of buyers or quality of buyers? (Traditional salespeople think quantity; customer-centric salespeople think quality.) Even if they try to focus on what they feel are qualified opportunities, their judgment may be clouded, and their opinions shaped, by the pressure to show activity.

Within a few more months, they will be required to provide their opinion as to which opportunities in the forecast will close, why they will close, and when. Opinion, opinion, opinion. Is it any wonder that many customer relationship management (CRM) systems are flawed, at best? Many companies gather the input for their CRM system by asking their salespeople to interpret the outcome of their calls. But in many cases, the weakest link in the chain is a salesperson's opinion of what constitutes a qualified opportunity.

Salespeople are also asked to give reasons—opinions—when fading prospects finally must be removed from their pipelines. The most common reasons given are product and price. In most cases, we believe, neither is valid. If "product" is cited as a reason for the loss after a 6-month selling effort—for example, "we can't run under UNIX"—we believe that questions such as the following should be asked of the salesperson: "How long did it take you to discover that the buyer needed UNIX support? How long did it take you to realize that we don't provide that support?" The hard fact remains that if the product is not a "fit," the opportunity was never properly qualified, and those 6 months of activity were wasted.

And yes, unless you are selling a commodity like pork bellies, wheat, or gold, price is likely to be a factor in your success (or lack thereof). But we believe it's not always—or even often—the *determining* factor. Buyers tend to use price as an excuse when delivering bad news to salespeople. Think about it: Very often, when a salesperson learns that a sale has been lost on the basis of price, he or she asks, "Where do we have to be?" In most cases, the buyer declines to give an answer. Sometimes, this is because the buyer has psychologically closed the door and doesn't want to reopen it. But many times, as noted, price is used as an excuse. It was only one of many factors that went into the purchasing decision.

Stated conversely, if price were the be-all and end-all, vendors could post their prices on the Web and do away with salespeople. Purchasers could make all their buying decisions based solely on price. But they don't—so clearly, other factors are involved.

After a salesperson has competed for months and then lost, the buyer tends to let him or her down easily. One of the easiest ways out is to blame price or product, and most traditional salespeople are happy to take these reasons back to their managers. How many professions have situations in which there is one winner and a four-way tie for the silver medal? The real reason most opportunities are lost, however, is that the losing salesperson got outsold.

The odds are high that "I got outsold" will never appear on a loss report (that is, the write-up of a lost prospect). And this, in turn, is one of the reasons most loss reports are exercises in futility. Companies that attempt to direct product development based on loss reports, therefore, are doing the equivalent of driving down the highway by looking through rearview mirrors distorted by the opinions of salespeople.

A while back, we worked with a company that sold software to help manufacturers schedule preventive maintenance on their production equipment. They were one of three or four major players in this particular niche. About a year before we began working with them, they offered only a Disk Operating System (DOS) version of their product, while two of their competitors had developed Windows support. Predictably, the most common reason cited by the salespeople to explain losses was the lack of a Windows version of the product. In fact, the salespeople complained to the point where corporate made the investment, developed the new offering, and withdrew support for the DOS version.

What happened next? The next round of loss reports highlighted the fact that many buyers were still running DOS, and couldn't use the new Windows product!

We undertook a pipeline analysis and found two major problems. First, reps were filling their funnels with unqualified opportunities. Second, their opinions about which transactions were winnable, and how they could be won, were simply wrong. The company's strategic direction—to develop a Windows product and to stop supporting the DOS version—was misled by the opinions (excuses?) of their salespeople.

Turning Opinions into a Forecast

As you may have surmised by now, opinions permeate most sales organizations. Their importance is magnified when people are asked to predict the future. This barbaric ritual is euphemistically referred to as *forecasting*.

If a salesperson is under the gun—in other words, if he or she is busy and hasn't made much progress with the pipeline—then forecasting is likely to mean spending a few minutes massaging dates, amounts, and percentages from the previous month's report, most likely late in the afternoon on the day the report is due. The poorer a person's year-to-date position against quota, the greater the temptation to inflate the forecast. In such cases, the report should carry a disclaimer patterned after the one on side-view mirrors: "Warning! Objects in forecast may be further away and smaller than they appear."

Salespeople quickly learn that monthly review meetings with their managers go much better when they have lots of accounts listed in their pipelines. Because there is no standard way to position offerings, it is up to each salesperson to list the accounts he or she feels are viable. First they persuade themselves of that viability, and then they persuade their managers. By the time they get to this second round of persuasion, they may be quite eloquent in arguing for an opportunity's viability. In fact, if these salespeople could sell to buyers and customers as well as they do to their managers, they would be 200 percent of quota every year!

Sales managers are required to give their opinions of their salespeople's opinions. They are measured in the short term by the aggregate of the pipelines of the salespeople reporting to them. Inevitably, their opinions are influenced by what they want to believe. They want to believe that the opportunities in the pipeline are winnable, and that all the salespeople will make their numbers.

The job of sales manager is a very difficult one, and most are subjected to a great deal of pressure to deliver revenue objectives. Salespeople's lives are better if they can either (1) show a strong pipeline or (2) defend a weak pipeline. First-level managers have exactly the same challenge when doing a pipeline review with their managers. For this reason, first-line managers want to believe the yarns being spun by their salespeople.

There's another reason not to stir the pot. If the sales manager is able to poke holes in a rep's funnel for several months in a row, his or her "reward" is to put the salesperson on a performance improvement plan, which in many cases must be overseen by the HR department. Writing and monitoring this plan requires a huge commitment of time and serves as a distraction from the task of achieving branch or district quotas. It is also an unpleasant task to finally realize that a potential hiring error was made.

Ultimately, moreover, if the salesperson is unable to achieve the established objectives, he or she will be terminated. Now the manager is faced with the task of recruiting, hiring, and training a new salesperson.

Does all of this influence how hard a manager drills down into a given rep's pipeline? We think so. All things considered, it is far easier for managers to believe their salesperson's overoptimistic assessment of the opportunities that are out there, soon to be closed.

The barbaric ritual continues all the way up the chain—from district, to region, to the vice president (VP) of Sales. Each level puts its happy spin on the figures and then passes them along. The accuracy of the forecast usually improves over this long journey; the major reason it does so, though, is that the statistical base behind the forecast is getting larger, and this generally leads to a more reliable final result. This forecasting activity happens either weekly (weakly?) or monthly, and culminates with the forecast from the senior sales executive that arrives on the desk of the CFO, who must project earnings for the quarter.

Virtually all companies have become skilled at controlling their expenses, so the largest variable in projecting profitability is top-line revenue. But CFOs have learned from experience not to take revenue projections from Sales at face value. In fact, not believing the projected total for a moment, CFOs tend to multiply the gross forecast by a heuristic factor—always less than 1, often written on a scrap of paper and then stuck in their top right-hand drawer—to take some of the sunshine out of the forecast. After making this adjustment, they tell the CEO what the results for the quarter will be, so that he or she can set earnings expectations for analysts and investors.

So, as we've seen, senior executives have good reason to doubt the accuracy of their forecast. On the occasions where it *is* accurate, that may be due to offsetting errors. For example, the ABC Company (95 percent probability) did not close, but the DEF Company placed a huge order for add-on business that was never factored into the forecast. The most important revenue number at so many companies turns out to be little more than a piling up of opinions, many of them extracted from people under pressure to protect their jobs. Unless and until organizations take responsibility for forecasting out of the reps' hands, this key number will continue to be unreliable.

In reality, monthly forecasts tend to be most useful as potential wake-up calls, alerting salespeople that their pipelines are thin and warning them that they've got to ramp up their business-development activities. When the revenue forecast starts looking overoptimistic and it appears that there could be a shortfall late in a quarter, the pressure (internal and external) intensifies. Salespeople are encouraged to close business, often by offering "Hail Mary" discounts. Even if the current quarter is salvaged, though, this too often becomes a vicious cycle, with the pipeline being flushed at every quarter end, and then having to be filled from scratch.

One of the most difficult aspects of forecasting is projecting when opportunities will close. If a salesperson forecasts the Acme Company to close in September, then in October, and then in November, and it finally closes in December, the forecasting accuracy is 25 percent, even though they got the business.

Too often, close dates have nothing to do with the buyer's agenda, but correspond to seller's agendas. Under the best of circumstances, closing before buyers are ready requires significant discounting. In the worst case, pressuring buyers prematurely can cause the seller's organization to either (1) lose the sale or (2) compromise pricing. In the latter case, if the order doesn't close, the seller can anticipate either having to honor the discount at a later time or having to talk their way around it.

Organizations spend a significant amount of time forecasting. Much time and effort are expended to create the forecast, and—in months where there is a shortfall—more time and energy may be expended defending the bad numbers and explaining how they were generated in the first place. (These resources should, of course, be devoted to selling, rather than finger pointing.) And in many cases, after the last dust settles, things return to normal, dates are shifted back, and the process is repeated. The quality of the pipeline remains fairly consistent, still reflecting the (optimistic, undisciplined) opinion of each salesperson.

Many libraries offer amnesty programs to their borrowers, whereby fines on overdue books are forgiven. The books come back, their borrowers are reinstated, and everyone starts with a clean slate. Sales organizations would benefit from the equivalent. They would benefit from getting rid of all the dead wood contained in the pipeline and starting from scratch, without unduly penalizing those who come clean.

One of the most extreme examples of dead wood in a funnel emerged during a workshop we taught for a company in Cleveland. We asked what was the longest sales cycle that the company ever encountered. Without hesitation, the VP of Sales said, "Seven years." Knowing that their average sale was about $50K, this seemed to be impossible, so we asked a number of follow-up questions. As it turned out, the company had, indeed, competed for a particular account for 7 years. During that period, they actually wrote four separate proposals.

The business initially was awarded to one of their competitors by a decision maker who was comfortable doing business with their major competitor. After 7 years, that decision maker left to join another company. At that point, in response to a fifth proposal, the buyer switched vendors.

Amazingly enough, during the entire 84 months, this "opportunity" appeared in the pipeline. We've already suggested the reasons for this: Salespeople take comfort in having a long list of buyers as they set out to convince their manager that things are going to be great. Removing a dead opportunity would create more problems than it would solve. A new prospect would have to be found to replace it. Embarrassing questions would have to be answered. Better to sell your manager on being unrealistically optimistic.

Aiming for Best Practices

As long as there is a system, there will be people who abuse it. This is as true in sales as in any other walk of life. In this book, we would like to propose ways to make the scenarios described above the exception, rather than the normal course of business.

The concept of "best practices" has been associated with virtually all aspects of business. Sales has been, and remains, the most notable exception. Most senior executives and investment analysts believe sales to be much more art than science, and therefore not amenable to a best-practices approach.

We believe this view can be changed—but only after companies provide direction to all their salespeople about how to have conversations with buyers about how to use offerings to achieve a goal, solve a problem, or satisfy a need. Unless and until this happens, companies will continue to be dependent on the opinions of their salespeople in the following areas:

1. How their offerings are positioned to buyers
2. What accounts and titles to call on once given a territory
3. What accounts should be included in their pipelines
4. What accounts will close, and why, and when
5. What the reasons are for losses
6. What enhancements to offerings are necessary to improve win rates

One thing we have learned from our years in the systems business is that reports are only as good as the quality of the input that goes into them. Consider again the disappointing results that most sales force automation (SFA) and customer relationship management (CRM) systems have delivered with respect to pipeline management. Why? Because the input to these systems consists largely of salespersons' opinions of the outcomes of sales calls they have made. When you add in the fact that product positioning is left up to individual salespeople, and that they often are under enormous pressure to justify their positions, you can see how problems get built into the system.

Automation without improved process only makes a bad system faster. In the following chapters, we will focus on the kinds of improvements that are necessary to make the sales process better.

In closing, consider what a misnomer the term *forecasting* is. If that were the objective, CFOs would just take the number they receive from their VP of Sales and run with it. Our view is that senior executives crave control. Doing this exercise weekly or monthly is a flawed attempt to give them an illusion of control. In point of fact, allowing salespeople to forecast abdicates control to people whose mission is to justify their jobs, not to predict what will actually close. Without process, opinions rule.

Success without Sales-Ready Messaging

Aᴼᴛᴇʀ READING THE PREVIOUS CHAPTER, you might well be asking: Aren't some companies successful despite their reliance on the opinions of their salespeople? The answer, of course, is yes. We learned a long time ago that using the words *always* and *never* in the context of selling techniques is (usually) a bad idea.

Throughout this book, we extol the virtues of what we call Sales-Ready Messaging. But some companies were succeeding long before this book became available. We think there are at least two explanations. The first is that a small number—roughly 10 percent of all salespeople—use a customer-centric approach intuitively. The second is that there are certain market conditions that make success without Sales-Ready Messaging possible. This chapter describes those conditions—and also explains why it is important for almost all companies to migrate toward supporting their salespeople in positioning their offerings.

Understanding the Early Market

The early success of start-up companies or new offerings can often be attributed to the existence of one or more of the following conditions:

- High percentage of early-market buyers
- Significant price/performance advantage in established markets

- Early successes with recognized industry leaders
- Entry into a hot market space
- A disproportionate percentage of customer-centric salespeople
- Strong outside factors (Y2K, government regulation, and so on)
- Offerings whose applications are obvious to buyers

Looks like a good list, right? But look again: With the exception of the last item, all of these factors are fleeting. The first condition is a good illustration: What happens when the supply of early-market buyers is exhausted? Because of the opinions problem described in the previous chapter, companies may be ill prepared to sell their offerings to mainstream-market buyers, who over the long run buy the lion's share of an offering and ultimately determine if revenue objectives will be met.

Geoffrey Moore has authored several books describing stages of market acceptance of offerings, and especially of new technologies. He offers an approach to changing Marketing's message as offerings mature. See Figure 3-1. The premise for much of Moore's work is that there are different types of likely buyers at different phases of an offering's life cycle. This may sound obvious and easy to act on, but it isn't. Even if Marketing recognizes the need to change its approach and is capable of doing so—two big ifs—how does it convey the message to the field sales reps?

We'd like to provide our views of the life cycle of an offering from a *sales* perspective.

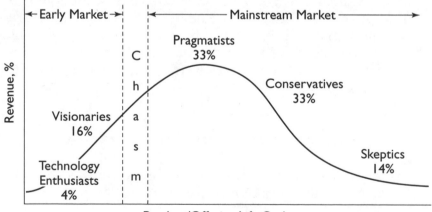

Figure 3-1 Market Acceptance of New Offerings (Geoffrey Moore, *Inside the Tornado*)

The early-market Innovators and Early Adopters are composed of technically savvy people who are willing and able to buy from companies with a limited track record and/or offerings that few organizations have implemented. In terms of technology, early-market buyers have the ability to visualize usages and view new offerings as potential competitive advantages, if they can implement them early enough in the offering's life cycle.

Why is this interesting to us? Because early-market buyers excel in determining applications for technologies that can give them a return on their investment in those technologies. In other words, they're doing what we contend traditional salespeople don't do. They focus on uses rather than features, and this is a talent that is in short supply in most selling organizations. Early-market buyers have defined and will continue to define start-up organizations' niches.

A few years ago, we were hired as consultants to a venture capital (VC) firm that had identified specific market segments for potential investments. One of their criteria was that companies had to have shipped to at least two customers; another was that the management team (and especially the CEO) had to have a strong track record. The VC team felt comfortable in assessing these areas, but also felt that there was a missing piece in most business plans. That missing piece was a clear statement of how the potential portfolio company was going to achieve its top-line revenue projections.

Why? In our experience, people with the ability to develop new technologies and build companies around those technologies are truly gifted individuals—but those gifts tend to show up in specific areas. The habits that make them great innovators are not necessarily those that will serve them well in the marketplace. Many are so enamored of their offering—their "child"—that they have what we call the *Field of Dreams* mindset: "If we build it, they will come." When challenged to talk about vertical industries, applications, and potential business uses—as opposed to technical artistry—some of these brilliant innovators get defensive, or even feel insulted. Converting their creation into a business offering somehow seems beneath them.

In many of the business plans we reviewed at the request of the VC team, little thought had been given to which industries could use this new technology, which titles would be involved in the decision to buy or not buy, how the offering would be used to achieve goals or solve problems, what business objectives could be achieved through its use— and so on, and so on. In other words, very little thought had been given to how the offering was actually going to be sold.

Typically, the revenue plans assumed the acquisition of a few customers in the first year. Future revenue projections consisted of pie charts showing growth in that market segment and assumed that the company would attain an increasing percentage of that growth, and the associated revenue, over the next several years. But the mechanics of getting there, from a sales standpoint, were sorely lacking.

Companies going down this track tend to create technologies in search of markets. And unfortunately, brilliance alone is not enough. Xerox provides a powerful and sad example of a truly brilliant research-and-development operation that failed to find the applications for many of its creations. The mouse, icons, and desktop that are now used on every PC were all developed by Xerox. And yet Xerox reaped very few financial rewards for all its innovations. If you build it, they may not come to *you*. They may go to the company that figures out how to show buyers how to use it and sells based on that application.

Let's look a little more closely at these early-market buyers, who have the rare ability to (1) grasp new capabilities and (2) visualize how those capabilities can be used for business applications at an acceptable cost. How do they work their magic?

In most cases, it's not easy. Within larger companies, early-market visionaries face a series of challenges, even after they have identified a new technology that they feel should be implemented. If they are unable to allocate unbudgeted funds, for example, they have the ability to champion a new approach and sell one or more people within their organization on the potential benefits of this new offering.

To succeed at this, of course, they have to know the right person to approach and the right way to make the case. Most decision makers up the ladder are likely to be risk-averse, and therefore ask the question: "Why don't we wait until some other companies in our industry validate the approach?"

Our experience suggests, however, that early-market visionaries control (or can get access to) adequate funds. As a result, most early purchases are made impulsively, without extensive debate. In other words, gut instincts play a much larger role than formal cost-benefit analyses.

Early-market buyers are willing to endure the inconveniences and disruptions that almost always come along with being first-generation customers. Potential problem areas include poor product reliability; inadequate training, documentation, and support staff; missing functionalities; and so on. Early-market buyers often participate in identifying these kinds of problems, and in making suggestions about possible improvements. In fact, these customers sometimes use their position to drive product development in directions that will be most advantageous to their own agenda. In such cases, they're unlikely to be worrying about what the requirements of mainstream-market buyers may be.

Assuming you want early-market buyers—and in most cases, you should—how do you find them? It's not easy. The best approach we've seen is to try to get exposure for new offerings by asking Marketing to create "buzz," and then to wait for the early-market buyers to find you. If your product is good and the buzz is adequate, they will find you. And when they do, you'll be in good shape, because early-market buyers buy. They don't need to be sold.

Beyond that, early-market buyers are often found at small to mid-size companies (or divisions of large companies) that (1) have minimal red tape and (2) aren't burdened by the need to get a consensus to make a somewhat adventurous buying decision. Like venture capitalists, these buyers understand and accept that some decisions will not achieve the desired results. Let's say that they make ten buying decisions. If two exceed expectations and six are moderately successful, they can easily tolerate two mistakes. They can be confident that the advantages accruing from those two good decisions will outweigh the write-offs.

When implementing a new offering, early-market buyers generally have the expertise to integrate the new technology into their current environment. Let's take a humble example on the retail level. An early-market audiophile assembling a sound system would research all options, focusing on recently announced offerings and also considering lesser-known companies. The best individual components would be chosen, and the task of integrating them would begin. The early-market audiophile would buy (or make) the necessary interface cables, and might even make a custom cabinet to house the system.

Understanding Mainstream-Market Buyers

Mainstream-market buyers, by contrast, would buy a consumers' guide, go to a national electronics chain store, and buy a standard package, complete with mounting brackets for the speakers, cables, prebuilt cabinet, instructions, and so on. The mainstream-market buyer is willing to pay extra to have the system delivered and installed. He or she may take out an extended warranty for extra peace of mind.

Few of them will admit it, but mainstream-market buyers don't want the latest technology. The concept of being first, or even early, is an unpleasant one. Their comfort zone lies being in the middle of the pack—

following, not leading. They focus on issues that the early-market buyer either doesn't consider or minimizes. For example:

- Is this a proven offering?
- What is the track record of this company?
- Who are the more established competitors playing in this space?
- Will this offering become a de facto standard for my industry?
- Who else in my industry is using it?
- What business results have others achieved?
- What will the return on investment (ROI) on this project be?
- What do industry experts think about this offering?
- Can we get consensus from an evaluation committee?
- What type of support will we get during implementation?
- Is my career at risk by committing too early in the product life cycle?
- Is making no decision better than making the wrong decision?

Prior to making decisions, mainstream-market buyers need to make comparisons. Getting a minimum of three bids, for example, may be corporate policy. If your offering is so unique that there are no vendors to compare it to, the evaluation may come to a grinding halt, because the mainstream-market buyers cannot validate that they are making the right decision.

If other vendors can be assembled, they may be more established than you are. If they don't have an offering ready, they may sow seeds of doubt with the buyer about committing early to a little-known company (i.e., yours) and a technology that has not been accepted as a de facto standard. Larger companies refer to this strategy as "sowing FUD" (fear, uncertainty, and doubt), and employ it to scare mainstream-market buyers into a "no decision" posture—giving them time to come up with their own offering.

Prior to signing, mainstream-market buyers may want a cost-benefit analysis of a potentially risky expenditure. In most cases, it will be incumbent on the vendor to help facilitate these calculations. Salespeople who don't fully understand how buyers can use their offering will have difficulty facilitating this analysis.

And finally, mainstream-market buyers often require references and reassurances that the early market doesn't ask for. Typical requests made by mainstream-market buyers prior to making a buying decision include

- Vendor contractual guarantees
- Your entire reference list to perform their due diligence

- Delayed payment contingent on performance
- Meetings with your senior executives
- Prototypes or free evaluations
- Headquarters visits

Crossing the Chasm

While early-market buyers can serve as a start-up's lifeblood for the first several months, longer-term revenue objectives (a much larger piece of the revenue pie chart) cannot be realized within this segment, which makes up only a small percentage of the overall market.

Companies remain in the early-market stage for offerings within vertical markets until they establish a beachhead consisting of a critical mass of customers who can provide credible references. These are invaluable in emboldening the initial mainstream-market buyers—the "early majority"—to evaluate and consider making a buying decision. Eventually, if all goes well, these buyers are followed by other groups of mainstream-market buyers: the "late majority" and—very late in the cycle—the "laggards."

Even in the case of horizontal offerings—that is, products that are applicable universally, rather than to a particular vertical segment—mainstream-market buyers respond best when selling organizations appear focused on their particular vertical segment. An example of a horizontal offering would be e-commerce software that applies to a wide range of businesses. If you are selling this product to a mainstream-market catalog retailer of clothing, for example, they are likely to be most comfortable with you if your company has already sold to other customers in their market segment. The fact that you've sold successfully to, say, a tire manufacturer isn't likely to carry much weight with them—even if the product is equally as applicable to selling tires as to selling clothes.

After the initial missionary sales effort—often accomplished through heavy involvement by the founders and intensive product redevelopment—the following months can be heady ones. Sales come more easily, and momentum is established. Customers are providing validation with their checkbooks, and this feels good. The sales team now begins a round of recruiting, to handle what they perceive to be increasing demand.

The company is now approaching the chasm between the early and mainstream markets. To get across this chasm, the company needs to be sure that at least two fundamentals are in place: (1) the new offering has been proven functional and reliable, and (2) there have been quantifiable results. With these two criteria met, and with a sales force that is up to the new challenge—a subject to which we'll return below—the company is ready to attempt to penetrate the mainstream market, which usually represents something like 80 percent of the market potential.

An example of the chasm can be seen in the artificial intelligence (AI) industry of the early 1980s. This industry comprised disruptive technologies that could be used in all sorts of ways. The early market (think tanks, universities, and so on) saw this potential and bought the products. Purchases were not usually based on near-term business applications; rather, they were made to allow organizations to explore. Many traditional salespeople who represented companies with a competitive product killed their quotas and cashed huge commission checks.

This wave of buying and euphoria lasted about 18 months. Then, suddenly the superstars couldn't achieve 50 percent of their numbers. While there certainly were other factors at work, one underlying problem was that the artificial intelligence companies failed to cross the chasm. They never showed the mainstream market why the offerings were needed, and how they could be used to achieve improved business results. Artificial intelligence has been recovering from this debacle ever since. Decades later, AI has made a modest reentry into the marketplace.

Unfortunately, getting across the chasm is not an optional exercise, nor can it be done at a casual pace. Failure to execute this phase of the larger business plan will adversely affect revenue. Delays may afford competitors an opportunity to catch up, and may fritter away whatever first-mover advantage the company may have had.

Postchasm Sellers

Mainstream-market buyers, as suggested above, prefer to follow rather than lead. In adopting that attitude, of course, they're simply being human. Mainstream humans crave predictability. We want to know what we're getting into. How often do you go to see a play, try a new restaurant, or read a book that you know absolutely nothing about? An enthusiastic recommendation from a personal acquaintance, or a trusted reviewer in a newspaper, dramatically increases the probability that you'll sample this new offering.

In fact, there are whole industries devoted to providing these kinds of recommendations and assurances. Think of all the movie critics, travel guides, consumer magazines, and so on that are alive and prospering.

We've already alluded to the need for a prepared sales force, able to align with and enable this more plodding and cautious buyer. A danger at this stage in a company's development is that success in selling early-market buyers often has been achieved by evangelizing a leading-edge offering, and by metaphorically challenging buyers to "be the first one on the block" to have it. But as they say of generals, the great temptation is always to fight the last war. Early-market buyers can make traditional sellers seem brilliant—that is, look customer-centric—because they buy. But in many cases, they buy despite the product pitches. For the mainstream-market buyer, the leading edge sounds too much like the bleeding edge—in other words, a thing to stay away from.

What of the sellers? In many cases, a good percentage of the initial salespeople hired were naturally customer-centric. They may have been recruited by the founders themselves, and incentivized (through the use of lucrative stock options) to take a high-risk, high-reward gamble. But as revenues grow and some of these top performers accept promotions into sales management, a shift begins to take place within the organization.

As the company begins to migrate from start-up to going concern, stock options for new salespeople become less generous. An initial public offering (IPO) can be great for those salespeople with founding stock; it does little for those who join the company after the IPO. Compensation similarly tends to become more bureaucratized and less lucrative. Senior executives, meanwhile, are preoccupied with building and running the business, and perhaps with keeping Wall Street happy. They are less likely to be recruiting salespeople personally and making sales calls.

The net result of all these changes? The sales talent that the company was able to initially attract and hire begins a downward spiral.

Newly promoted managers—that is, those who were responsible for early sales results—now are responsible for hiring new salespeople. In many cases, this is a task for which they are ill prepared and temperamentally unsuited. Even if they were customer-centric salespeople in their former incarnations, how do they evaluate the skill sets and chances of success of candidates they interview? Will insecurity in their new positions tempt them to hire less talented people who won't be a threat? In our experience, the answer is often yes. Many 10s (highly talented people) hire 9s, who hire 8s, and so on.

Winging It

The major difficulty with the selling environment we've described so far is that few companies develop a repeatable way for traditional salespeople to navigate buying cycles with mainstream-market buyers. Instead, they offer disparate silos of product and industry knowledge, backed up by more or less irrelevant sales collateral. Ultimately, in the absence of a workable structure, salespeople have no choice but to wing it. Revenue growth stagnates, and no one can explain how or why.

Contrast this with other occupations. For example, you won't find plumbers or electricians winging it. They are required to take courses and get certified. Most serve an apprenticeship, working under someone who is experienced. Finally, jobs have specifications showing which materials will be used, drawings that define how the work will be done, on-site supervisors or postjob building inspectors who monitor quality, and so on. All these factors combine to create a structure designed to ensure that (1) the worker is competent and (2) the outcome is predictable and satisfactory.

Why do so many salespeople wing it? We believe it's because in most cases, there is no clearly defined structure within which salespeople can operate. Expectations (beyond achieving quota) are vague; a definition of a standard sales process is almost nonexistent.

Don't believe us? Based on your own experience in sales, try this experiment: Get out your laptop, and take a moment to write down the steps you follow in selling to a prospect. (If you aren't in sales, ask someone who you believe is a competent salesperson to perform this exercise for you.)

Now look at that document. If your son or daughter were just starting a sales career, how helpful would this description of selling be? Does it give specific direction about how to sell? If your son *and* your daughter went off to sell the same product based on your document, how similar would those two sales efforts be?

The underlying reason most traditional salespeople wing it is that their sponsoring organizations haven't codified the selling process. So—as discussed earlier—the positioning of offerings is abdicated to salespeople, even though it never appears (and doesn't belong) in their job descriptions.

What about the Naturals?

As we've already pointed out, some salespeople are exceptionally talented, in the sense of being naturally customer-centric. Our best guess is that they make up about 10 percent of the sales population. These are gifted, intuitive salespeople, with the remarkable ability to transform (mostly irrelevant) product training into a coherent message—one that is tailored to the title and function of the person they are calling on.

To reiterate: Calls made by customer-centric sellers are conversational. These salespeople relate to buyers, establishing their credibility by asking intelligent questions. Rather than leading with offerings, customer-centric salespeople ask questions. They seek to understand a buyer's needs, so that they can focus on the parts of their offerings that provide a fit. By so doing, they are preparing buyers to want what they are going to offer, later in the conversation.

Naturally customer-centric sellers are the only salespeople who are capable of doing an adequate job of positioning offerings without Sales-Ready Messaging. Their opinions of what is qualified and what will close can be taken to the bank. (Even customer-centric sellers, we should note, may have trouble forecasting when opportunities will close.) They rarely waste time—yours or theirs—on unqualified opportunities.

Customer-centric salespeople need minimal coaching. After completing new-hire training, they find the best product and support people, and pick their brains to understand what this offering allows the buyer to do. Customer-centric sellers make their first sale quickly, and most make their numbers the first year. In subsequent years, they almost always exceed whatever quota they are assigned.

Some organizations, having spotted this pattern, conclude that the best approach is to recruit and hire only naturally customer-centric salespeople. Two problems: First, there are not enough to go around. And second, customer-centric sellers are selective about the types of companies they join. They know how good they are. As a rule, they seek smaller companies. They like to be recruited and interviewed by senior executives. They want situations with equity and highly leveraged compensation plans, reflecting the difficulty of selling the first several accounts. They do not want to be managed, they hate red tape, and they like to have the freedom to do whatever it takes to get the business—even if that sometimes means stepping on toes internally. This means, therefore, that companies that don't fit this description have to either develop their own customer-centric salespeople or do without.

When asked to summarize the difference between customer-centric and traditional sellers in a single word, we respond, "Patience." Customer-centric salespeople are patient; traditional sellers are not. Once a buyer shares a goal or reveals an organizational problem, traditional salespeople launch into a "here's what you need" product pitch. This creates problems at several levels:

1. Most people don't like to be told what to do or think. This is especially true when the person telling you what to do is a salesperson—who almost always has a quota to meet, and therefore can't be seen as an objective party.
2. When assaulted by a "spray and pray" pitch, buyers are likely to realize that there are features in this offering that they don't need. The conclusion that the offering is too complicated, and therefore too expensive, may not be far behind.
3. By failing to ask good questions and listen, the traditional salesperson fails to understand the buyer's current environment and the reasons he or she cannot accomplish the goal or solve the problem being discussed.
4. Similarly, the traditional salesperson has no way of discovering if the offering is a good fit with the buyer's needs. The buyer hasn't been allowed to describe his or her current situation. Failure to understand the customer environment leaves the door to misset expectations wide open.

Customer-centric sellers, by contrast, are patient. They ask buyers *why* they are having trouble accomplishing the stated goal. They dig into the barriers that are standing in the way of a solution. By so doing, they can home in on the capabilities of their offering that may actually help the buyer.

Punished for Success

Imagine that a company has grown to the point where it is time to open a new branch office. The decision has been made to promote a salesperson from within the company to be a sales manager. Whom do you think they'll turn to? Do you think they will promote a salesperson who has struggled to hit 100 percent of quota, year in and year out? Or do you think they will promote someone who has consistently exceeded quota?

Almost universally, companies promote their top-performing sellers. This may seem like the right thing to do, but in fact, it most often creates a whole new set of problems:

1. A top-producing salesperson is removed from a territory, and sales and relationships may suffer.
2. In the absence of a sales structure, as described above, a top-producing salesperson is likely to make a rotten sales manager, and may make life miserable for those reporting to him or her.
3. This may be the first job in which the top-producing seller fails. Many first-year sales managers go from a hero (top-performing salesperson) to a zero (bottom-third performance as a manager). As a result, he or she may ultimately leave the company.

The skill set needed to teach traditional salespeople to be customer-centric is vastly different from the skill set needed to perform as a top-producing salesperson in a territory. Customer-centric salespeople have an Achilles heel, which rarely shows up until they are promoted to sales manager: They don't know what has made them successful. They were intuitive; it "just happened" for them. They have never broken down what they do into understandable (teachable) components.

For that reason, they tend to tell their direct reports what to do, not how to do it. They've never been asked to be articulate about their work; now they're expected to be. Imagine former NBA star Michael Jordan becoming a coach. He tries to explain to an average basketball player how to do a 360-degree turn while hanging in the air, switch the ball from the right to the left hand, go under the basket, and put reverse spin on the ball so that it will carom off the backboard and drop into the hoop. Unlikely! As an individual performer, Jordan does his thing, and the rest of us admire his artistry and athleticism.

Think about the athletes who become outstanding coaches. Many of them were average players, at best. It didn't come naturally for them. Because they lacked the talent of a Michael Jordan, they had to plod along and learn all aspects of the game. As a direct result, they set themselves up to be better teachers. Average performers are process-friendly. They are more likely to be patient with other average people, and therefore, they are more likely to help them improve.

The newly promoted top producer, as described above, has always hated the administrative aspects of selling. Now, thanks to this promotion, he or she is expected to spend 20 to 30 percent of his or her time performing these tasks. Promoting a top-performing salesperson to sales manager is analogous to "promoting" a Top Gun pilot to air traffic controller. It's taking them out of a realm in which they are almost certain to succeed, and putting them into a realm in which they are almost certain to fail. In effect, it's punishing them for their past successes.

A Changing Context

Meanwhile, our former Top Guns find themselves in a changing context. As the ranks of salespeople swell, the percentage of top performers declines. The company begins the task of creating and implementing policies, procedures, and structure.

As the landscape shifts to the mainstream market, new sales managers may start to find that they no longer have the same flexibility in pricing and terms that they enjoyed when they were enticing early customers to sign. The customer base is changing, too. As we've seen, early-market buying behavior is driven by a small number of participants, sometimes even by one primary supporter. A high percentage of early customers were small to mid-size companies.

Now, senior management is determined to pursue larger transactions at larger companies. These are very different beasts, with multiple layers of management, infrastructure, and so on. Mainstream-market buying involves a larger number of people, often through a committee structure, and often entails the need to gain consensus. (In some cases, a majority prevails, but in the worst case, decisions must be unanimous.) Even in a case where the committee concludes that an offering is viable, there may be a delay until other options are considered—for example, a request for proposal (RFP) that is distributed to multiple vendors. Mainstream-market buyers are pragmatists. They believe in due diligence. As a seller, you may even be punished for your uniqueness: Mainstream-market buyers sometimes defer a decision indefinitely because they are unable to evaluate alternatives.

Meanwhile, as the sales organization grows, the Marketing department expands (or is organized for the first time). Its objective is to shape the way prospects are approached by standardizing product presentations and brochures. There is an attempt to codify how offerings are sold. What began as handwritten notes on a cocktail napkin by the founder early in the company's history is now a glossy six-color brochure, bursting with high-end graphics and ambiguous terms: *leading edge, robust, synergistic, scalable, seamless, state of the art*, and so on.

These marketing efforts are often flawed because they tend to be based on successes with early-market buyers who didn't need to be sold. The deliverables to the field are product-intense, treating offerings as nouns rather than verbs. But the strengths embraced by the early market—and now highlighted in the newly created collateral materials—may be out of alignment with the concerns of pragmatic buyers. In fact, they may raise issues that will be barriers to getting buying decisions made.

In this changing context, the danger lies in not knowing when or how to change the selling approach. Leading with features was (sometimes) acceptable with the early-market buyers. But leading with features when approaching mainstream-market buyers is deadly poison. Telling them that this is the latest technology, and that they'll be the first on their block to have it, is simply too scary for them.

The 72 Percent Zone

Now let's look at Figure 3-2. If you create a standard two-by-two grid, segmenting salespeople and buyers into two categories, you come up with four possible buyer/seller combinations.

This grid shows how 100 percent of all selling situations are distributed across our four combinations. For example, if early-market buyers are 20 percent of selling situations and customer-centric salespeople are 10 percent, then that combination results in 2 percent of the overall total.

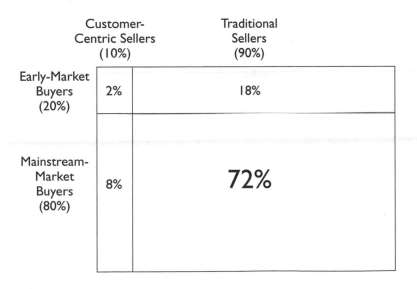

Figure 3-2   Who Ends Up Selling to Whom?

In other words, 2 percent of selling situations consist of customer-centric sellers calling on early-market buyers. This situation yields the highest ratio of success. In fact, it may be overkill, because the early market typically buys; it doesn't have to be sold.

Similarly, 18 percent of selling situations consist of traditional sellers calling on early-market buyers. Let's assume the traditional salesperson is capable of delivering the standard PowerPoint presentation that describes the new offering as if it were a noun. Early-market buyers are willing to endure a "spray and pray," and are also capable of determining if this offering can be used to their benefit. Despite the fact that the salesperson cannot describe how the offering could be used, the vendor still has a high probability of a sale. The biggest challenge, in this case, is finding those early-market buyers.

In 8 percent of selling situations, customer-centric sellers are calling on mainstream-market buyers. This is the best use of a customer-centric seller's talents. The mainstream-market buyers need help in understanding what the offering will enable them to do, and how they will benefit as a result. The customer-centric seller has the ability and patience to navigate through the buying cycle and maximize the chances of getting the business.

The most disturbing fact that emerges from this chart is that 72 percent of the time, salespeople who are selling risk (that is, focusing on technology and features) are calling on people (mainstream-market buyers) who are highly risk-averse.

Buying cycles with this combination are arduous, at best. In our 72 percent zone, a far higher percentage of sell cycles end with no decision. For example, in our experience, information technology vendors selling to the mainstream market win about 15 percent of opportunities that go to the end of a decision cycle, and another 15 percent of the time, a competitive vendor wins. But in a discouraging 70 percent of these situations, buyers make no decision at all.

In the late 1990s, vendors of technology had the huge advantage of the looming Y2K threat, which forced mainstream-market buyers to make decisions in a hurry. Absent that kind of external pressure, these buyers would have been far less likely to move—and the salespeople of the day would have had far less reason to be smug.

We worked with a CEO who concluded that there *was* no early market for his company's offerings—that is, no easy sell. He then took it a step further: He also concluded he had no customer-centric sellers within his sales organization. His calculation of who was calling on whom was simple: 100 percent of his sales situations were the least desirable—traditional salespeople calling on mainstream-market buyers, which can be considered as having the inept call on the unable.

Figure 3-3 is simply another way of illustrating that the majority of a potential market is postchasm and that therefore potential buyers are unable to understand on their own why they need a new capability or technology, or how they might use it. For companies selling technology, delays in crossing the chasm can be devastating. While most everyone would agree that delays provide competitors time to catch up and adversely affect overall market share, many have not considered the impact of price erosion as a technology goes through its life cycle. Companies with unique offerings can command a premium, but as other companies enter the market, there is a tendency to migrate toward commodity pricing. In the late stages of a product's life cycle, reduced pricing is often the tactic to stay competitive with newer technologies. Companies failing to cross the chasm are adversely affected by both lower market share and margins.

We tell our clients that if they start preparing to sell to the early majority (the pragmatist) from day one, they can virtually eliminate the chasm and change the shape of the bell curve in Figure 3-3 by bringing in mainstream-market sales sooner. Note in Figure 3-4 that the duration of the product life cycle does not change but that now the categories of buyers can be sold to concurrently rather than serially. By empowering traditional salespeople to have conversations about usage with Key Players, Marketing can accelerate acceptance and market share at higher mar-

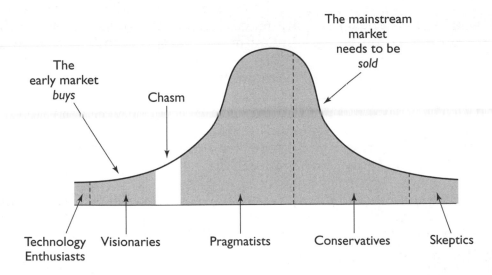

Figure 3-3 Waiting for the Mainstream Market to "Get It"

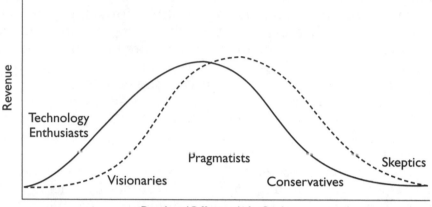

Figure 3-4 Eliminating the Chasm: Helping the Mainstream Market "Get It" by Incorporating Sales Ready Messaging into Product Launches (Solid line curve = without chasm; broken line curve = with chasm)

gins. If time to revenue is the question, then Sales-Ready Messaging from day one is the answer.

What happens when a company fails to drive top-line revenues? The most common result is mutual finger pointing by Sales and Marketing. We believe that both Sales and Marketing have failed to do their jobs. Traditionally, there is a great deal of tension, even conflict, between these two functional areas. Later in this book, we'll explore this relationship more closely, and offer a definition of an appropriate interface between Sales and Marketing.

In summary, there are circumstances in which new offerings can enjoy success even without Sales-Ready Messaging being made available to their sales organization. As markets and sales organizations mature, however, penetration of the mainstream market almost always proves to be more challenging (a.k.a. "hard rock mining"). To sustain success, companies have to realize how different mainstream-market buyers really are, and act on that insight.

Mainstream-market buyers don't buy; they need help in understanding how an offering can enable them to achieve a goal, solve a problem, or satisfy a need. So, companies can maximize their chances of prospering if they enable their growing number of salespeople to have conversations with buyers in a way that positions offerings more consistently, leveraging best practices.

CHAPTER 4

Core Concepts of CustomerCentric Selling

CUSTOMERCENTRIC SELLING EMPOWERS SELLERS to execute Sales Ready Messaging to help their buyers visualize using their offerings to achieve a goal, solve a problem, or satisfy a need.

In our conversations with selling organizations, we believe that most of them would benefit from *reframing the concept of selling*.

Why? Because by changing the way people think about the sales function, the idea of selling becomes palatable to people who otherwise would never view themselves as salespeople. Over the years, we have helped large numbers of engineers, scientists, accountants, and consultants become successful salespeople by allowing them to do what they like to do naturally—that is, help their clients achieve goals and solve problems.

Is this sales? Sure. But it's not traditional selling, which is viewed as distasteful to many people who would otherwise make excellent salespeople.

A client who sells enterprise information technology recently asked us to help them fine-tune their hiring model. We studied the backgrounds of their top salespeople going back 10 years, and discovered that seven of the top ten salespeople came out of some form of customer support. This was a validation of something we had long believed: that people who enjoy helping their customers use their offering to achieve goals and solve problems make excellent salespeople.

Many clients ask us, "Which is better: hiring an experienced salesperson and teaching him or her our product or teaching an employee who already knows our product how to sell?" Good question. We believe the answer lies in the individual. If the experienced salesperson believes that selling means persuading, convincing, closing, and so on, then he or she is very likely to create more of the bad experiences that buyers disdain—this time in your company's name. If the existing employee likes to help people, has the confidence to approach strangers, and knows how to use the product offering, then we vote for teaching that person how to sell.

Think of the frame of mind of the traditional persuading/convincing salesperson in the minutes just before an initial meeting with a prospect. What is he or she thinking? Most likely, "What can I sell this person?" Or maybe, even worse, "What do I need this person to buy?" And how long do you think it takes the prospect to sense this and to start to feel uncomfortable?

But what if the seller's primary agenda is finding out whether the prospect has a goal, problem, or need that the seller might be able to help with? And what if the seller is actually willing to leave if he or she doesn't have anything to offer in this particular context? Again, we believe that reframing the concept of selling will cause the sales call—and the entire relationship—to be far more productive and rewarding for all parties.

In this chapter, we present thirteen core concepts that collectively begin to reframe the concept of selling. They are the following:

- You get delegated to the people you sound like.
- Take the time to diagnose before you offer a prescription.
- People buy from people who are sincere and competent, and who empower them.
- Don't give without getting.
- You can't sell to someone who can't buy.
- Bad news early is good news.
- No goal means no prospect.
- People are best convinced by reasons they themselves discover.
- When selling, your expertise can become your enemy.
- The only person who can call it a solution is the buyer.
- Make yourself equal, then make yourself different—or you'll just be different.
- Emotional decisions are justified by value and logic.
- Don't close before the buyer is ready to buy.

You Get Delegated to the People You Sound Like

Sales executives have complained to us forever that their salespeople don't (can't?) call high enough. Many of them lament the fact that their sellers prefer to call on the potential users of their offering, rather than on the decision makers who can actually buy the product or service.

What happens when sellers do get an audience with a decision maker? In many cases, they present product features and functions to someone who has no interest in or time for such a presentation, and they get delegated. They get delegated to someone else in the organization who shares their interest in product features and functions, but—almost by definition—lacks the power to buy.

Why does this happen? As we've already seen, part of the problem probably lies in the product training the salespeople received. If they are trained in the hundreds of features and marketing hype of their offering, then isn't it reasonable to expect them to regurgitate features and hype, regardless of the buyer's title?

Most senior executives will allocate about 30 minutes to a sales call with a salesperson who has proved competent enough to get an appointment with them. But few executive calls last a full 30 minutes. If the seller begins expounding on technology, features, platforms, network architecture, and so on, senior executives are quick to delegate them to the people in their organization who *care* about technology, features, platforms, network architecture, and so on. In many such cases, it would have been far better not to have called on the executive at all. Your company's position may have been compromised in the eyes of the buyer. Access to decision makers is a high-risk, high-reward proposition.

When we work with Marketing departments to create Sales-Ready Messaging—that is, messaging that allows sellers to converse with decision makers—one of the major difficulties we face is the shortage of people in our client organizations who know how decision makers (by job title) view the use of their offerings.

This is true whether you're talking with Product Development, or Marketing, or Sales. There is a notable exception, however: The people who understand how their customers think about using the product tend to be the professional-services people. Why? The answer is clear: because it is their job to help customers achieve goals, solve problems, and satisfy needs through the use of their offering.

It's not that complicated. Our goal in CustomerCentric Selling is simply to help our clients develop Sales-Ready Messaging—messaging that will enable their salespeople to have peer-to-peer conversations regardless of buyer title, in turn creating visions in the buyer's mind of using their offering to achieve goals, solve problems, or satisfy needs.

Take the Time to Diagnose before You Offer a Prescription

If you went to see a physician with a goal (losing weight) or a problem (lower back spasms), you would expect the physician to ask you a series of specific diagnostic questions. Your trust and confidence in the physician would increase with each intelligent, probing, on-target question he or she asked you. When you have confidence in the diagnostic process, you are far more likely to have confidence in the prescription.

Why should selling be any different?

What we are talking about here is *process*. The ability to ask diagnostic questions is a key differentiator between great salespeople and traditional salespeople. Customer-centric sellers do this intuitively. Traditional sellers need help not only with content, but with process as well. They need help with the process of asking the right questions to learn how the customer operates today, and the associated costs of the current method.

In many of our consulting engagements, we help Marketing develop the diagnostic questions about (1) the buyer's current situation and (2) the potential usage of the offering to help the buyer achieve a goal, solve a problem, or satisfy a need. Most human beings (particularly, it must be said, male human beings) do not appreciate unsolicited advice. But if the potential buyer is being asked intelligent questions that he or she is capable of answering, the advice that emerges from that process is, in a very real sense, solicited advice. The buyer has participated in, and partly directed, the conversation that developed both the diagnosis and the prescription.

People Buy from People Who Are Sincere and Competent, and Who Empower Them

When we do role-playing exercises in our workshops, we stress that it is equally important for our attendees to take the part of buyers as it is for them to play the role of sellers. This is the best way for them to learn to think like a buyer. What they tend to discover through that process is that buyers want to deal with sellers who (1) are sincere, (2) are competent, and (3) allow the buyer to participate in the conversation. This is a welcome change from the "Here's what you need" approach taken by traditional salespeople.

In today's competitive market, a salesperson must be sincere and competent merely to get the opportunity to compete. But that's just the price of admission. Lots of companies know how to recruit sincere and competent salespeople (at least of a traditional sort). We submit, therefore, that conversing with buyers is the most sure-fire way for sellers to differentiate themselves from the pack.

The key to further differentiation lies in making sure that buyers retain ownership of their goals, problems, and needs. One of the quickest ways for a seller to lose credibility with a buyer is to look the buyer in the eye and say that a particular offering is going to "solve your company's problems." Solving the company's problems is what the buyer and his or her colleagues are paid to do, day in and day out. They don't want to hear that someone who drops in once a month, or once a year, is going to meet all their needs. Experience has taught them that no company, salesperson, or product can take responsibility for achieving the desired business result.

Many technology companies believe they can win simply by putting a superior product on the table and talking up its features. But think about it: Doesn't this force the buyer to lose control of the conversation and talk about what *you* want to talk about? Yes, if you are selling to truly expert buyers, you can win with a superior product. But did you really sell anything? Or did you simply take an order from a buyer who was smart enough to figure out how to use your product? And if it were the latter, why wouldn't this savvy buyer simply purchase on-line next time, and cut you (and your associated costs) out of the loop?

It's a simple concept, but a critically important one. The buyer must own achievement of the goal. If your buyer concludes that you first understand the current situation, goals, or problems, then—and only then—you have earned yourself the opportunity to help your buyer understand how he or she can achieve the goal, or solve the problem, with the specific capabilities of your offering.

Don't Give without Getting

Almost all sales involve some kind of negotiation. And like sales, negotiation is not an event; it is a process. In this process, we believe, the seller should strive to create a reciprocal relationship. He or she should get something in return for giving something. We call this our "quid pro quo philosophy."

This begins as a psychological adjustment: how the seller looks at himself or herself. The seller should remember that he or she is not a supplicant, looking for a handout or a favor; instead, he or she is providing a valuable service to the buyer (assuming, of course, that the offering actually can help the buyer solve a problem or meet a goal). We've already talked about how the buyer's time is valuable. Well, so is the seller's time. We believe that if a salesperson gives a buyer an hour of time, he or she has the right—and even the obligation to get something in return, before giving up another hour.

What's the practical benefit? If quid pro quo becomes a habit early in the relationship, sellers can become more effective negotiators and deliver more profitable business.

When our potential clients try to assess whether to engage us and implement CustomerCentric Selling, many wind up focusing their cost-benefit analysis on this area of discounting. Once our client decision makers understand our quid pro quo philosophy, many realize that the entire Sales-Ready Messaging and sales process implementation will more than pay for itself if sellers can reduce discounting by 1 percent.

The math isn't complicated. Let's say that the total cost of one of our standard sales-training programs is between $3000 and $4000 per salesperson. If each of those salespeople who has an annual quota of $2 million can reduce discounting by 1 percent, that's $20,000 a head. And, of course, this is the proverbial gift that keeps on giving, in that once salespeople understand quid pro quo, they keep on thinking and acting that way.

You Can't Sell to Someone Who Can't Buy

Or, stated more positively, "You can sell only to someone who can buy."

Many salespeople end up in the free education business. Think about knowledge workers in corporate America—engineers, software developers, scientists, and so on. How do they become educated in new technologies and new ways of doing business? By salespeople who spend their time and effort presenting their offerings. The problem is that the vast majority of knowledge workers embrace learning, yet can't buy. The length of the sales cycle is often inversely proportional to the level at which it is initiated.

This is most severe with breakthrough products and services. If you are first to market with a new concept or technology, then by definition, no budgets exist to buy what you are selling. This means you have to gain access to the very small minority of people who can spend unbudgeted funds. We were working with a large software company in the mid-1990s. Of the 14,000 people on their payroll, only four could spend unbudgeted funds.

For sellers selling continuous-improvement products and services, they still have to get to the person who can spend budgeted funds. This is where homework pays off. Ideally, your prospect is both the user of your product or service and the head of a department that already has the money budgeted.

Bad News Early Is Good News

This particular core concept of CustomerCentric Selling is for salespeople who have long sell cycles. Prior to hiring us, it is not uncommon for our clients, when initiating opportunities, to have 9-month sell cycles, in part because in the enterprise sales environment, the selection process usually requires the evaluation of multiple vendors. When a corporation is considering a large purchase, it typically wants three or more quotations. For vendors reacting, it will be a short sales cycle with little or no chance of winning. In many such cases, the buyers knew from the start which vendor they wanted to buy from, but they still had to get others to bid. In other words, these buyers are simply going through the motions to demonstrate to senior management that they did sufficient due diligence.

If you are not the predetermined vendor, bad news early is good news. The worst thing a salesperson can do to him- or herself and the company is to go the distance and lose. This feels a little counterintuitive, but it's true. Two vendors win in every predetermined sales cycle: the company that is awarded the business and the company that has pulled out early, giving itself the chance to pursue other winnable opportunities. All the other vendors invited in go the distance, only to be awarded a silver medal.

Again, the key is to do your homework, keep your ear to the ground, and be realistic about your chances of success. A salesperson has to qualify opportunities, which in many cases means disqualifying opportunities—including those buyers who are simply putting them through the motions. Sales managers, too, have a role to play. They can help their salespeople recognize bad news early and disqualify nonopportunities.

No Goal Means No Prospect

When meeting buyers for the first time, the salesperson's primary focus should be to build rapport and trust. Without rapport and trust, it is unlikely that buyers will share their goals and virtually certain that they will not admit problems to a salesperson.

When we help our clients define their sales process, we suggest that an opportunity should go from inactive to active status when the buyer shares a goal. In Mike's previous book—*Solution Selling, Creating Buyers in Difficult Selling Markets* (McGraw-Hill, 1994)—a prospect was defined as a buyer who has admitted a problem. This may sound easy, but it's not. Over the years, we've discovered that there are very few sellers (particularly young sellers) who are able to get senior-level executives to admit critical business problems.

Sometimes the solution lies in focusing on goals rather than problems. Experience has taught us that it is far easier for salespeople to get a buyer to share a goal than to admit a problem.

Let's look at it from the other end of the telescope. We—the authors—are both in our fifties. You will have a much easier time getting one of us to share that he would like to lose a few pounds (goal) than to admit that he is getting fat (problem). In fact, there are cases where the salesperson should help the buyer turn the admitted problem into a goal, since it's more fun to talk about goals than about problems.

A sales cycle begins once a buyer shares a goal with a seller. The seller now has the opportunity to use our solution development process (or their own) to ask a series of questions to understand the current situation, and to empower the buyer with usage scenarios that will help the buyer understand how he or she can achieve the goal by use of the seller's offering. But without a goal, there can be no solution development and therefore no prospect.

Goals may have longer-term value as well. In longer sales cycles, sellers often get to a point where they are working with delegatees—lower-lever implementers—who may get lost in the details of evaluating particular features. In such cases, the seller may find it helpful to refocus the implementer on the previously stated goals of the business buyer.

People Are Best Convinced by Reasons They Themselves Discover

We believe that with the benefit of a strong selling process and the belief that prospects have IQs above room temperature, sellers can allow buyers to reach their own conclusions.

Customer-centric salespeople leverage their expertise by asking questions, rather than making statements. We provide our clients with a dialogue model for asking questions and Sales-Ready Messaging in the form of a Solution Development Prompter. This enables the seller to facilitate an intelligent conversation with the buyer about a specific goal. The process of asking questions helps buyers discover their own reasons that prevent them from achieving a specific business result.

Expert buyers are able to convince themselves that they should buy something, because they figure out on their own how to use the proposed offering. But most buyers *aren't* experts, and therefore need help buying. By using a process that allows the buyer to feel that he or she is in control, by helping rather than pressuring, and by using content that is aimed at the buyer's specific situation, sellers can shape their customer's experiences. They can lead the buyer to discover the solution, and therefore own it.

When Selling, Your Expertise Can Become Your Enemy

Have you ever noticed how once you know something, it is difficult to have patience with or empathy for people who don't know what you know?

This can be a curse for salespeople, and experienced salespeople can be most cursed. They've seen it all before. When they see a solution to the buyer's need, they get enthusiastic and impatient, and start projecting their solution onto the buyer. (More on solutions below.) They forget their own learning curve, stop asking questions, and start telling: "What you need is. . . ."

In the late 1970s, the Xerox Corporation hired Neil Rackham to study the behavioral habits of their best salespeople. Rackham discovered that newly hired Xerox salespeople went through a quite predictable performance curve over time. Their sales performance steadily improved from their date of hire through about their 18th month—and then, inexplicably, suddenly declined.

Why? Eventually, he concluded that it took these sellers 18 months to become "experts." After a year and a half, they understood every goal, problem, or need that their product set would address, in every combination and permutation. Given that expertise—plus, of course, the sincere desire to help their buyers and make a sale—they began going too fast for their buyers, like clockwork in about their 19th month. A buyer would begin explaining his or her situation, and the overeager seller would see a perfect fit for the Xerox solution, and start telling the prospect why he or she needed this product.

It's a paradox. Of course your clients want expert salespeople. (That's what this book is all about.) At the same time, if your salesperson is tempted to use his or her expertise as a club on the buyer, a lack of expertise can make for a better sales call. Without expertise, your seller's only course of action is to ask questions. As a buyer, do you prefer salespeople who ask or who tell?

The Only Person Who Can Call It a Solution Is the Buyer

We've already talked about solutions. We believe that *solution* is one of the most misused words in the English language, certainly within the sales profession.

The *American Heritage Dictionary* defines a solution as "the answer to or disposition of a problem." But isn't it enormously presumptuous for someone with the title "salesperson" on a business card to announce to a buyer that he or she has the solution, even before the buyer has shared a single goal? Is it surprising that buyers find this offensive?

In our CustomerCentric Selling workshops, we take a different approach to solutions. We believe that a salesperson can't and shouldn't define a solution. Only the buyer can call something a solution. The seller can help the buyer get there, but can't get there first. When the seller—using the right process and content—leads the buyer to conclude that he or she needs the specific capabilities the seller has posed, only then do we have a solution. Because the buyer said so.

Make Yourself Equal, Then Make Yourself Different— or You'll Just Be Different

When salespeople are in competitive situations, they frequently fall into a trap that is set—usually unintentionally—by their buyer.

It goes like this: The buyer, usually not a decision maker, is required to interview multiple vendors, but is predisposed to go with Salesperson A's product. More or less innocently, he or she asks Salesperson B how his or her offering compares to that of Salesperson A.

At this point, Salesperson B—along with something like 90 percent of all salespeople in the universe—responds with something like the following: "Mr. Prospect, I'm so glad you asked that question. Here's how our product is different from Salesperson A's offering!" And from there, on to the specifics.

Uh-oh! Salesperson B is describing how his or her product is different from the one the prospect likes the best—before trust has been established, before goals have been articulated, before diagnosis has occurred, and before the buyer has become convinced of the seller's expertise. Think about it: The *worst* thing Salesperson B can do at this point in the relationship is to contrast his or her offering to Salesperson A's. After losing, should the buyer be asked to help fill out the loss report?

Instead, Salesperson B could have asked: "What are you hoping to accomplish?" If the buyer responds with a goal, the seller now has a prospect (see above). Now the seller can use patience, process, and content to establish credibility, diagnose the current situation, and pose some usage scenarios that will differentiate the product from Salesperson A's. We have found, with client after client, that you have to get on an equal footing from a personal, competence, and capability standpoint first, before you differentiate your offering. Otherwise, you'll just be different— and you'll lose.

Emotional Decisions Are Justified by Value and Logic

Buying is almost always an emotional act. Depending on the specifics of the situation, those emotions may or may not have to be justified—but they're still there.

When a buyer decides to buy from a particular seller, it is an emotional decision. Equally, when a buying committee decides to buy from a particular vendor, it is an emotional decision. When a buyer decides to pay an asking price rather than holding out for a lower price, it is an emotional decision. When a buyer decides to buy from a person or company he or she is comfortable with, rather than shopping for the lowest possible price, it is an emotional decision.

If the buyer answers to no one, and does not care what other people think, then he or she can buy strictly on emotion. The rest of us, though, need some kind of logic to explain to peers, superiors, subordinates, friends, or family why we chose to buy what we bought.

An acquaintance of ours bought a very expensive, stunningly beautiful, fun-to-drive German car. We asked him why. His rationale included things like *it will be a classic, it will go up in value, it has an aluminum body and will never rust,* and so on. All very logical reasons, right? The truth is, he bought that car because he loved it at first sight, wanted to drive it, and felt he looked more handsome driving it. If a close friend asked him why he bought that car, the emotional reason would flow along with the question: "Don't I look good in it?" If a stranger asked, most likely the logical reasons would be offered.

In our CustomerCentric Selling workshops, we teach salespeople to be prepared to sell to both logic and emotion. A non-decision maker will make an emotional decision to buy from a salesperson first, but then should be armed with the logical reasons so that the buying decision can be defended.

Don't Close before the Buyer Is Ready to Buy

We like to ask our audiences if any of them have ever gone out with the intention of getting a particular order on a particular day, and failed to get it. Almost everyone who has been selling for more than a couple of months (and responds honestly) raises his or her hand. We then ask them to quote their buyer's reasons for not signing on the dotted line that day. The reasons do not vary much from workshop to workshop:

- He needs to get someone else's approval.
- The contract is still in legal.
- The CFO has not approved it yet.
- They are working on their implementation plan.

- They are still waiting for another proposal.
- We are not on their approved vendor list.
- They're still on the fence.

And the dreaded

- Something's come up.

But what was *really* going on here? In most cases, the seller was asking for the business before the buyer was ready to buy. This is a big mistake. We tell sellers that once they close the first time, their relationship with their buyer will never be the same. It will be either better or worse, but it won't be the same. And almost without exception, it will be better if they were ready to buy, and worse if they weren't.

Sellers are often justified in blaming their own management for closing prematurely. It was the final 10 days of the quarter, and management is pressuring the sales force to see what opportunities they can pull in from the next quarter to this one. Again, big mistake: The saddest situations we see are salespeople who sincerely want to help their buyer achieve a goal, solve a problem, or satisfy a need, but are pressured by their management to close early. In many cases, this trades a long-term relationship for potential short-term gain, and increases the likelihood of a significant discount.

We live in the real world, and we understand that there are exceptional circumstances under which it's necessary to attempt to close early. When this is the case, the sales manager needs to acknowledge that this is the situation and explain why he or she is asking the salesperson to accelerate the buying process. But this should be the exception, rather than the rule. When management pressures salespeople to close early at the end of each quarter, there's a structural problem, and it's likely that larger future gains are being traded away for smaller near-term gains.

Before asking a buyer to buy, sellers should ask themselves:

- Have I documented the buyer's goal(s)?
- Have I diagnosed the buyer's current situation?
- Have I documented how the buyer's goal(s) can be achieved by using my offering?
- Have I helped the buyer cost-justify the decision?
- Have I documented what will happen between signing my order and having our offering fully available for the buyer's use?

- Have I provided the buyer proof that our offering and organization are for real?
- Have I asked the buyer about and mapped out organizational decision requirements—legal review, approved vendor list, and so on?

The salesperson should have some version of this list in mind very early on. He or she should be prepared to share it with the sales manager, if and when pressure comes down the pipeline, and explain which preconditions to a sale haven't been met yet, and why. And sometimes, being able to respond to these questions or most of them—with a "yes" helps the salesperson get comfortable with the idea of moving up his or her timetable for closing.

Defining the Sales Process

THERE ARE LOTS OF PEOPLE OUT THERE—most likely a majority of people—who believe that selling is really an art.

This belief is sustained, in part, by the existence of customer-centric salespeople with innate skills who make selling look so easy. But there are two problems with this assumption. The first is that, as we've already seen, there aren't enough customer-centric salespeople out there to go around—perhaps 10 percent of sales professionals.

The other problem is that it presents a self-fulfilling excuse for not getting better. If selling is an art, and I'm not an artist, then I'm off the hook, right? All I can do is plod along in my traditional selling mode and hope for the best.

We don't agree. What if we could codify the "artful" behaviors of the customer-centric sellers? What if we could build those behaviors into our sales processes and messaging? The truth is that all salespeople, and in particular traditional salespeople, can become more customer-centric, and can produce at higher, more predictable levels. In fact, we have found over the years that a traditional seller following a good process is likely to outperform a naturally talented seller who is winging it.

Sometimes we cite the example of two different kinds of musicians—those in a jazz trio and those in a symphony orchestra. The jazz musicians improvise, in real time. They rarely play the same piece the same way twice. But if you dig a little deeper, you find that there is a great deal of structure and discipline behind most of their improvisation. Meanwhile, the musicians in the orchestra try their hardest to play a Mozart piece (for example) perfectly. For the most part, the members of the orchestra couldn't write music like Mozart's. (No slight intended; how many of us can?) But because Mozart's music has been codified, they can replicate it, and brilliantly.

Naturally talented sellers are very similar to jazz musicians. We can launch a new company with a few naturally talented salespeople (the jazz guys), but to build it big enough to go public and capture its share of market, we will need to teach traditional salespeople (the orchestra) to execute a customer-centric sales process. We have to teach the orchestra to play a little jazz. At the risk of overworking the metaphor, we have to look for the structure that underlies the jazz.

In the enterprise selling world, there are many complicating factors—multiple decision makers, platform sales, commodity sales, relationship sales, application sales, new-name sales, add-on sales, sales through channels, and so on. When we work with our client organizations, one of our first tasks is to help them document, define, and understand all their sales processes. In other words, we help them codify their selling behaviors for the different selling situations they encounter.

Is this necessary? We think so. Many companies define the *what*, in other words, the things that *should* be done at each step in their sales process. Most are not so good at codifying messaging that guides the behavior of their sellers and provides the *how* for these same steps. Unless you establish a set of standards or rules—the how—at each step of the selling process, you have to depend on unreliable data (i.e., the opinions of those around you) or data that come far too late (i.e., your closed orders). If management can proactively assess the quality of what is in the pipeline and help salespeople disqualify low-probability opportunities earlier, pipelines won't be filled with hopes and dreams. Without a process, conversely, management tends to be a series of autopsies performed on dead proposals or lost orders. With process, corrective surgery might have been possible, and the outcome could have been a win.

Have you thought about your sales process? CRM works best for companies with well-defined processes already in place. Automate chaos and it's still chaos.

Larry Tuck, editor of *CRM* magazine, 2000

Defining the Sales Process

Many companies have established milestones and believe they have process. For traditional sellers, however, this is analogous to giving a destination without a map or directions and occasionally asking if they are going the right way. To chart a different course, it will be necessary to establish some definitions that we can build on:

Process: A defined set of repeatable, interrelated activities with outcomes that feed another activity in the process. Each outcome can be measured, so that adjustments can be made to the activities, the outcomes, or the process itself.

Sales process: A defined set of repeatable, interrelated activities from market awareness through servicing customers that allows communication of progress to date to others within the company. Each activity has an owner and a standard, measurable outcome that provides inputs to another activity. Each result can be assessed, so that improvements can be made to (1) the skills of people performing the activities and/or (2) the sales process.

Sales pipeline milestones: Measurable events that take place during a sales cycle that enable sales management to assess the status of opportunities for the purpose of forecasting. Ideally, most of these milestones are (1) objective and (2) auditable.

Sales funnel milestones: Measurable events that take place on specific opportunities that enable sales management to assess the quality of selling skills and the quantity of activity needed at the salesperson level. Again, these milestones are (1) objective and (2) auditable.

Because of the predominant perception that selling is more art than science, few companies have sales processes that traditional sellers can execute. We believe that this deficiency is the single most significant factor contributing to the disappointing results achieved with sales force automation (SFA) and customer relationship management (CRM) systems. As suggested in the above definitions, the chances of building and sustaining an executable and therefore successful sales process are slim in the absence of the following prerequisites:

1. Pipeline milestones
2. Repeatable process
3. Sales-Ready Messaging
4. CustomerCentric Selling skills
5. Consistent input
6. Auditable input

SFA and CRM systems are among the most common sales-process management techniques today. The allure of these SFA and CRM systems is that they supposedly give companies better control over their sales efforts, culminating in more accurate forecasting. But most companies attempting to implement SFA or CRM have had only one of these six components in place—the pipeline milestones—and even this tends to be updated based mainly on the opinions of salespeople.

We'd like to drill down further into three of the remaining five areas with two goals in mind: (1) defining the component and (2) offering suggestions as to how to fill any voids that may exist. Then, later in this chapter, we'll return to the pipeline milestones.

Repeatable Process

We've already introduced this idea. What is the "code" that allows the traditional salesperson to become more customer-centric? What constitutes success, and how can more people achieve it?

We should point out at this juncture that most companies have more than one sales process. For example, the selling activities will vary when selling major accounts, national accounts, mid-size accounts, add-on business, professional services, contract renewals, and so forth. Most people quickly realize that one size does not fit all; in fact, it can be a recipe for disaster to impose a single sales process on all sales. (Salespeople are fully within their rights to complain about being asked to kill a mosquito with a cannon.) Later in this chapter, we will address how to handle these different types of sales.

Consistent Input

The majority of the input to SFA/CRM systems consists of salespeople's opinions of the outcome of sales calls they make. By definition, this input is subjective and variable. Compounding the problem is the fact that the positioning of offerings falls almost exclusively on the shoulders of individual salespeople.

Consider how odd this situation is in the larger context of a business enterprise. How many other functional groups get to make this kind of report on their work, without fear of contradiction? How many other numbers that are critically important to the corporation have so much subjectivity built into them?

Auditable Input

As noted above, many companies have defined milestones—that is, clearly identified steps in a sell cycle that are used to determine where the company stands vis-à-vis a given opportunity. But asking traditional salespeople to tell what milestones they have achieved invites them to provide the answer they think their manager wants to hear, and in some cases do so in order to secure their position for another quarter. Unless or until milestones have components specific to job title and business goal that can be audited by someone other than the salesperson, input will continue to be variable. More on this topic later in the chapter.

The Trouble with the Data

We don't mean to imply that companies implementing SFA/CRM systems have failed to realize any benefit, especially in the realm of improvements in forecasting accuracy. Indeed, many have experienced some success in that area. But in many cases, part of the difficulty with these implementations has to do with poorly managed expectations about how much forecasting accuracy will increase, and when.

A few years ago, while working with a CRM vendor, we asked the vice president (VP) of Sales if the company "ate its own dog food" (i.e., used its own software to forecast). This question elicited an enthusiastic *yes!* from this executive. He then went on to say that he usually came within 5 percent of his quarterly forecast—a level of accuracy most sales executives can only dream about. We asked for details, and within seconds, he had his laptop fired up so that he could share his forecasting secrets with us.

He showed us that the company had defined seven milestones in its sales pipeline. Beginning with the first month that a salesperson started reporting on his or her pipeline, the software heuristically captured close rates at each of the milestones. When it came time to forecast, the software took each salesperson's gross pipeline and applied that salesperson's unique factors to the dollar volume represented by each of the seven milestones. In this way, he achieved his enviable forecasting accuracy.

We then asked: "Are your salespeople telling their prospects that if they use your software package, they will achieve a similar degree of forecasting accuracy?" He acknowledged that, as we hoped and expected, they were.

Next, we began to dissect how his miraculous results were being achieved, and the degree to which other companies would find them replicable. The hard fact was that it would take months or years for other companies to gain the historical close rates by salesperson that were the key component in our client's ability to predict revenue. Ironically, the only reason he could be so accurate with his forecast is that the software tracked historically how inaccurate (i.e., overoptimistic) his salespeople tended to be, in that they overstated their pipelines at each of their seven pipeline milestones. Any new users of this CRM system—in other words, all the new purchasers of the software—could only assign estimates of close rates at various milestones. Most likely, these would be across the board for all salespeople, and would become homed in at the individual salesperson level only over time.

Even with the software in place and defined milestones, moreover, forecasting accuracy could continue to be adversely affected by a range of internal and external factors:

- When salespeople leave, their historical data are no longer relevant.
- When new hires join, there are no historical data.
- Salespeople who are below quota are liable to overstate their pipeline.
- New offerings don't have the benefit of historical data.
- New vertical industries present new challenges.
- A changing economic climate can undercut the relevance of historical data.
- The changing fortunes of clients within the product segment can similarly undercut historical data.
- Offerings by competitors may raise the bar.

Fire Drills and Hail Marys

Under the *best* of circumstances, the analysis of the pipeline is based on input from the sales organization. Notable by its absence is any input from the buyer (which, as you'll see in later chapters, could give sales management a way to audit where the buyer stands in the buying cycle, and therefore provide a sanity check). With or without a CRM system, leaving the buyer out of the picture often means that the timing of asking for the business is much more a function of when the company wants (or needs) the order than of when the prospect or customer is ready to buy. In other words, it is rarely customer-centric.

Many companies spend the last few days of nearly every quarter attempting to squeeze out business in order to make their numbers. Many senior executives leave their calendars open during the last week of the quarter, allowing them to embark on "closing junkets." The tool commonly used to get buyers to commit earlier than planned is substantial discounting. Some buyers are so offended by this approach ("I was naïve to assume that the initial price they quoted was real!" or worse, "They must think I'm an idiot!") that they ultimately decide not to do business with a company that employs these kinds of traditional closing techniques.

One difficulty with selling in this fashion is that it tends to turn into standard operating procedure. Emptying the pipeline at the end of March is likely to transform April and May into the months for rebuilding the pipeline, but not closing much business. This culminates in another high-pressure close toward the end of June. Another difficulty is that savvy buyers learn to delay buying decisions, in the knowledge that they will get the absolute best price at quarter's end.

Are you skeptical that such "fire drills" are commonplace among established and reputable companies? Consider the following quote by Computer Associates' chief financial officer, Ira Zar, from an article in *Forbes*:

> Negotiations [at Computer Associates] came down to the last day of the quarter, with Hail Mary discounts of up to 55 percent fairly common in the business. In the quarter ended September 30, 2000, CA did $1 billion of its $1.6 billion in revenues in the last week. We ended up trading phone calls at 11 at night.

Prior to our working with them, one company entered the last quarter of a particular year with a chance to achieve $300 million in revenue—a threshold they had never before attained. Senior management then decided that this target was within their reach, and instructed managers and salespeople to close everything they could (i.e., go as low as necessary) so that the goal could be achieved. The good news is they succeeded, booking a few million dollars beyond the magic number. At the subsequent January kick-off meeting, jackets were distributed to everyone with that record year's revenue figure embroidered on the sleeves. The meeting proceeded with a general sense of satisfaction, accomplishment, and even euphoria. Success was in the air!

Then came the bad news. As a division of a larger company, the company received its quota from on high. The objective assigned by the parent company for the following year was $360 million—a 20 percent increase over the record revenue that had just been delivered. As you might expect, virtually nothing closed in January and February, as a result of emptying the pipeline in December. The company finished the first quarter with bookings below 50 percent year-to-date. Ultimately, it stumbled its way toward matching the revenue delivered the previous year—but not before both the chief executive officer (CEO) and the VP of Marketing were relieved of their duties midway through the second quarter. With 20-20 hindsight, the results were predictable, as the company effectively had a 10-month year to produce the revenue. You can imagine the resulting impact on profitability.

Even without being instructed to do so by their management team, many traditional salespeople are guilty of closing prematurely, often attempting to close the wrong person. Attempting to close non-decision makers (and close them prematurely) can cause several bad things to happen:

- The person being closed on may end up feeling inadequate or insignificant.
- You may convey the stress you are experiencing to the buyer, even to the point of appearing desperate.
- The person may become a messenger to the decision maker about your discounted pricing.
- If the decision maker is serious about doing business, the discount you provide to the person who cannot buy may become the starting point for negotiating further concessions.
- If the order is not closed during the quarter, you may have set an expectation of pricing that you may be unwilling or unable to meet, based on your situation when the decision can be made early in the next quarter.
- You may lose the transaction because of your bad behavior.

A sales process should contain a specified time to close that was agreed to by the buyer. Senior management can attempt to accelerate orders at their own risk.

Shaping Your Perception in the Marketplace

In most cases, companies think of their sales process as a way to control cost of sales, facilitate management of the sales force, and forecast top-line revenue more accurately.

These are all valid objectives, of course. But we take things one step further. We believe that a sales process should create a framework for relating to customers and prospects. Think about it: Many organizations develop reputations and are assigned a personality by their behavior in the marketplace. Companies become known as aggressive (Siebel and Oracle), predatory (Microsoft), arrogant (Accenture), and so on. How does this happen? In part, it happens through corporate policies, public utterances of the CEO, and similar high-level actions. But we believe that the behavior of the company's representatives in the field deserves at least as much credit (or blame).

By extension, we believe that it is possible to shape the marketplace's opinion of you by designing a customer-centric sales process that reflects the way you want your customers and prospects to be treated. In other words, the CEO can create a blueprint for customers' experience that will influence the words that salespeople use when developing buyer needs and setting expectations. We believe with equal or even slightly inferior offerings, companies can make the way their salespeople sell a differentiator. These organizations can win on sales process.

What Are the Component Parts?

A customer-centric sales process needs to cover all the steps, from market awareness through measuring results achieved by customers. It should define and comprise:

- When buying cycles begin
- The steps involved in making a recommendation
- The steps necessary to have the buyers understand their requirements
- The steps needed for buyers to understand how your offering addresses their goals and problems
- An estimated decision date documented to confirm the buyer's agreement

- Built-in feedback loops, to permit a rapid adjustment to timing issues, competitive pressures, client feedback, market issues, and external events (e.g., 9/11, Y2K)

One way of structuring a sales process is to define an appropriate set of pipeline milestones, as mentioned earlier. Consider, for example, the following set of milestones in a typical sales process:

- Access to decision maker
- Return on investment (ROI) completed
- ROI agreed to by prospect
- Billable event
- Customer resources committed
- Budget allocated (whose?)
- Meeting with Information Technology (IT)
- Business issue(s) shared or admitted
- IT technical approval
- Corporate visit
- Implementation plan
- Executive call
- Professional services call
- Specific titles called on
- Non-IT champion
- Demonstration
- Proposal submitted
- Reference site visit
- Site survey
- References provided
- Verbal agreement
- Client financials received
- On-site survey
- Financials requested by prospect
- Pilot agreed to
- Competitors identified
- Projected decision date
- Price quotation
- Compelling reason to buy
- Contracts submitted to legal
- Call made by services staff
- Contracts approved

- Billable education
- IT approval of cutover
- First-level manager call
- Trial
- Project start date defined
- Credit approval

How do you identify milestones? In addition to drawing on your own experience and process, as well as the list above, we recommend analyzing transactions from the past year or so to determine if you can isolate common factors and patterns in opportunities that you've won and lost. By so doing, it is often possible to identify and incorporate specific best practice events and use them as milestones. This can allow organizations to begin to institutionalize their best practices within a sales process and improve win rates on opportunities in the pipeline.

One company we worked with sells software, and would not allow opportunities to be qualified past a certain level unless the salesperson had made calls on business people outside of the IT department. This milestone was created because history showed that many sales cycles that began within IT ended suddenly, and unhappily, as soon as a request for funds was made without having built a business case that end-users could present to their line of business executives. On the more positive side, another client discovered that when prospects came for a corporate visit, they had an 88 percent close rate on those opportunities. Guess what recommendation we made that became a step in their sales process?

These milestones allow salespeople and management to better understand where they are in a given sell cycle. Just as important—or maybe more important—they provide insight into whether opportunities are qualified, and therefore worthy of resources. As noted in earlier chapters, many traditional salespeople take comfort in having quantity, rather than quality, in their pipelines. They are competing to keep busy, rather than to win.

Key steps in every sales process must be documented in order to be auditable. In other words, there must be a letter, fax, or e-mail from the salesperson to the buyer that summarizes key conversations. Such documentation serves multiple purposes:

1. It maximizes the chances that both the salesperson and the buyer understand where they are.

2. It allows consistent internal messaging by the buyer, within his or her organization.
3. It allows the first Key Player in a committee sale to communicate his or her vision clearly to peers and superiors.
4. It minimizes the chance that the salesperson is overoptimistic ("happy ears").
5. Most important, it allows the manager to audit and grade the opportunity.

Note that not all milestones need to be auditable. Your goal should be to define those critical ones that will allow you (or your sales managers) to grade opportunities. This is the only way to get away from the unbridled optimism (i.e., in salespeople's opinions) described earlier.

Senior management must take ownership of the customer experience and the corresponding sales process, in part by defining deliverables based on the size and complexity of a given transaction. If this is not done by management, salespeople will do it in a more informal manner—often at the annual kick-off meeting—in ways that undercut the sales process. Consider the following imaginary (but entirely plausible) exchange:

Salesperson 1: *What was your largest transaction this year without following the process?*

Salesperson 2: *$60,000.*

Salesperson 1: *Wow, mine was $30,000.*

Salesperson 3: *Got you both. Mine was $85,000!*

The simple fact is, salespeople tend to resist following a process. As a rule, they don't like documenting their sales efforts. And—still in the spirit of generalization—they like to boast of their successes outside the process, which they tend to see as bureaucratic and intrusive. In the conversation above, a policy decision has been made informally by staff who have no authority to do so.

Consider for a moment how much money it costs an organization to compete on a major transaction and lose. According to Gartner Group, the cost per sales call by a salesperson working for a high tech company is about $450, when all compensation and costs are factored in. On a major opportunity, if you were to add in management calls, support people, demonstrations, plane trips, and so on, the cost to compete on a major opportunity over the course of 6 months could easily be $30,000.

Seen in that context, is it reasonable to require that the salesperson be able to document where he or she is in the opportunity, so that the sales manager can determine if it is qualified and warrants the allocation of additional resources?

Salespeople (especially those who are not year to date against quota) intuitively know how much needs to be in their pipelines to keep their managers off their backs. When their pipelines are thin, salespeople become less selective about what they are working on. Along with the compromise in quality of opportunities comes an increasingly unbridled optimism. Here's another dialogue that may sound familiar:

> **Salesperson:** *As you know, boss, things have been slow for me the last 4 months. I've been in a slump. But this is my month! Grab onto my coattails, because we're going to have a huge month!*
>
> **Manager:** *Let's run through your forecast.*
>
> **Salesperson:** *O.K. Unexpectedly, I received an RFP this week. It looks like it was wired for us. They're going to make a decision by the end of the month. I figure it to be about an 80 percent chance. I just spoke with the ABC Company. The proposal has been sitting there for 90 days, but my friend in the account says management is getting serious again. And there's another one sitting out there! . . .*

Most likely, this salesperson will continue in this vein until the manager is persuaded that things are O.K. And most likely, that won't be too difficult, because managers want to believe. Optimistic forecasts from the sales force, as noted earlier, permit the sales manager to make his or her own forecast more optimistic. And—on the downside—asking a salesperson to leave is likely to cause disruption, distract the sales manager from more important tasks at hand, and perhaps reflect poorly on the manager.

We've presented these two dialogues in part to underscore the critical importance of having a process and managing to it. Discipline and structure are as important to sales as they are to basketball, military maneuvers, and the opera. Yes, creativity and spontaneity have their place—but not in a conversation between a salesperson and a manager of a publicly traded company about what opportunities make up the revenue forecast.

By reviewing progress (or lack thereof) against defined and auditable best practices, managers can assess the probability of winning a particular opportunity, and help salespeople do something that they are loathe to do themselves—that is, withdraw from low-probability opportunities. (For a salesperson, removing a low-probability account from the forecast generally means that a replacement will have to be found by prospecting, which is an activity that many salespeople like less than a root canal.) The role of salespeople is to *build* pipeline by executing the sales process; the role of the manager is to *grade* that pipeline, with an eye toward disqualifying. Managers should own the quality of the opportunities they allow their salespeople to spend time and resources on.

By invoking and sticking to a strong sales process, managers should be able to increase the percentage of winnable situations in the pipeline.

More Than One Process

A common misconception is that companies have a single sales process. In fact, most organizations have multiple offerings, serve different vertical industries, and engage in several different types of sales. Some examples include

- Add-on business with an existing client
- Sale of professional services
- Renewal of a maintenance agreement
- Sale to a prospect
- Sale involving a partner
- Sale through a reseller
- Major account
- National account

Given this diversity of transactions, many companies find that one size (or process) does not and cannot fit all of their selling situations. We suggest defining customer-centric steps and deliverables for your most complex sale, and then determining subsets of steps and deliverables for smaller transactions.

Targeted Conversations

In our view, a sales cycle can be distilled into a series of conversations between the seller and the buyer(s) for each defined step in a sales process. But the emphasis is on the *buyer*—that is, someone who is qualified and empowered to buy. This means that conversations have to be targeted. Sales-Ready Messaging involves defining the titles or functions of people within a prospect whom salespeople will have to call on in order to get their proposed offering sold and installed.

Once those titles have been identified, a menu of business issues for each title should be developed. As explained in our previous discussions, a buying cycle does not begin unless or until the buyer shares a goal that your offering can help them achieve. Once you have a title and a business objective, you are in a position to have a targeted conversation.

See the Targeted Conversations examples in Figure 5-1. This simply lists four titles at a prospect company and assigns a total of eight goals to them. Obvious? Perhaps. But we've seen most salespeople start making sales calls without this kind of structured and focused approach.

Another advantage of developing this kind of list is that it can include inputs from more than just the salespeople. In fact, people at many levels in the selling organization can contribute. In addition, targeting conversations permits a more consistent positioning of offerings, because the responsibility for positioning no longer falls solely on the shoulders of the salespeople. And finally, we find that targeting conversations tends to push conversations up higher in the hierarchy—and the higher in the organization a salesperson calls, the shorter the potential menu of business issues, the more predictable the ensuing conversation, and the more likely the sale.

Title	Goal
VP Finance	Achieve profit projections with accurate sales forcasting
VP Finance	Reduce the cost of sales
VP Sales	Improved forecasting accuracy
VP Sales	Shorten start-up time for new sales reps
VP Sales	Increase the number of B and C reps who make quota
VP Mktg	Provide sales-ready messaging to sales force
CIO	Support implementation with limited resources
CIO	Secure customer/pipeline data from competition

Figure 5-1 Integrating Marketing and Sales Targeted Conversations for Selling: Sales Force Automation

The Wired versus the Unwired

Here's a piece of traditional sales wisdom: "Winners never quit, and quitters never win."

Nonsense. We believe that most organizations don't quit often enough, or early enough, when the odds are against them. Without a defined sales process, they don't know that the odds are against them.

Consider the case where a firm receives a "wired" request for proposal (RFP) that requests responses from ten vendors, and a sales manager authorizes the 60 hours needed (by multiple people) to prepare a response. (By *wired*, we mean that the fix is on, and the process is not truly open.) Would you agree that the salesperson who generated the initial interest, and shaped the RFP's requirements with a bias toward his or her own organization's strengths, has a 90-plus percent probability of getting the work? We would.

Now let's say that six other organizations choose to respond. What probability will the salespeople from those six firms enter on their respective forecasts? In most cases, the win rate on unsolicited RFPs is less than 5 percent. But if a salesperson were honest and assigned a 5 percent probability to this effort, his manager would almost certainly ask why 60 hours should be spent in crafting such a careful response to such a low-percentage opportunity.

Experienced salespeople skirt this issue by assigning even the wildest long shots at least a 50 percent probability. If you think about it, being a salesperson is one of the most measurable jobs in the world (percentage of quota obtained), but one of the least accountable. The 60 hours are spent, and when the order goes somewhere else, that opportunity quietly falls off the radar screen. In this example, even though only one favorable decision could possibly be made, six organizations within the vendor community have acted as if they all had at least a fifty-fifty chance at getting the contract.

This points out the fact that in defining your sales process, it may make sense for your organization to define two RFP processes. One should be for RFPs that your company has proactively uncovered and driven. A second one could be defined for RFPs in which you have been mainly reactive—that is, not well positioned to influence any of the requirements in the RFP prior to your receiving it.

To give you an idea of win percentages: We worked with a company selling enterprise software that had an entire department that did nothing but respond to RFPs. The previous year, they had reviewed their records and divided RFPs into proactive and reactive initiation. They discovered that in 1 year they had responded to 143 unsolicited RFPs that required an average of 75 hours—and got the business a grand total of three times! Long story short: Responding to RFPs that you did not initiate can be a huge drain on your resources. Consider segmenting your sales process, and investing your limited resources where they'll give you the most return.

Further Segmentation Opportunities

For companies having multiple divisions with independent sales forces, and/or those using value-added resellers (VAR's), it may be helpful to take a step back and decide who you want calling, and where. While this seems fundamental, sales organizations tend to evolve over time, and they sometimes get out of touch with a changing reality. A fresh look— a "clean sheet of paper" approach—can be helpful in stepping away from the trees and looking at the forest.

One account we worked with sold engineering software, and over time had developed an extensive reseller channel. They shared with us their desire to migrate their direct sales force from departmental technical sales to Fortune 1000 enterprise sales. After better understanding their direction, we attempted to segment their territories and markets and how they were being covered. We ultimately came up with a grid (see Chapter 17 and Figure 17-1) with the key demarcations they wanted:

1. Sales below $10,000 should be handled by their Telesales group.
2. Transactions with F1000 companies should be sold by their direct sales force.
3. Transactions with non-F1000 companies below $50,000 should be done by resellers.
4. Non-F1000 transactions over $50,000 should be handled jointly.

After defining these thresholds and where they wanted people to be calling, we asked the firm's sales executives what their coverage looked like currently. They sheepishly admitted that they had the small company/ small transaction quadrant covered jointly, transactions over $50,000 with small companies were rare, and virtually none of their direct salespeople were capable of executing an enterprise sale to the F1000. Further investigation uncovered the roots of the problem:

1. Their traditional salespeople were comfortable leading with product and talking to engineers, but were unable to relate to business people.
2. Their compensation plan provided an override on business sold by resellers in the direct salesperson territories. Some direct salespeople were making a great living by doing nothing more than overseeing the efforts of their assigned partners, and hadn't closed any business of their own in over a year.

The executives realized that in order to achieve the desired coverage, it would be necessary to train their salespeople to make higher-level calls, and that the compensation plan had to change. Due to their concern about the potential loss of many of their direct salespeople, we suggested a 12-month weaning period, during which the override would be phased out. This approach allowed the pipeline on larger accounts to be built. Turnover was minimal, and a high percentage of direct salespeople who were either unable or unwilling to make the adjustment to large account enterprise sales voluntarily joined reseller organizations—a favorable outcome for all concerned.

This situation was discussed, and an approach to resolving it was completed, in about an hour. We don't claim to be geniuses, and in fact, none of the concepts came close to being rocket science. But we think the example underscores the fact that most sales processes evolve over time and that a fresh look is often a good idea. (And in many cases, inviting in an outsider for a new perspective turns out to be productive.)

The Clean Sheet of Paper

When it comes to sales process, an occasional "clean sheet of paper" look is a good idea.

Take, for example, a company that starts with a few salespeople and co-founders selling the first few accounts, then evolves into a $250 million organization using both direct and indirect sales. The VP of Sales was the first salesperson hired all those years ago. A wonderful success story, all around—and yet, in our experience, the company could derive a great deal of benefit from a third party facilitating a session to evaluate (1) where the business is heading, (2) what markets they are attempting to penetrate, and (3) who is calling where.

Just as offerings, markets, and sales situations are dynamic, sales processes, too, must be reviewed and adjusted on an ongoing basis, if they are to reflect how your salespeople sell. A review is advisable, and milestones should be either verified or modified by analyzing the results. This may be done as often as quarterly, for a relatively new market or offering, or on an annual basis for mature organizations.

As suggested above, consider reviewing your top five wins to highlight best practices in selling. And as unpleasant a task as it may be, review your toughest five losses as well, in an attempt to see if your process needs to be changed.

Process Is Structure

Our view is that a sales process represents the management team's best understanding of how buying cycles take place, and how to fit into those cycles.

As with most processes involving human behavior, there can and will be exceptions that must be made under certain circumstances. While some sales methodologies treat selling situations as being black or white, experience has taught us there are many, many shades of gray.

If the potential usages of your offerings are highly variable (i.e., consulting, professional services), process becomes more important. The worst-case scenario is a salesperson calling on a buyer who has a wide spectrum of responses and reactions without a plan of how to handle the call. In one sense, sales process tries to put structure around the number of sales calls made during a sales cycle.

Without sales process, every situation is an exception based on the seller's opinions. Despite the potential benefit of repetition, everything gets done "once in a row." This can be costly at several levels:

1. Salespeople are determining when and how to compete. These are people whose compensation is based on gross revenue, without regard for the amount of resources required either to win or to lose. Their qualification skills in filtering out low-probability opportunities tend to be proportional to their year-to-date quota positions. For someone behind quota who is working marginal opportunities, things are likely to get worse, not better.
2. Without putting structure around sales situations, selling organizations lack the ability to drill down and better understand the

kinds of circumstances that are likely to result in unsuccessful sales cycles—or, conversely, are likely to lead to sales.

CEOs frequently proclaim to the investment community that their firms embody "best practices." Unfortunately, we rarely hear this claim made in regard to sales—probably because most companies don't do so, and wouldn't dare to claim to. In fact, when it comes to sales, they're not even sure that best practices exist. (It's an art, right?)

We believe that a milestone-based road map that can be audited is absolutely essential. Sales is less an art, and more a craft. While the design and implementation of an effective sales process are formidable tasks, the upside—having better control over top-line revenue generation—can be absolutely invaluable.

CHAPTER 6

Integrating the Sales and Marketing Processes

IN MANY CASES, the difference between a company that is enjoying success and one that is struggling is the degree of integration and cooperation among the functional departments. If the relationships among Engineering, Manufacturing, Purchasing, Finished Goods, Accounting, and so on, are poorly defined, you can have anything ranging from disorganization to chaos. CEOs are hired, in part, to create and maintain effective relationships among functional organizational "silos," and—in the best of cases—to break down the walls between those silos. And most CEOs will tell you that they're pretty good at that role.

Our professional experience has focused us on the interface between two of these functional areas: Sales and Marketing. (We'll use the generic term *marketing*, but in this and subsequent chapters, our focus is on product and tactical marketing rather than, say, institutional marketing, strategic marketing, or consumer packaged goods marketing.) We believe strategic marketing means looking at the convergence of market factors, technology trends, productivity improvements, and the like and asking questions like "Who and where do we want to be 3 years out? Five years out? What decisions must we make today to position ourselves for where we want to be in the future?" Tactical marketing's mission is to figure out how to achieve today's revenue targets with today's offerings.

In the business-to-business (B2B) world, our experience tells us that the interface between Sales and tactical marketing is often neglected, and frequently tenuous—limited, in some cases, to a lead's being passed from one to the other. On the face of it, this most common touch point is a weak reed to lean on. Imagine if the VPs of Sales and Marketing were each asked to define a lead. How closely do you think those two definitions would resemble each other?

If we dig deeper, we believe the root cause of the problem between Sales and Marketing is a lack of formal awareness and process to gather knowledge about how customers use their offerings to achieve goals, solve problems, and satisfy needs. In most organizations we work with, product development is also culpable. How many technology companies have been founded by a technologist who created a solution that was looking for a problem?

Later in this book we are going to show you how to create an organization's "core content"—content that will enable business conversations with decision makers and influencers. Content that will enable Web visitors to understand how they might use your offerings. Content that will permeate the rest of your tactical marketing vehicles—white papers, brochures, advertising, trade shows, and so forth—and make its way into your customer and sales training.

We believe that a key component of creating B2B core content is tapping the experience of our client's customer service people and professional services people. These are the people who are responsible every day for helping customers use their offerings to do their jobs and satisfy their needs. They have the customer usage knowledge we need to help them create Sales-Ready Messaging.

In virtually all organizations, Sales and Marketing are expected somehow to collaborate. These two functions within an organization ultimately drive top-line revenue, and yet few companies have a working definition of how they are supposed to interact. Further complicating things is the fact that in many organizations, marketing activity is neither clearly defined nor readily measurable. This overall lack of clearly defined roles and responsibilities contributes to what is frequently a strained relationship. In the extreme, when revenue targets and market share numbers are not achieved, the result is a rash of finger pointing.

An all too typical example of how each side views the other, when things get testy:

> **Sales on Marketing:** *Ivory-tower big-picture people with no clue as to what customers need!*

> **Marketing on Sales:** *Overpaid order takers who will promise almost anything to get the business!*

The executive to whom both functions report—most often, the CEO or another senior-level person—is sometimes called on to "referee" their relationship, especially after the finger pointing sets in. This is a difficult and unpleasant role. Who's to blame for the fact that revenue objectives are not being met? We've already seen how selling (in most organizations) is a pretty haphazard activity. And inside the walls of the organization, the assessment of Marketing's performance is almost entirely subjective.

Often, in the early stages of our interactions with a client CEO, we find an opportunity to ask him or her to describe Marketing's role as it relates to sales. Usually, there's a long pause, meaning that the executive doesn't have a ready answer to this question. (There would be no similar pause if the question focused, for example, on the relationship between engineering and manufacturing.) After some hemming and hawing, we tend to get responses like the following:

- They support sales.
- They position our offerings.
- They generate leads for sales.
- They create collateral for our offerings.
- They run our seminars and trade shows.

From the CEO's perspective, the good news is that over the past several decades, many companies have made huge progress in establishing clear and effective processes to govern the relationships among Accounting, Engineering, Manufacturing, and so on. The bad news is that Sales and Marketing have resisted this kind of progress. By any measure, this is an enormous lost opportunity. These two functions define, almost exclusively, the company's relationship with its customers, and ultimately are responsible for driving and achieving top-line revenue. Think how much a business could benefit from putting processes in place that would get these two functional silos—traditionally uncooperative—to (1) work together, and (2) work for the good of the customer.

A Natural Integration

We believe this is possible, because we've seen this transformation take place in literally dozens of different settings. Here's a necessary first step: Marketing must view itself as the front end of the sales process, rather than the back end of product development.

Sound simple, or like some sort of psychological sleight of hand? Not really. Before two groups can coordinate their efforts, they need to settle on one or more common objectives. We've already described Customer-Centric Selling as a way of helping buyers achieve a goal, solve a problem, or satisfy a need. Well, shouldn't that also be Marketing's objective, as well—to help potential customers understand how they can achieve a goal, solve a problem, or satisfy a need with the company's offering? If, in addition to creating the "view from 30,000 feet," Marketing could contribute effectively to the conversations that salespeople have with their prospects and customers—the "view from three-and-a-half feet"—all would benefit.

But this can't happen unless Marketing joins forces with Sales. To restate the imperative stated above: Marketing has to believe that they are the first car on the train of sales, rather than the last car on the train of product development. Marketing has to learn to face the customer, learn from the customer, and enable the customer, rather than look toward the lab.

Many marketing executives, of course, claim that they are already supporting Sales. They are handling messaging; generating leads for Sales (but what really *is* a lead?—see Chapter 9); creating collateral for product and service offerings, seminars, and trade shows; and, of course, cranking out PowerPoint presentations for senior executives. But the evidence suggests that whatever they're currently doing, it's not working. Feedback from the American Marketing Association's Customer Message Management Forums indicates that between 50 and 90 percent of the collateral prepared by Marketing is not used by salespeople in the field.

Clearly, something new is needed. We suggest that the first change needs to be a shift of affiliation within the organization. This is primarily a psychological shift, but it can also take many procedural and even physical forms. (How is the organizational chart drawn? Whose office is next to whose? Which departments are physically adjacent?)

A second step is to formally charge Marketing with the responsibility for developing and maintaining the company's core content—in other words, its sales messaging. Sales-Ready Messaging must be created to support targeted conversations with decision makers and decision influencers. As stated in earlier chapters, this cannot be accomplished with product information, it requires product *usage* information positioned specifically for decision-maker job titles within targeted industries. We strongly recommend to many of our clients that they consider creating the post of chief content officer. This is an individual who takes responsibility for all product usage messaging—the positioning of an organization's offerings at all levels and through all channels.

In today's business environment, most companies are trying to eliminate positions, and we don't make this recommendation lightly. But think about the potential benefit that grows out of this kind of change. We now have a way to begin a natural, organic integration of the Marketing and Sales functions: Both Marketing and Sales share the common mission of helping customers achieve goals, solve problems, and satisfy needs through the use of the company's offerings.

The sales and support teams in the field are closest to the customers and prospects. If a tool doesn't work in making a call, they're the first to know. They therefore have to serve as constructive malcontents—meaning that they have to suggest how messaging tools can be improved and kept up to date. They have to bring back from the field new insights into how offerings are actually used, and not used, by customers.

Marketing, meanwhile, must own the content. It owns the responsibility for achieving consistency of message and dissemination across multiple sales channels, multiple product lines, and so on. In the past 10 years we have seen technology increase the touch points that are now available to Marketing. Consider email, Web sites, Webinars, banner ads, CDs, and so forth. Adding the responsibility of Sales-Ready Messaging dramatically increases the scope of Marketing's job, which is the reason we believe the title chief content officer is more appropriate.

Learning from the Web

For a number of reasons, we love the Web.

One reason, relevant to this chapter, is that it tends to put Marketing directly in touch with buyers. Think about it: In most organizations, Marketing owns the Web site. Every day, dozens—or hundreds, or thousands—of visitors show up on the organization's electronic doorstep. Some are only window-shopping, of course. But in many cases, they are trying to buy.

True, they may have gotten there as a result of a salesperson making an in-person sales call or a demand creation campaign. But now they're at the doorstep, and ready to be influenced, if the Web site is up to the challenge. As a result, the Web is giving organizations—and specifically marketing groups within those organizations—the opportunity to develop a rich and nuanced understanding of what customers want to accomplish. In addition to information dissemination or even order fulfillment, Web sites can be designed to help Marketing learn: "How do you use our products?" "What were you able to accomplish?" "How would you like to use our products in the future?"

This understanding can profoundly influence subsequent messaging (and ultimately, perhaps, research and development, product development, and engineering). When Marketing relates directly to buyers by means of a Web site, they begin to understand the necessity for facilitating the buying process with meaningful electronic dialogs. You don't handle an objection on a Web site; instead, you make it easy for buyers to get good answers to and work through their questions. You don't close a sale on the Web site; instead, you make it easy for buyers to take action to satisfy their own needs. When the Web visitor hits "enter" and buys, it may be because Marketing was able to facilitate the buying process. In other words, in the electronic manifestation, Marketing has acted exactly like an effective, customer-centric salesperson.

The Web is not the answer to everything, of course. In most enterprise selling situations, for example, salespeople are necessary. But think how much more effective Marketing can be, in providing tools and collateral to support enterprise selling, when they have had sustained, iterative contact with the customer base through the Web. They are far better prepared to develop Sales-Ready Messaging to support all the many conversations that add up to an effective customer-centric sales process.

Toward a Selling Architecture

Sales-Ready Messaging, as we've already noted, means empowering salespeople to have meaningful conversations with decision makers and decision influencers about how they can achieve a goal, solve a problem, or satisfy a need through the use of the offering. Sales-Ready Messaging also empowers Web visitors to understand how they can achieve a goal, solve a problem, or satisfy a need through the use of the offering. When you combine this effective core content with sales process, you gain the capability of codifying, or architecting, sales conversations and sales cycles.

As we've already seen, many organizations are currently struggling to implement customer relationship management (CRM) systems. With Sales and Marketing integrated at the salesperson level, the desired return on a company's CRM investment now becomes achievable. But in real life, most CRM systems are failing because the sales force automation (SFA) component is failing. We believe that by integrating product usage messaging with defined sales processes, the manual sales productivity system can now be automated. We have developed "best practice" sales processes for multiple industries. With the SFA component enhanced with sales process and just-in-time Sales-Ready Messaging, CRM systems can begin to produce tangible, measurable results.

And this is a big deal. The CRM business is in trouble. There is a huge amount of CRM "shelfware" out there. CRM software companies are being forced by their market to become CRM solution companies. Recognizing this gap, at least two CRM vendors (Siebel Systems and Onyx Software) acquired sales training companies in the late 1990s. If sales processes can be integrated with marketing processes, which include Sales-Ready Messaging, CEOs can gain control over generating top-line revenue, and organizations can improve their relationships with their customers.

In subsequent chapters, we'll describe the components of a sales process that allows sharing of best sales practices, defines the relationship between Sales and Marketing, facilitates creation of Sales-Ready Messaging, allows managers to ensure pipeline quality while assessing and developing their direct reports, and ultimately results in an improved ability to forecast revenue at the opportunity level.

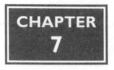

CHAPTER 7

Features versus Customer Usage

IN THIS CHAPTER, we're going to pick up on a theme introduced earlier: the need to focus on how a customer might use a product—growing out of conversations about that customer's needs—rather than on a presentation of a product's features.

Here's a question you might want to ask us, at this point: Is CustomerCentric Selling applicable in a range of situations? For example, is it applicable when a product is viewed as a commodity with no distinguishing features?

Our methodology is based in large part on our recent experiences, many of which have involved selling information technology at the enterprise level. But the principle of positioning offerings applies whether you are trying to make an enterprise sale for an intangible offering, selling the phone company's services, or helping a bank that is trying to cross-sell additional features or services directly to consumers.

Over the years, we have worked with a wide range of companies in a variety of industries. These have included professional services providers, retail banks, companies offering credit card sales to merchants, overnight delivery services, and temporary housing providers, to name a few. All benefited from our approach, even in cases where the offering was only one of many in a crowded field of entries. In fact, our experience suggests that in situations where the offering is perceived as a commodity—that is, interchangeable with the competition—the most powerful differentiator is the buyer's experience with the salesperson or sales process.

The Pinocchio Effect

As noted in earlier chapters, traditional sellers tend to lead with product—that is, to push hard on what they perceive to be the distinguishing characteristics of their offering. But this approach is fraught with peril. It often fails, for example, to establish a salesperson's competence. It short-circuits meaningful discussion of the buyer's needs. It may lead to premature price discussions, causing sticker shock, and ultimately result in no sale. Many traditional salespeople fail to realize that only those differentiators that the buyers agree they want or need are applicable.

Part of the problem is the seller's familiarity with the offering—most often thought of as a great asset. Think about how traditional salespeople learn about their products. In many cases, newly hired salespeople are sent off to what their employers call *product training* during their very first week on the job. In many organizations, this instruction is referred to as *sales training*, but it should not be, in our estimation. This training is frequently conducted by the Product Marketing department.[1]

More and more companies are building infrastructures in Product Marketing. In many cases, these efforts lead to what might be called a Pinocchio effect: The product begins to take on a life of its own, aside from any customer-related considerations. The apparent mission of Product Marketing is to talk about what "it" will do—"it" being the product. It will lower your inventory costs, it will build your market share, it will improve your profitability, it will reduce your employee turnover . . . (feel free to fill in any unsubstantiated claims your Pinocchio can accomplish).

This is backward. At the end of a call made by a customer-centric seller, the buyers shouldn't be focusing on what *it* can do for them; they should be focusing on what *they* can do with it. The conclusion is inescapable: The focus of both salespeople and buyers should be on product usage, not product features.

---

[1] In this case, we'll use the specific term *product marketing*, rather than the broader *marketing*.

Features and Benefits

What's a feature? For our purposes, a feature is an attribute of a product or service. Features include things like size, weight, color, material used, modules, and specifications. Product Marketing people take artistic license with these facts, adding adjectives to heighten the feature's presumed sex appeal and thereby make the product even more irresistible. This is where words like *robust*, *seamless*, and *integrated* begin to creep in.

The primary problem we have with sellers being taught to lead with features is that this approach counts on the buyer's knowing whether or not the feature is useful and therefore relevant. Yes, there are hundreds of thousands of salespeople who lead with product features in their sales pitches every day, and yes, in a lot of cases, it actually works. But it works best when buyers already understand how to use the proposed product or service, understand the value of using it, trust the seller, and trust the seller's company.

Information or Irritation?

Let's say that you are a satisfied BMW customer, and you go into a BMW dealership shopping for your next Beamer. You already know the product line, already trust the company, and already have a pretty good idea of which model you are interested it. Up comes the salesperson, and begins lecturing you on the way-cool new features of something called "I-Drive." As a buyer, can you get past this feature presentation? Probably. You'll listen for a while, take a test drive, and—all else being equal—you'll buy your BMW. Were you impressed by the salesperson or by I-Drive? Not really. How much selling was done here? Not much. You came in the door as an expert buyer, and you bought. If you didn't buy, has the salesperson earned your loyalty? Wouldn't you buy the same car for $500 less from another dealer? The seller has missed an opportunity to become part of your buying decision.

So is it a good idea for salespeople to spew features? Almost never. The expert buyer already knows about, or knows enough not to care much about, I-Drive. As for the rest of the buying population—most people, in other words—those who do not understand I-Drive might not ask for an explanation that could expose their ignorance to someone they don't trust. They could be intimidated, and start to distance themselves from the salesperson. Most people have their own version of I-Drive in their buying past. For example: Have you ever been told that the car you are thinking about buying has an overhead camshaft? Well, do you know or care what an overhead cam is, or how that feature might be useful to you? How about a McPherson strut? Does that sound like something you might put to good use? Could you explain the usage or value of these commonly spewed features at a cocktail party?

The CustomerCentric definition of selling is "helping a buyer achieve a goal, solve a problem, or satisfy a need." So what do we do if we're not BMW—if our buyer has no clue as to why he or she might need our product, or how to use it? Presumably, our product has some features that are of interest. So how do we position our features to nonexpert buyers?

The first step in a buying process, of course, is having someone decide to look. Assuming that our business-development efforts succeed in stimulating some measure of curiosity or interest on the part of prospective buyers who we believe should be looking at our offering, what then? They will stay interested only as long as they are curious about what we are selling, understand the importance of our offering to them, or have hope for a solution from us. If we launch into a feature presentation, we will lose most nonexpert buyers very quickly. They will stay interested only as long as they perceive the conversation, and therefore the seller, to be relevant.

Many salespeople experience a 6- to 12-month learning curve when they join companies selling enterprise solutions. In those weeks and months, they frequently get their heads stuffed full of product features—which in the case of a complex product may number in the hundreds or even the thousands. Then they go out into their territories and attempt to convey their personal versions of that vast mental archive in a 30-minute presentation—and are surprised, and frustrated, when their prospects don't get it. How well can CEOs sleep when they come to the realization that each of their 200 salespeople has developed his or her own boiled-down version (opinions?) of what the company sells?

In most cases, the buyer who doesn't get it isn't stupid. So what's going on in a buyer's head when he or she encounters a seller describing a product as a noun (versus a verb)? Here are some of the questions a buyer may be asking:

- "Is the salesperson trying to sell me?"
- "Am I supposed to understand what the salesperson is talking about?"
- "Why is the salesperson telling me this?"

- "Why does the salesperson think I would be interested in *that*?"
- "Am I supposed to take the salesperson's word for it?"
- "Are these facts or opinions?"

In situations like this, buyers defend themselves with objections. Dozens of sales courses over the years have had modules on handling objections, as if an objection were an ailment or character flaw in the buyer. Many companies have taught the "feel, felt, found" approach. When encountering objections, the seller takes three steps:

1. "I understand how you feel."
2. "Others have felt that way."
3. "But they found that (insert phrasing indicating that the buyer is mistaken in having the concern mentioned)."

The fact is, most objections that salespeople encounter are salesperson-induced. Sellers invite objections by the way they present their offerings.

Even some sales approaches that seem customer-friendly are really "spray-and-pray" presentations in disguise. In early Xerox sales training, for example, salespeople were taught to talk about benefits: "Because of Feature X, dear buyer, you can expect to get Benefit Y!" But strangely enough, Xerox's sellers were not encouraged to find out what the buyer wanted to accomplish before they made their initial benefit statement. In that sales culture, therefore, the alleged benefit of a feature resided mainly in the mind of the seller.

And Xerox was not unique in this regard. We sometimes ask our audiences the question, "What sales culture did you grow up in?" Most large selling organizations have their subtle sales-culture idiosyncrasies, but virtually all of them encourage presumptuous benefit statements by sellers to buyers.

The Power of Usage Scenarios

Our experience has taught us that great salespeople rarely have to close, and that great sales calls are conversations, rather than presentations. Customer-centric salespeople are able—usually with very little help from their Marketing department—to translate the feature knowledge they are given by Product Marketing into usage scenarios. These are simply hypothetical examples that are highly relevant to the buyer and that the seller can use to conduct intelligent conversations. They somehow just roll off the tongue of a customer-centric salesperson.

As noted, those are the lucky 10 percent. But what about the other 90 percent? What about salespeople who are unable to do the feature-to-usage-scenario translation on their own?

Let's say we have a seller in his late twenties who is going to make a sales call on a senior executive in her mid-fifties—let's have her be the Vice President of Sales of a Fortune 1000 company. The seller's mission is to convince the buyer to spend hundreds of thousands of dollars on a customer relationship management (CRM) system, which is an application she does not fully understand. How can we help this young seller relate to this buyer? How can we help him have a conversation, rather than make a presentation?

One of the features of the CRM application is control over access to specific data—that is, who can see what—in a company's database. Most likely, an expert buyer can understand this feature and relate it easily to his or her own use. Most senior executives, however, are not adept at understanding how software can help them achieve their business goals. What can the seller do?

Well, most senior sales executives understand high employee turnover. Suppose the seller asked a question like, "What if you heard through a reliable source that one of your top salespeople was going to leave to go to work for your competition?" If the executive expressed interest, the salesperson could then pose another question: "Would it be useful to you to be able to go into your CRM system and suspend that person's access to your prospect and buyer data—from any location, even if you were traveling?"

This is an example of converting a feature into a usage scenario. It works because it is so specific. It shows the prospective buyer how the data security feature could be used by the executive to protect company assets in the event of employee turnover. Usage scenarios help buyers visualize how they could use the seller's offering to solve a problem, achieve a goal, make money, or save money.

The above example involves a complex enterprise software sale. What about simple retail sales? Would converting from product presentations to usage scenarios also be preferable?

We gave a presentation at a Silicon Valley marketing executive symposium at the Stanford Business School. At the end of our talk, a senior vice president of a retail bank approached us with the idea of trying out our ideas in a banking context. Specifically, their issue was cross selling. At that time, the average number of bank products (savings account, checking account, ATM card, CD, and so on) for a retail bank buyer was 2.2. His bank was below average—at 1.9—and he was under heavy pressure to increase cross selling.

First, we needed to learn how they were currently selling before we could suggest any changes. We were observing one morning when a couple from out of state came into a branch near one of the campuses of the state university system. They had their daughter in tow. After a brief wait, they were steered toward the desk of a 23-year-old retail banker, whom we'll call "Sarah."

"Our daughter will be going to school here," the father told Sarah. "We want to open up a checking account for her."

Sarah immediately brought out her sales kit, which included details about the four checking account plans. She detailed each, and asked the buyers if they were prepared to select one. Then she remembered the new corporate priority—cross selling—and asked politely, "Would you also like a savings account?"

No, thanks, said the father, they did their banking back home in Iowa. They simply needed a local checking account for their daughter while she was in college.

We told the bank that this was one approach to cross selling, but that we thought there was room for improvement. The bank's marketing head decided to let us try out our ideas on a pilot basis. After we studied how consumers actually used each of the bank's products, we developed usage scenarios, and (in a predetermined pilot region) trained their retail people in the use of these scenarios.

Here is an example of adopting a customer-centric approach to cross selling: A couple from Nebraska visited a branch office to open a checking account for their daughter, who would be attending school near the bank. This time, before working through the specifics of the checking account, the retail banker asked a number of usage-scenario questions. For example:

- When you are back in Nebraska, would it be useful for you to be able to check on your daughter's balance by using the Internet?
- When you are back home, would you like to be able to transfer money from your bank account there to your daughter's account here simply by using the Internet?

- If your daughter has a roadside emergency, would you like her to be able to get emergency funds anytime she wants—but still not have her hand in your wallet?

Good questions, right? Questions that you would like to be asked by a representative of a bank that you're doing business with, and that demonstrates customer-centric expertise in dealing with circumstances like your own. Well, guess what happened: Through the use of these kinds of usage-scenario questions, cross selling in the pilot region went up 100 percent. In truth, the bank had no product differentiation whatsoever from its competition. The difference lay in patience, process, and content—in architecting the buyer's experience with the seller. It lay in shifting from feature selling to customer-usage selling.

Another, slightly more complicated, example of converting from feature to customer-usage selling involved the call center of a telecommunications company in a large metropolitan area. When new residents moved into the area, they typically called to set up their phone service—service initiation. We're willing to bet that almost everyone reading this book understands what call waiting is, and what it enables you to do. But imagine it's the early 1990s, you *don't* understand call waiting, and someone is trying to sell it to you. Chances are that you'll have to ask some follow-up questions before you get it—and maybe even buy it. Even then, the phone company would hope mightily that you would keep that service for at least 6 months, so that they could break even.

Let's assume that a call center representative of a phone company today were speaking with a retired couple in their late seventies or early eighties. During the service-initiation process, the call center representative asks a series of "do you want . . ." questions regarding the company's various products: call forwarding, voice mail, call waiting, paging, and so on. If a free trial were offered, might people say yes to these features?

The problem for the phone company arose when many of these services were discontinued 3 to 6 months after initiation. The phone company needed these additional services to stay installed for at least 6 months to break even on them; after that, the arithmetic was good. So how do you keep new services installed? Customers must realize the value of the services and understand how to use them.

In the case of our client, our analysis revealed that many buyers didn't know *why* they needed the additional services they were saying yes to, or *how* they would use them. Some elderly purchasers of call waiting were calling customer service complaining that their phones "keep on beeping." Others objected strenuously when their phone bills went up in the fourth month—perhaps forgetting that the premium services that they had subscribed to (and that they had never used) were offered free of charge for the first 3 months.

In designing an approach to this customer issue, we first developed a simple spreadsheet of available features (the y axis) and their related buyer issues (the x axis). We then worked through a series of diagnostic questions and usage scenarios for their customer service representatives to use while taking orders during service initiation.

Example

Call center representative

> Have friends or family tried to reach you while you have been on the phone?
>
> Have they been frustrated by busy signals?
>
> Have you missed, or been delayed in receiving, important calls?

If (and *only* if) the buyer says yes to these questions, the call center representative then asks:

> "If someone attempts to call you while you are already on a call, would it be useful if you could hear a tone, and—at your option—click the receiver to put the first call on hold, take the incoming call, and when finished, click the receiver to resume your original call?"

If the buyer answers with a yes, the call center representative can then close the sale:

> Our Call Waiting feature provides this capability at a cost of only $4.95 per month. Would you like to try it for 30 days, at no charge?

It's not rocket science, right? But it works. By taking the time to ask a few simple questions about need and customer usage—and, not unimportantly, to educate the consumer about the usage and value of particular services—the company was able to cut discontinuances dramatically. And, we should stress, the company was able to deliver services to people who understood and appreciated them, and were willing to pay for them. A win-win outcome, all around.

The Shared Mission

In simple terms: What we propose to our clients is the reinvention of their marketing efforts away from Product Marketing and toward what might be called customer-usage marketing.

The core enabler in this reinvention process is the CustomerCentric Selling Solution Development Prompter, to be explained in subsequent chapters. Once the theme of customer usage replaces the traditional emphasis on product features, all kinds of good things can start to happen across multiple marketing vehicles. These include, for example:

- Prospect and customer correspondence
- Product development
- Advertising
- Success stories
- White papers
- Web site
- Trade-show strategies
- Demand-creation strategies
- Buyer training
- Sales training
- Professional-services training

When Marketing becomes focused on customer usage, it shares a mission with Sales: helping buyers discover how they can achieve their goals, solve their problems, and satisfy their needs through the use of their company's offerings. For companies without this shared mission, CEOs will continue to lose sleep at night, knowing that the forecast consists of the opinions of sellers who each developed their own boiled-down version of what they're selling.

CHAPTER 8

Creating Sales-Ready Messaging

SELLING AT ITS BEST consists of a series of conversations with buyers. During these conversations, the salesperson's objective is to uncover and understand the buyer's needs, problems, desires, and goals. As the salesperson learns about the buyer's circumstances, he or she also begins to position the company's offerings. An additional benefit of a competent diagnosis is that the root causes of why the buyer cannot achieve a goal, solve a problem, or satisfy a need are clarified.

Selling organizations would dearly love to influence and steer these conversations. But this seems like an impossibly ambitious and far-reaching objective—so ambitious, in fact, that most such organizations that have considered it have dismissed it out of hand. In this chapter, we lay out a strategy to accomplish that goal.

No, you can't anticipate all potential interactions with buyers at all levels. You can't "boil the ocean," as the saying goes. (And most likely, the salesperson who went in with the boiled ocean crammed into his head would be a poor conversationalist.) So our approach is to help the salesperson orchestrate conversations with targeted decision makers and influencers about specific business issues addressable with their offering. After having such a buyer share a goal, we help the salesperson follow one of a number of flexible scenarios.

Looking at this issue from another perspective, companies that fail to step up to the challenge of influencing sales conversations are abdicating an enormous degree of responsibility to their salespeople. They are asking their salespeople to interpret and communicate the capabilities of their products single-handedly.

So let's begin with the three conditions that must exist in order to have an effective sales conversation about an offering:

- The buyer's title (or function) and vertical industry must be known.
- The buyer must share a business goal or admit a business problem.
- The seller's offerings must have capabilities that a targeted buyer can use to achieve a goal, solve a problem, or satisfy a need—and, of course, the seller must understand and articulate those capabilities.

Given these three conditions, we believe, organizations can help their traditional salespeople have these kinds of sales conversations. They can create Sales-Ready Messaging—a way of approaching a conversation that greatly increases the chances of success.

A Caveat

We will return to this premise throughout the remaining chapters, but we want to offer a caveat at this point: The higher within an organization a salesperson calls, the more predictable the conversation. Traditional sales managers will respond well to this observation, of course, since they're always begging their salespeople to shoot higher.

But we're making the same point for a different reason: The higher in the organization you call, the smaller the number of business objectives you are likely to encounter. This sounds a little counterintuitive, but it's not: In general, senior people worry about a finite number of important issues. Conversations with senior management tend to be shorter, more conceptual, and less technical—which in many cases means they're more interesting and more productive.

And looked at from the other end of the telescope: There is a level within every target organization below which people tend to have personal goals or agendas, but these are not usually issues their organizations are willing to fund. Architecting dialogues at these lower levels is nearly impossible. These people may want to learn all about your offerings, but they don't usually have either (1) the title or (2) the business goals. Without these prerequisites, Sales-Ready Messaging is impractical.

In the enterprise-solution world, of course, conversations eventually must take place with technical people and end-users. Our concern is when in the sales cycle these meetings take place. If they constitute the initial meeting, brace yourself for a long sales cycle, and one that can fall apart at any one of several places. If, by contrast, your initial conversations are with targeted business people who share with you their goals, your meetings with the people who report to them will be more productive. After having high-level conversations, calls on lower-level buyers can be more focused by having the buyer understand senior management's goals as they relate to the offerings being discussed.

In still other words: We advocate, and are attempting to illustrate, a top-down approach to sales. The structured approach described in this chapter lets salespeople spend far less time with people who can't, or are not going to, buy. Whenever possible, we advocate calls being made on people who can't buy only after qualifying one or more people within the organization who can.

Titles plus Goals Equals Targeted Conversations

We typically initiate our Sales-Ready Messaging projects by asking our clients a fairly basic question: "What are the typical job titles or job functions of the decision makers and influencers your salespeople will have to have meaningful conversations with?" Or, phrased differently, "Who is in a position to cost-justify, fund, buy, and implement your products and services?"

The first step in answering this is to list your vertical industries. Even if you have horizontal offerings, bear in mind that mainstream-market buyers (as described in earlier chapters) like to feel that the selling organization understands and has done business with their industry.

For each industry, make a list of the titles (or functions) a salesperson is likely to call on in order to get your offering sold, funded, and implemented. This exercise often will be dependent on the size of the potential transaction and the size of the prospect organization. For now, let's concentrate on large transactions to large organizations, since you can scale down this process at any time.

The difficulty of this task is directly related to the complexity of the offering. In some instances, salespeople enjoy the luxury of calling on just one person who can make the decision. For enterprise sales, the challenge ramps exponentially as the number of people and the accompanying number of business issues increase. Having said that, most of our clients find this to be a fairly easy exercise. They can do it from memory, because they encounter the same job titles in sale after sale.

Answering the next questions, though, usually requires more thought: "For each of these job titles, what goals or business objectives should they have in that function? Which of those goals are addressable through the use of your offering?"

Every goal in your list should be a business variable that your company's offering can help a particular title achieve. Ideally, the goal should be monetarily based, as the financial benefit of achieving the goal will be used to determine if the cost of the offering can be justified. Put another way, a business should be willing to spend money to achieve a goal.

Let's imagine that you are selling an enterprise-wide CRM system to a large company. Your amended list might look as follows:

CEO	Achieve revenue growth targets
	Improve company image
	Improve share price via improved forecasting
	Shape customer experience
CFO	Improve profitability by lowering cost of sales
	Lower IT cost for providing a single view of the customers
	Improve forecasting accuracy
VP Sales	Increase revenue through improved win rates
	Shorten sales cycles
	Improve cross selling
	Increase close rates by tracking leads
	Improve forecasting accuracy
	Reduce start-up times for new salespeople
VP Marketing	Increase market share
	Track results by campaign to justify programs
	Reduce expense of collateral
	Deliver JIT Sales-Ready Messaging to the field
CIO	Support end-users
	Protect valuable company data
	Reduce IT expenses
	Achieve service-level commitments

In this example, the objectives of the CIO are especially telling (and this turns out to be true in many cases). Buyers generally need the opportunity to quantify solutions. But how would someone determine, for example, if it would be worth $1 million to better support end-users? The only way to make that business judgment would be to go out and get the perspectives of the end-users—certainly possible, but not an easy task. So the goal that the CIO's office is best able to quantify is that of staying within budget, and that may turn out to be your most fertile ground. Focusing on staying within budget, however, does not bode well for funding new initiatives.

Creating this merged list—job titles with associated goals—sets the stage for what we call Targeted Conversations. But before those conversations can begin, more homework needs to be done.

Next Step: Solution Development Prompters

As a next step with our clients, we usually begin to develop questioning templates, which we call Solution Development Prompters, or SDPs.

We recommend that Marketing take responsibility for developing these materials and maintaining them. They represent the core content of a company's Sales-Ready Messaging, and they give selling organizations the ability to influence the conversations that their salespeople have with buyers. Simply put, they constitute a sort of road map for a salesperson—a tool that he or she can use to lead a specific job title to a specific vision of using the company's offering to achieve a specific goal.

Unlike a movie, where the writer and director exert full control over the interactions among the actors, no dialogue between a buyer and seller will go absolutely according to a script or a plan. Instead, our approach is about increasing the odds in the salesperson's favor by setting the stage for a Targeted Conversation. If a seller can approach a call with a clear idea of (1) who he or she is talking to and (2) where he or she hopes the conversation will wind up, the chances improve. On average, the seller will make better calls.[1]

Solution Development Prompters, as noted, are the core content of a company's Sales-Ready Messaging. So it may surprise you to learn that the messaging in SDPs takes the form of questions. Why? Because ques-

---

[1]The phrase "better calls" involves a subjective judgment, but in Chapter 12, we'll show you a more objective way to debrief and assess calls.

tions keep salespeople from "telling." As long as they are asking intelligent questions that their buyer is capable of answering, they are not selling (at least in the buyer's mind). They are consulting. This is a welcome change for the buyer, and also for the seller.

We believe the role of the salesperson is to become a buying facilitator by leading the buyer with questions that are biased toward their particular offering. SDPs help develop "buyer visions" that have a bias in favor of your offering.

Some people have difficulty with the term *bias*, feeling that it implies a manipulation of the buyer. We disagree. When we talk about creating a bias, we mean that the salesperson should be making an attempt to help the buyer put his or her stated goal in a context in which the seller's offering will help the buyer achieve that goal. It's something analogous to trying on a new pair of running shoes to solve the problem of recurring blisters. If the shoe fits, great. If the seller's offering doesn't fit the problem as defined by the user, then the "opportunity" should be disqualified.

Here's another analogy: Let's say you injured your back, and you consulted with three doctors—one trained in the United States, another in China, and a third in Sweden. Most likely, their methods of treating you would vary enormously, based on their training and experience. And most likely, each would attempt to create in you a bias in favor of his or her specific therapies. Are they manipulating you? No. They are offering solutions based on how they have been successful in treating similar conditions in the past. They are attempting to help you solve your problem (very patient-centric). And ultimately, you will choose your doctor based on the trust and confidence the doctor created during the diagnosis.

Once you have created your Targeted Conversations List for a given offering, you are ready to create Sales-Ready Messaging, in the form of SDPs. You do this by assembling four components: offering, industry, title, and goal. Using an example from the list developed above, the result would look like the following:

Offering: CRM Software
Industry: Fortune 1000 Company
Title: CFO
Goal: Improve forecasting accuracy

The next step is to position your offerings. With the CFO's goal of improving forecasting accuracy in mind, you now identify all the features of your CRM software that could be used to achieve this goal. As you do so, keep in mind that up at the CFO's 30,000-foot level, multiple features are likely to merge into one overarching feature, and/or that there may be features that are vital to users but will be of no interest to a senior executive. We recommend distilling your features down to your top four.

That said, here is an example, with the features that could be helpful to a CFO wanting to improve forecasting accuracy highlighted in italic type:

Password administration

Single view across platforms

24/7 access

Contact information

Account history

Cross selling

Standard milestones

Political mapping

Electronic coaching

Historical close rates

Lead tracking

Passing of leads

Analysis of past campaigns

And so on, ad nauseam

This may seem like a small step, but we believe it is a significant one. It is the start of positioning the CRM offering in a way that is targeted on a specific conversation—and is being done on behalf of the salesperson. In the same way that a tailor takes a client's measurements prior to an initial fitting, this is an attempt to put some structure around the prospective conversation by identifying the parts of the CRM offering most likely to be relevant to a CFO who wants to improve forecasting accuracy.

Nearly as important are the features *not* chosen for a potential conversation. They have been eliminated because they have little potential relevance to the topic of forecasting accuracy. Note, too, that they probably are not of interest to a CFO under most conceivable circumstances. Discussing them with a CFO is likely to confuse the buyer, waste time, and/or cause a seller to be delegated to a lower level. Even though this exercise so far has done executive buyers of the world a tremendous service, there is still work to be done.

Back to the Usage Scenario

A problem remains. If a salesperson simply blurted out "24/7 access!" to a CFO, that probably wouldn't be successful. Most likely, the phrase would mean more to the seller than to the buyer. Feature names (nouns) don't help buyers understand how the features can or could be used (verbs). Therefore, an additional step is needed to convert features into usage scenarios, as introduced in the previous chapter. Here again there are four components:

Event: *The circumstance causing a need for the specific feature.*

Question: *Asking versus telling doesn't feel like selling to the buyer.*

Player: *Who (or what system) will take action to respond to the event.*

Action: *How the feature can be used, stated in terms buyers can understand and relate to their job title. The description of the action should be specific enough so buyers can visualize how the result will be achieved. Terms used in a call with a CIO, for example, would be different from those used when calling on a CFO.*

Let's take a closer look at the feature 24/7 access to create a usage scenario for a conversation with a CFO about the goal of improving forecasting accuracy:

Event: *When trying to determine the status of large opportunities,*

Question: *Would it be helpful if*

Player: *You*

Action: *Could access your pipeline via a laptop, anytime, anywhere, and review progress against standard milestones, without needing to talk with anyone in your sales organization?*

Please note that the action refers to the ability to "access pipeline information via a laptop." This degree of specificity and concreteness is deliberate. If it simply read, "could review progress against milestones without needing to talk with anyone in your sales organization," the CFO probably would have no way of understanding how this would be accomplished.

In other words, the salesperson would be asking the CFO to either (1) imagine how it might work or (2) trust that it would work. But buyers—especially those who have authorized previous expenditures that haven't performed as advertised—are likely to be very skeptical. (They will be short on imagination and trust.) And keep in mind that we want all buyers to be able to articulate what they are buying and why, if asked by another person within their organization to explain the offering. "I can use my laptop to access specific opportunities in the pipeline even when I am on the road," the empowered buyer can say with confidence.

Here are the other three features selected for a discussion with a CFO about forecasting accuracy that have been converted to usage-scenario format:

Event: *After making calls,*

Question: *Would you like*

Player: *Your salespeople*

Action: *To be prompted on their laptops to report progress against a standard set of milestones for each opportunity in their pipeline?*

Event: *On demand from any location,*

Question: *Would it be helpful if*

Player: *Your sales managers*

Action: *Could access the pipeline database for their salespeople, evaluate the status of specific opportunities, and email suggestions to reps to improve their chances of winning the business?*

Event: *On an ongoing basis,*

Question: *Would it be useful to you if*

Player: *The system*

Action: *Could track historical close rates for each salesperson by pipeline milestone, and apply them to each of the salesperson's opportunities to predict revenue?*

The next step would be to sequence these usage scenarios. This is usually driven by the order in which the buyer would be likely to encounter them. In this example, you want to lead the CFO to a vision of creating an accurate monthly forecast. The right sequence, therefore, is: pipeline milestones, electronic coaching, historical close rates, and 24/7 access.

Note that the feature we considered first—24/7 access—winds up being the last in the sequence. This kind of reshuffling is quite common, and illustrates the importance of approaching this task systematically.

The Templates

Let's formalize this template—in part to emphasize that salespeople need structure for using Sales-Ready Messaging to make calls, and in part to underscore the systematic nature of our approach.

The header information in the blank Solution Development Prompter (SDP) template (Figure 8-1) contains the prerequisites for the targeted sales conversation (offering, vertical industry, title, goal). Figure 8-2 shows the partially developed SDP that we are building for the CFO of a software company whose goal is improving forecasting accuracy. The right column has been populated with the usage scenarios we developed earlier that were relevant to the buyer's goal.

But what's that column labeled "Diagnostic Questions" on the left of Figure 8-2? We have just created four usage scenarios that *might* be used to enable a CFO to visualize how he or she could improve forecasting accuracy. But the real test for this system comes when a salesperson tries to determine which of these usage scenarios a CFO would agree he or she needed, during a structured conversation. Consider how important the diagnostic process would have been in the selection of a doctor earlier in this chapter. In sales, since the diagnosis is so critical, does it make sense to abdicate this step to traditional salespeople?

For each usage scenario, therefore, we now create corresponding best practice diagnostic questions for the salesperson to ask in order to determine if the buyer has a need for the usage scenario described in the "event, question, player, action" (EQPA) question. In addition, it is helpful to seed questions that can be used to determine the potential value of a usage scenario to the buyer.

Diagnostic questions are used to better understand how the buyer is performing a function today—e.g., forecasting—and, ideally, the cost of doing it the way he or she is currently doing it. At the same time, good

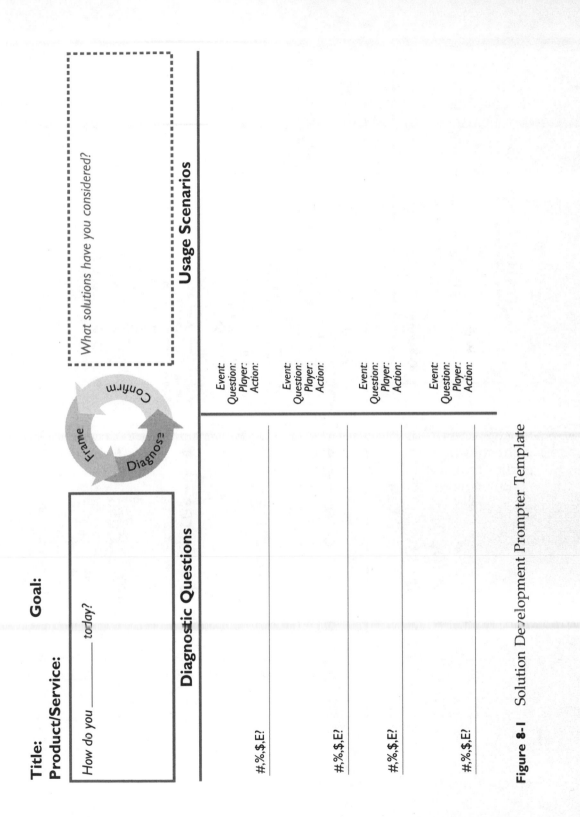

Title: **Goal:**
Product/Service:

How do you _____ today?

What solutions have you considered?

Frame — Confirm — Diagnose

Diagnostic Questions   **Usage Scenarios**

#,%,$,E?   Event:
                     Question:
                     Player:
                     Action:

#,%,$,E?   Event:
                     Question:
                     Player:
                     Action:

#,%,$,E?   Event:
                     Question:
                     Player:
                     Action:

#,%,$,E?   Event:
                     Question:
                     Player:
                     Action:

Figure 8-1 Solution Development Prompter Template

Developing Solution Development Prompters

Targeted Conversation:

Title: VP Finance

Goal: Achieve profit projections with more accurate revenue forecasting

Offering: Enterprise SFA Software

Potential Usage Scenarios

Pipeline milestones →

Event: After making calls
Question: Would it help if
Player: Sales reps
Action: Could be prompted to report progress against a standard set of milestones for each opportunity in their pipeline?

Electronic coaching →

Event: When reviewing a salesperson's pipeline
Question: Would it be helpful if
Player: Sales managers
Action: Could access, from any location, a central database, evaluate the status of opportunities, and email suggestions to reps to improve the chances of winning the business?

Historical close rates →

Event: On an ongoing basis
Question: Would you like
Player: The system
Action: To track historical close rates for each rep by milestone and apply them to the pipeline to predict revenue?

24/7 access →

Event: When evaluating the status of large opportunities
Question: Would it be beneficial if
Player: You
Action: Could access a centralized database via your laptop anytime/anywhere and review progress against milestones?

Figure 8-2 Solution Development Prompter-in-Progress

diagnostic questions help the seller build credibility, in the same way that a physician you meet for the first time builds credibility with you by asking insightful, intelligent questions that you are capable of answering

Now refer to Figure 8-3. This fills in the Diagnostic Questions column with the questions that a competent diagnostician would ask a buyer. (Remember: These are good questions only if the person with whom you're having the conversation can answer them—the point is *not* to embarrass someone with unanswerable questions.) Every conversation is different, and *no* conversation would follow the script outlined in Sections 1, 2, 3, and 4. Conversations have to follow their own flow; otherwise, they're not conversations. But if you look at these questions, you'll get the idea.

How many usage scenarios will a given CFO want to engage? The answer lies between zero and four. (Zero means you're not calling on a qualified buyer as relates to forecasting accuracy; four approaches the upper limit that can be dealt with in a conversation that's scheduled for a half-hour.) Later, we'll describe a structured way for salespeople to navigate through SDPs so they can lead the buyer to understand why he or she is having difficulty achieving a goal (diagnostic questions) and what is needed to achieve the goal (usage-scenario questions).

So we've now completed the first SDP. Additional SDPs would be created for each remaining goal on the menu for CFOs. After that, this same process would be repeated for each title/menu that is specific to an offering and vertical title. The final result is Sales-Ready Messaging to enable sellers to have targeted conversations with the titles needed to sell, fund, and implement an enterprise CRM system.

Closing Observations

Is this a significant effort? Absolutely. But we believe the result is well worth that effort. If properly prepared, SDPs provide a more consistent positioning of offerings by all salespeople, and should help your sales effort overall.

A few other observations about creating SDPs:

- They get easier to prepare after you have created the initial ones, because usage scenarios tend to be reusable for multiple targeted conversations.

Title: VP Finance   **Goal:** Achieve profit projections with more accurate sales forecasting

Product/Service: SPA

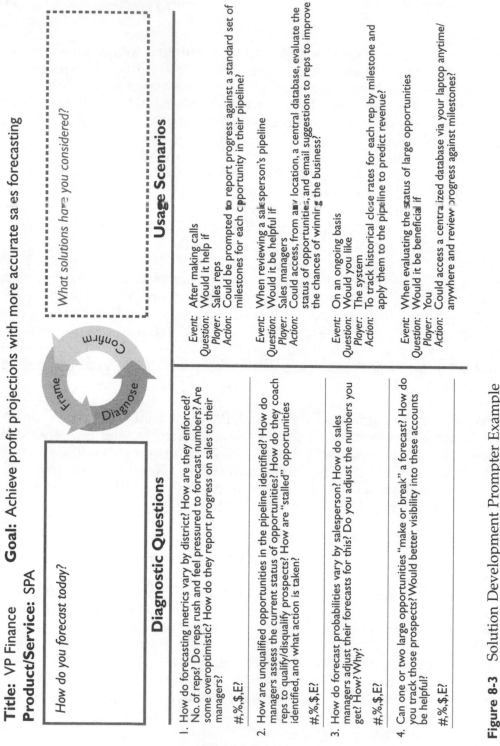

What solutions have you considered?

How do you forecast today?

Diagnostic Questions

1. How do forecasting metrics vary by district? How are they enforced? No. of reps? Do reps rush and feel pressured to forecast numbers? Are some overoptimistic? How do they report progress on sales to their managers?

   #,%,$,E?

2. How are unqualified opportunities in the pipeline identified? How do managers assess the current status of opportunities? How do they coach reps to qualify/disqualify prospects? How are "stalled" opportunities identified, and what action is taken?

   #,%,$,E?

3. How do forecast probabilities vary by salesperson? How do sales managers adjust their forecasts for this? Do you adjust the numbers you get? How? Why?

   #,%,$,E?

4. Can one or two large opportunities "make or break" a forecast? How do you track those prospects? Would better visibility into these accounts be helpful?

   #,%,$,E?

Usage Scenarios

Event: After making calls
Question: Would it help if
Player: Sales reps
Action: Could be prompted to report progress against a standard set of milestones for each opportunity in their pipeline?

Event: When reviewing a salesperson's pipeline
Question: Would it be helpful if
Player: Sales managers
Action: Could access, from any location, a central database, evaluate the status of opportunities, and email suggestions to reps to improve the chances of winning the business?

Event: On an ongoing basis
Question: Would you like
Player: The system
Action: To track historical close rates for each rep by milestone and apply them to the pipeline to predict revenue?

Event: When evaluating the status of large opportunities
Question: Would it be beneficial if
Player: You
Action: Could access a centralized database via your laptop anytime/anywhere and review progress against milestones?

Figure 8-3 Solution Development Prompter Example

- While Marketing should take responsibility for the creation and maintenance of SDPs, it also requires significant involvement from the sales organization.
- The true test of an SDP is whether it can be used in making a call. If it cannot, salespeople must offer constructive feedback on how it needs to be modified.
- At executive levels, anticipate that a salesperson has only 15 to 20 minutes to have a discussion. This means limiting the number of usage scenarios to a maximum of four (perhaps with a fifth in reserve).
- A single usage scenario may require integration of multiple product features.
- SDPs are indexed by vertical market, title, and business goals and objectives. Therefore, they are geared more toward management discussions than toward product presentations. If you are selling a complex offering with 847 features, eventually someone in the organization will want to know about all of them—and maybe more—in discussing potential future enhancements. SDPs won't be useful in these calls, which are often associated with due diligence.

But we'd turn this on its head by asking a key question: "Where in the buying cycle are these detailed feature discussions taking place?" If they are during the first meetings in an enterprise sale, it may take months of effort to get in front of the right person. It is far better to have these "due diligence" meetings take place after you have generated interest at business/executive levels.

- Whenever possible, SDPs should bias buyers toward usage scenarios that represent a company's strengths against competitors that either (1) are in the account today or (2) are likely to be invited to compete at a later time.
- SDPs should be developed for offerings besides product. As an example, software companies should create templates for selling professional services and ongoing consulting. We work with a company selling copiers and printers that has an SDP for positioning leasing (which is more lucrative for them than a straight purchase).
- In the same way that your marketplace and offerings change, SDPs are dynamic, not static, and must be maintained and updated over time. Sales-Ready Messaging is more a journey than a destination.
- New product or service announcements should be accompanied by (even preceded by) the preparation of SDPs.

- Outside help may be necessary, in preparing SDPs. Many people working for a company get so steeped in their offerings that they find it hard to create SDPs; conversely, people unfamiliar with a company's offerings often have an easier time of it. If the ultimate objective is to facilitate a dialogue with an executive who is unfamiliar with your offerings, you may find that hiring an outside person to pick the brains of your smartest people is a good investment.
- With salespeople directed to higher levels, qualification becomes easier. Most senior executives will not waste their time or their staffs' time. If they point or delegate you to others after being empowered to achieve a goal, they are serious about evaluating your offering.
- Some of our clients find that in calling high, SDPs can span multiple offerings. This is a shift from selling product by product at lower levels. In some cases a single usage scenario at a decision-maker level can cover an entire offering. The call on the next level down may consist of an entirely separate SDP to have a more detailed discussion.
- In creating SDPs, it is sometimes impossible to establish competitive differentiators. Consider for a moment multiple vendors selling CRM systems. To make it easier, let's assume all offer client-server applications. If salespeople are making calls at the highest levels (CEO, CFO) and having conceptual discussions, the conversations (and therefore the SDPs for any such CRM company) would be similar. Differentiators may have to be introduced at slightly lower levels.

**CHAPTER
9**

Marketing's Role in Demand Creation

IN PREVIOUS CHAPTERS, we've been advocates for a new psychological stance for Marketing. Marketing, we've said, should think of itself as being the front end of the sales process, instead of the back end of the product-development process. Why? Because we believe that this is a prerequisite for more closely coordinating efforts with Sales.

Marketing is a huge function, and it comprises many activities that are beyond the scope of this book. So as we look at Marketing's role in demand creation, let's explicitly limit our scope. We intend to focus on Marketing's direct support of salespeople by attempting to create demand for qualified buyers to generate leads and move new opportunities into salespeople's funnels. We will *not* look, for example, at Marketing's efforts to build brand recognition and awareness or its strategic planning for future offerings.

Leads and Prospects

Most Marketing departments allocate a large part of their budget to creating demand for their offerings, in one way or another. In some of those organizations, salespeople are not expected to do much heavy lifting as relates to prospecting or business development. In such cases, they are dependent on leads, a nebulous term that reflects (1) the poorly defined relationship between Sales and Marketing and (2) a lack of understanding about what a good prospect is.

Let's start with this second issue. Does your company approach demand creation systematically? If so, are you learning enough from your customer base to leverage how they've used your offerings to achieve goals, solve problems, or satisfy needs?

Here's an exercise you might want to try. Figure out, in rough terms, the entire potential of your territory, district, region, or total target market. By potential, we mean the total number of people or entities that could benefit from using your offerings. Once you've established that figure, estimate what percentage of the people or organizations in that universe are currently conducting evaluations for offerings comparable to yours.

What do we mean by an evaluation? Here are five important criteria that suggest that a legitimate evaluation is underway:

1. The buyers have identified a business goal they want to achieve or a problem they want to solve that you believe can be addressed by your offering.
2. One or more decision makers are involved.
3. Requirements are documented.
4. A buying decision will be made within your average sell cycle.
5. Budget for the project has been earmarked.

As they conduct this exercise, most vendors conclude that only a small percentage of their potential prospects meet these criteria. (Most people find that between 0 and 10 percent of their potential market are currently evaluating.) In other words, there aren't many legitimate evaluations going on out there.

At the same time, though, they discover something very interesting: The majority of prospects that are not actively evaluating have goals that are similar to those of the prospects who are. This begs the question: Why would a buyer not attempt to improve an important business variable? Our experience suggests that there are three common answers:

- The company or buyer is unaware that it is possible to improve the business variable.
- The company or buyer is aware that the variable could be improved, but doesn't consider it to be a priority (including a budgetary priority).

- The company or buyer failed in previous attempts to achieve the goal, and is reluctant to try again.

So if the vast majority of your targeted marketplace is not looking to change, that's bad news, right? Yes and no. It's bad news if your organization knows only how to be reactive. But it may be good news if your organization knows how to be proactive—that is, how to cause buyers to begin considering change. Two advantages come to mind immediately:

- There is a huge, untapped pool of prospects out there.
- If you help initiate an evaluation, there's every chance that if the buyer ultimately considers other alternatives, you will be "Column A"—the vendor whose offering is perceived from the outset as the best match with the requirements of the buyer, and therefore is the standard against which other competitors are measured.

Many salespeople believe the best way to build a pipeline is to find and pursue active evaluations. Why? They are qualified in that budget, perceived need, and timeframe have already been established. We suggest that the real marketing challenge is to target potential decision makers (people who can spend or allocate unbudgeted funds) who are not looking to change with your Sales-Ready Messaging. If you disagree, please keep an open mind while reading the next section.

The Bottom Line on Budgets

Having already singled out salespeople, many companies steer their salespeople toward finding opportunities where buyers already have active evaluations underway. They do that by making budget an early qualification question that sales managers ask.

Is that smart? Let's examine why companies have budgets, and what salespeople can learn from the budgeting process.

Let's first agree why budgets are a way of life for buyers and sellers: Senior executives must predict and deliver a bottom line to investors. The two major variables are top-line revenue, which is speculative, and spending, which is more controllable.

Going into a fiscal year, would it be prudent for a chief financial officer to give, say, the top 20 executives in the company permission to spend whatever they felt was necessary to run their functions within the business? If he or she did so, it is possible that toward the end of the first quarter, it would turn out that each manager had spent $1 million more than what was expected. The CFO would then have the unpleasant task of informing the chief executive officer that the company was $20 million over on the spending side—which would in turn mean that the CEO would have to alert investors that earnings projections were not likely to be achieved. So budgets are established to control the expenditures of people within the organization, and to allow the CEO and CFO to sleep at night.

If given the choice between reporting missed earnings due to a revenue shortfall or due to a budget overage, most CEOs would opt for the former (and in a heartbeat). Even the most hard-nosed analysts and investors recognize that the CEO exerts only a tenuous control over revenue generation. These same people, however, would view the failure to control spending as a sign of gross executive incompetence.

That's the theory: Budgets are set at the beginning of the year and are cast in stone, and everybody sleeps well. The reality, though, is very different. In real life, companies retain a great deal of control over how they will spend their money, month-to-month or week-to-week. If a compelling case can be made that expending unbudgeted funds will (1) increase top-line revenues by (significantly) more than the cost of the outlay or (2) cut costs to a similar degree, most companies can find the necessary funds.

So—to bring this back to the perspective of the salesperson—if a buyer claims not to have budget, so long as the target organization doesn't have insurmountable financial or other constraints, the salesperson and manager should conclude that he or she is not calling high enough within the prospect organization.

Here's a real-life example from our own experience of how funds can be freed up for unbudgeted expenditures: A vice president (VP) of Sales who had attended one of our workshops told us after the session that he wanted to conduct an internal workshop for his staff, but he couldn't authorize the funds. He asked us to do an executive overview of our methodology for his VP of Marketing, his CFO, and his CEO. This entailed a flight to Utah, so we agreed to do the overview if he would defray our travel expenses, which he agreed to do. (Quid pro quo in action.)

Near the end of our discussion, the CEO asked how much it would cost to implement a sales process in his company. Because he already had a vision of how the process could be used and the accompanying value, we reviewed pricing with him.

After discussing costs, the CEO turned to his CFO, Ed, and asked how the company's cash flow looked. Ed gave the answer that all good CFOs give when asked that question in front of a salesperson: "Things are a bit tight." The CEO turned to the VP of Marketing. "Caroline," he asked, "of the three trade shows we plan to participate in this year, which one provides us the least value?" She quickly identified the laggard. On the spot, with the concurrence of his colleagues, the CEO decided to skip that trade show, thereby freeing up funds for the sales-training program. The CEO told us to work out the details and contact him with any questions, and then left the meeting.

In other words, when you call on decision makers, budget alone does not prevent buyers from going forward. Having said that, of course, even the most senior decision makers can't print money, so if they set a new priority, it is likely that some other project may have to be deferred or cancelled. This is part of the reason so many buying cycles wind up with no decision.

So salespeople not only compete with other vendors, they also compete for "mindshare" of business executives who have to decide how best to invest their company's limited capital, and how to adjust allocations that have—in most cases—already been fought for through the previous budgeting cycle.

Starting Out as Column B

We've already alluded to the advantages of starting out as Column A— that is, of being the vendor whose offering is perceived from the outset as the best match with the requirements of the buyer.

We believe salespeople who are called into or stumble on opportunities where buyers already have budget for the project should assume that they are not Column A. (The vendor who has initiated the evaluation that led to this opportunity is Column A, and will continue to enjoy this position unless or until another vendor is able to change the buyer's requirements.) In creating demand, therefore, we believe it is vitally important to cause organizations that are not currently looking to change to start looking to change.

Let's examine how much better your chances are as Column A versus Columns B, C, D, and so on, the inhabitants of which we sometimes refer to as "silver medal" vendors. Have you ever noticed that only one vendor gets the order (gold medal)? The other four are told: "We liked your proposal best, but I'm sorry to tell you we awarded the business to another vendor. You came in second." Here is a scenario that may be familiar:

A salesperson sits at her desk, debating whether to work on overdue expense reports or make some cold prospecting calls, when the phone rings. A prospect in her territory begins the call:

> I'm Ray Jones, project manager for XYZ Company. The reason for my call is that we are going to make a buying decision within the next month. I already have budget approval for the project. We've heard good reports about your company and products and would like to give you a shot at earning our business. We'll need a demonstration, price quotation, references, and a proposal as soon as possible. You should be aware that this ultimately is my decision, so there's no point in looking for ways to go around me. How soon can we meet to discuss these items?

In the wake of this kind of call, most traditional salespeople would feel fortunate to have been invited to compete for the business. The appointment would be scheduled for the earliest possible time, the salesperson's manager would be informed that there was a "hot one" in the funnel, and this opportunity would appear on the salesperson's next forecast. The pricing, references, demonstration, and proposal would be expedited to meet the prospect's tight timeframe. Everyone in the selling organization would be feeling a little giddy.

Before we allow ourselves to get *too* excited, however, let's examine the sequence of events that most likely preceded the call's being placed to the salesperson. (This is a composite, based on lots of stories like this that we've heard.) Is this a hot prospect?

Six months ago, Salesperson A uncovered a requirement for a product that XYZ Company had never considered, which meant that no budget had been established for this purpose. The sales cycle started at a lower level within the organization. After months of effort and education, a base of support and an overwhelming business case was built for Salesperson A's product, which cost $100,000. The internal champion could see the value of buying the product, but needed to obtain approval for an unbudgeted expenditure.

After the business case and an attractive payback were presented, the CFO said: "You've put a lot of effort into this evaluation, and it sure looks as though the benefits far outweigh the costs. What other vendors have you looked at?" The internal champion answered, truthfully, that no other alternatives had been considered. "Well," the CFO continued, "our corporate policy is never to consider just one vendor for a purchase of this magnitude. Get other quotes so we can make product and pricing comparisons. And by the way, please don't bring any salespeople in to meet with me. How soon can you perform this analysis and get back to me?"

After this meeting, the internal champion at XYZ Company has a sense of urgency about completing the requested analysis. To get funds allocated, he must perform due diligence by considering other options. But how objective will his evaluation really be? Naturally enough, he wants his initial vendor recommendation to be the chosen alternative. After all, Salesperson A initiated the sales cycle, showed strong potential payback, and spent months developing a relationship. The internal champion may confess to Salesperson A that he is required to look at other vendors, and solicit her advice on which ones to consider. What he may not fully understand is that Salesperson A also anticipated that her prospect would be instructed to look at competitors, and has prewired (biased) the requirements list to play to her product's strengths.

What does this list (see Figure 9-1) look like? The requirements column on the left is filled out first: a detailed description of the only product that has been evaluated to date. Column A is just to the right of this column. It is filled in completely, and—not surprisingly—it is more or less an exact restatement of the requirements column. To the right of Column A are blank columns for Competitors B, C, and D to fill out. The internal champion is now ready to call and invite the silver medalist candidates to bid on the business, provided they can pull all the numbers together by the deadline.

How well will the competitors compare? If Salesperson A's product is price-competitive, Competitors B, C, and D have little chance of getting the business. If Salespeople B, C, and D ask for the opportunity to meet the CFO—who could potentially change the requirements—they will be denied that opportunity. Even if one of them were successful in adding new features to the requirements list, weighting factors could still be used to ensure that Column A would win. If a lower bid comes in, Salesperson A may be given a clandestine opportunity to sharpen her pencil after all quotes are received. In other words, Competitors B, C, and D have been invited to compete, lose, and ultimately help the internal champion do business with the vendor he wanted from the start. In most cases, the reward for Columns B, C, and D is the silver medal.

Requirements[1]	Column A[2]	Column B[3]	Column C[3]

[1]Often vary by buyer.

[2]Vendor whose offering best matches the requirements. Can change during a sales cycle.

[3]Winning vendor often is known before others are invited to bid.

Figure 9-1 Vendor Evaluation

Column A's internal champion next schedules a follow-up meeting with the CFO. Although multiple alternatives are shown, there is a clear choice. Reallocated money for Column A is approved. Vendors B, C, and D are thanked for their responsiveness, complimented on doing an excellent job, and told that it was a difficult decision, but that they were not chosen this time. All three are told that they came in second, and that if future requirements arise, they'll be invited to bid. The losing vendors remove XYZ Company from their forecasts as a competitive loss, feeling—correctly, in many cases—that they could have turned the situation around, if only they had gotten into the account sooner.

In short: When you are told early in a sales cycle that the budget has been approved, you should *always* assume that your competition has set the criteria. The prospect has already started to evaluate the merits of comparable products or services being offered, and has obtained cost estimates. If this were not the case, how could they possibly know already how much money to budget?

Being called by prospects with preapproved budgets and tight deadlines for providing demonstrations, pricing, references, and proposals should warn you that you are being asked to provide a column. If the answer to the question, "Is there a budget?" is yes, sales managers may want to ask an additional question: "Whose numbers did the prospect use for obtaining budget approval?"

In our client engagements, we try to get our audiences focused on the advantages of being Column A, as opposed to being silver medalists. One way we do so is to ask them to look back on the competitions they've won over time, and to estimate the percentage of those wins that represented situations in which they started as Column A.

Most people wind up giving a number in the 80 percent range. Flipped the other way around, this means that they have a 400 percent better chance of success if they can proactively cause people to look to change. Yes, individual salespeople should prospect to fill their funnels, but Marketing also has a critical role to play as the front end of the sales process.

It should be noted here that the perceived average sales cycle for a company could be misleading. Even if you are calling high, when you are Column A, a fair amount of time is needed to get to the point of having a closable order. When you are coming in as a potential silver medalist, the good news is that it will be a short sell cycle (Column A has already done most of the selling). The bad news is that the sales cycle is likely to have an unhappy ending.

Marketing and Leads

If you want to start a buying cycle where none exists already, it is necessary to get mindshare. With decision makers, as suggested in previous chapters, this will not usually be accomplished by leading with your offerings. What we suggest, instead, is leading with business issues to generate curiosity and interest. Leading with business issues offers organizations the benefit of higher entry points into prospect organizations, leading to shorter sales cycles and quicker access to mainstream-market buyers because the buyers are now being shown product usage or potential results rather than starting with your offerings.

Which issues? Well, let's revisit the Targeted Conversations List—containing a menu of goals by offering, vertical industry, and title—that we created in the previous chapter. Using that tool, we would now like to offer a definition of a lead that Sales and Marketing can agree on, because the three components of a lead are the same as the Targeted Conversations List:

- Vertical industry
- Title (or function)
- Business goal identified

In our model, an organization (or salesperson) cannot begin selling until a Targeted Conversation buyer expresses a goal that can be achieved or a problem that can be addressed with an offering. When that happens, you have a legitimate lead that Sales and Marketing can agree is qualified. For companies with no standard definition for a lead, how meaningful is the process of tracking close rates?

We'd now like to discuss the various avenues that most marketing groups currently use in an attempt to generate interest—brochures and collateral, trade shows, seminars, Web sites, and so on—and how these approaches can be improved (by leading with either business goals or business problems) or replaced.

Brochures and Collateral

Just as traditional salespeople feel compelled to "spray and pray" when contacting prospects, so do most brochures and collateral literature. Many are little more than product specifications, often with some graphics and a sampling of nebulous terms (seamless, robust, synergistic, leading edge, and the like) thrown in to make them slightly more readable.

But this is silly. When you go fishing, you choose a specific location, type of bait, type of hook, and method (trolling, casting, and so on), all based on the particular type of fish you are attempting to catch, right? Why would you not do as much, or more, when trolling for prospects?

Here's a useful exercise: Pick up a piece of collateral that is likely to be sent to a prospect, and turn the pages. As you do, ask yourself:

- What level within the organization would want to read this?
- Can this level allocate unbudgeted funds?
- What business issues does the collateral attempt to raise?
- What action is it intended to prompt?

Yes, there is always a role for strong technical information—but is it something you want to lead with, in attempting to get an entry point into a prospect organization? In most cases, the answer is no. Brochures with extensive technical detail are best at (1) answering a deep question from an expert, (2) informing those who are not decision makers about your offerings, and (3) reinforcing credibility that you've built up in other ways.

Another generally deadly approach is to provide traditional salespeople with glossy "pocket folders," that is, large folders into which smaller brochures, letters, and business cards are inserted. In many cases, when a prospect asks, "Can you send me some information?" traditional salespeople start emptying out their drawers of printed material. The result? Five dollars in printing out the door and a three-dollar charge for the mailing, at the end of which buyers feel that they have received too much information (TMI) and therefore don't read much (or any) of the material. (We hear this story all the time as we follow up on clients' salespeople.) This, in turn, prompts the classic response from the prospect's assistant: "I'm sure she's seen it, and if there is any interest, she'll get back to you."

We don't recommend putting this prospect on your forecast. Does it belong there?

Of course, Marketing can reduce this exposure to some extent by being selective about the types of collateral it produces. But in addition, we suggest that when they receive requests for information, salespeople respond by asking for a brief discussion to better understand the buyer's area of interest, so that they can send only material that is germane. It doesn't hurt to be explicit about this: "We have lots of offerings with different capabilities, and we'd prefer not to subject you to saturation bombing. What, exactly, do you want to know about?" Another alternative is to ask the buyer: "What are you hoping to accomplish?"

Here are some possible alternatives to spec sheets and too many brochures falling out of pocket folders:

- Menus of business goals or problems
- Success Stories
- Sample cost-benefit results achieved by customers

Note that the menus of business goals or problems can be taken directly from a Targeted Conversations List, as described in the last chapter. The point of the menu approach, of course, is to allow sellers to use examples of common business problems to lead the buyer into a discussion. It's often easier for the buyer to say, "Hey—we have this same problem!" than to say, "Let me describe this odd problem we, and only we, seem to be having."

Success Stories are one of the oldest techniques in the sales profession. For understandable reasons, buyers are much more comfortable if they are not among the first to buy the seller's offering. Keeping in mind the concept of product usage and Targeted Conversations, consider the CustomerCentric Selling Success Story format in Figure 9-2.

Note that the first two components (Key Player and Goal) are from a Targeted Conversations List. Once a seller gets a buyer to share a goal, the next element is a "contributing reason" for the customer's not being able to achieve the goal. This reason is naturally aligned with a capability. The benefit statement now allows the seller to finally say, "We gave him that capability," and then finishes with the actual benefit derived from the customer's use of the offering.

In Figure 9-3, we have reproduced an actual CustomerCentric Selling client Success Story. This particular client sells a host of manufacturing productivity-enhancing products and services, and the Key Player and goal are from their Targeted Conversations List. The contributing reason is aligned with one of their key capabilities: early warning notifications. After their salesperson delivers a benefit statement, she can then finish by quantifying the actual financial benefit.

Note that this Success Story was crafted by Marketing, published by Marketing, used by the Training department in training salespeople, and

1. Key Player (industry/title)	From Targeted Conversation List
2. Goal	From the menu of goals
3. Contributing reason	Prior to implementing your offering, cite a reason they could not accomplish their goal. This reason should come from the left side of the Key Player's SDP.
4. Corresponding capability	Choose the capability from the left side of the SDP that addresses the corresponding reason cited.
5. Capability statement	State that you or your company provided the capability.
6. Quantified results	Share quantified results that were achieved, and be sure they link to the goal being discussed.

Figure 9-2 Success Story Components

finally used by the salespeople when engaging potential new prospects. This is the kind of collaboration that leads to sales success.

The third alternative to the standard collaterals listed above is sample cost-benefit results achieved by customers. These can be extremely powerful tools, because they let customers speak to customers, without any intermediation by the salesperson.

"We worked with a *(VP Sales of a software company)*[1] who wanted to *(improve his forecasting accuracy)*.[2] Forecasting was difficult because *(qualifications varied by salesperson and there was no standard way of assessing progress in an opportunity)*.[3] His salespeople updated forecasts when pressed for time at the end of the month. He said he needed a way to *(define milestones for the whole company so after making calls, the salespeople could sign onto a Web site and be prompted to update the status of opportunities against a standard grading system)*.[4] *(We provided him with this capability)*.[5] Over the last 6 months, *(his forecasting accuracy improved by 35 percent)*.[6]"

1. Key Player (industry/title). 2. Goal. 3. Contributing reason. 4. Corresponding capability. 5. Capability statement. 6. Quantified results.

Figure 9-3 Establishing Credibility: The Success Story

Trade Shows

By now, it should be clear that we don't approve of vendors leading with offerings. So you can guess how we feel about the ways in which many vendors—especially technology vendors—display their wares at trade shows. Product, feature; product, feature; product, feature; and so on. Suffice it to say that there's almost always room for improvement. The exception, of course, may arise in the case of an early-market offering, where just putting your product in front of early-market buyers—and letting them figure out how to use it—may be a valid short-term approach to getting help in understanding how your offering can help a buyer achieve a goal, solve a problem, or satisfy a need.

But let's assume that you're not pursuing Innovators and Early Adopters. So first things first: Exactly what are you trying to accomplish by participating in a trade show? Are you trying to generate leads? Many Marketing departments pound their chests in triumph after a trade show generates 500 "bingo cards" requesting information. But the hapless salespeople who follow up on these so-called leads soon discover that 95-plus percent of them are dead ends. They turn out to be consultants just trying to pick their brains, college students interested in the technology or looking for employment opportunities, window shoppers, trinket gatherers, and so on—in other words, people who may be intrigued by your offering, but can't buy.

If you were to take the total cost of participating in the trade show (including all personnel) and divide by the number of bingo cards generated, you might be shocked at how expensive these leads are—especially in light of the fact that many or most are not leads at all. And it gets worse: According to Gartner Group, a face-to-face call by a high-tech salesperson costs over $400, when all costs are taken into account. So if you called on just one in five of those 500 bingo-card contacts, you'd be out another $40,000!

Remember, too, that your initial contact becomes your point of entry into an organization. In the case of an enterprise sale, entering at the user level almost guarantees a long sell cycle. You'll probably spend a lot of time, along the way, with people who can't say yes, but can say no.

We suggest taking a different approach to trade shows. Just as companies can differentiate themselves with a sales process, we believe they can do the same with trade shows. When seeking mainstream-market buyers, consider scaling back your participation in traditional trade shows. Choose shows that business people are more likely to attend.

Get a small booth, and resist the temptation to load it up with equipment. Use prominently displayed quotes, or likely menus of goals or problems, to get Targeted Conversation attendees (who are not necessarily thinking about change) to slow down, enter your booth, and share a business goal. This puts your staff in a position to begin asking intelligent questions that the prospect is able and willing to answer.

If demos are appropriate, we suggest asking interested prospects if they'd like to see the offering. If they agree, fill out a card with (1) their goal and (2) the capabilities they'd like to see. Direct them to a suite away from the floor, where they can have refreshments and make phone calls. When they're ready, they visit the suite and give the card to one of your staff, who can then tailor the demo to the specific capabilities the buyer is interested in seeing.

Seminars

In a newly assigned territory, or in the case of a new announcement, a seminar can be an effective way to jump-start pipelines. Seminars take time and effort to coordinate, but they provide an opportunity to sell one-to-many, and therefore should not be overlooked. So the goal should be to structure them in a way that provides maximum benefit. Again, the ultimate goal here—as with the tools and techniques suggested above—is to get buyers who were not looking to change to realize the potential benefits of change, and initiate an evaluation. Your prospect pool gets bigger, and you're in Column A.

An important first step is to bring together a group of attendees who have something significant in common; for example, they work in the same industry, or do more or less the same job. A good way to do this is to feature one of your customers—preferably from a familiar company—who holds the same position and is willing to share a problem that your offering has helped them solve. When it works, this is a win-win-win: Your customer is flattered, the attendees can readily relate to material presented by someone with credibility who speaks their language, and you get access to a pool of prospects.

Little things count for a lot. Schedule your seminar for first thing in the morning—before people go into the office—and limit it to between 1 and 2 hours. Prepare your invitation carefully: It is very important in laying out the agenda and setting expectations. If you hope to attract an executive audience, spend enough money on invitations so that it looks like an executive event.

Consider preparing a menu of goals or problems that are likely to be relevant to this target audience, and include that menu—and a preaddressed envelope—along with the invitation. Encourage them to highlight topics that they would like to have covered during the session. (You may want to post this menu on your Web site as well, so that invitees can do their highlighting electronically.) You can tabulate the results in advance of the seminar, and thereby maximize your alignment with the audience.

Follow-up is just as important as the invitation—and maybe even more so. Call the people you've invited, and ask if they plan to attend, if they have looked at the menu, and if they have any questions that you can address. Above all, see if you can get them to commit. Then be sure to call the day before—under the pretense of getting head counts for refreshments—and confirm that they still plan to attend. You don't want a half-empty room, and sometimes it's worth making a full room (of high-potential people) the responsibility of one of your more reliable and creative people.

Start the session with a brief overview of your company—no more than 5 minutes, tops. If you were able to collect and pretabulate the menu of business issues before the meeting, present them now. Otherwise, build a menu on a flip chart by asking for suggestions, and then use that menu to settle on two or three goals that are of general interest. (Assure your guests that concerns that are not dealt with at this session can be revisited one-on-one at a later date.) In some cases, you may want to use a Success Story to prime the pump. Or, you may want to survey the entire room to pin down common reasons why attendees can't achieve the results they are looking for. After the session, you may have demos set up (if appropriate) that are focused on the specific capabilities that were discussed and presented.

Your objective, again, is to get them looking to change. We don't believe that one-on-one selling is appropriate at seminars. On the other hand, if you can get a business card and an associated goal or objective, this sets the stage for a follow-up phone call or meeting that can quickly determine if there is an opportunity to pursue.

Advertising

In too many cases, advertising ignores the most basic rule of Customer-Centric Selling. It treats offerings as nouns, instead of verbs. It ignores or undervalues business issues as a way of generating interest.

While the subject of advertising is large enough to justify volumes all on its own, let us suggest two CustomerCentric approaches for advertising:

- Attempt to create "results envy" by having buyers realize that people in their own industry, and with the same job function, are achieving improved results through the use of your offerings.
- Use a "hurt and rescue" approach, getting people to realize that there is a business problem that they are now experiencing, and that they have a means to control it.

In all cases, try to focus on the action you want buyers to take as a result of seeing your ad. Options would include, for example, visiting your Web site, calling a toll-free number, contacting a local office, sending in a response card, and so on.

Web Sites

We don't have to belabor the obvious: When it comes to the Web, the bloom is off the rose. The widely shared expectation that Web sites would be able to sell anything to anyone, 24/7, has been brought crashing to earth by mediocre results. True, an ever-increasing amount of *buying* takes place on the Web, but very little selling (or need development) actually goes on. Most Web sites are nothing more than electronic brochures. They lead with product, and they treat it as if it were a noun. In fact, it's difficult even to point to a model "selling" Web site.

What went wrong? It has a lot to do with the evolution of the relevant technologies. Web sites began as one-dimensional and static, mainly because of the limitations of modem speeds and twisted-pair capacities. Interactivity was a far-off dream. With the advent of high-speed Internet connections, these barriers have been overcome for many applications. A recent development, product configurators, can lead potential buyers step-by-step to a purchase recommendation—in other words, through a crudely interactive process.

So although technology has eliminated many barriers, the interactions still tend to be plodding and mechanical. We have yet to see a Web site that begins to simulate the work of a CustomerCentric salesperson. Perhaps it's unfair to expect a machine to interact with a person as well as another person would, especially since computers are still largely limited to seeing the world in a binary, on/off way. But Web sites do hold the potential to have dialogues with buyers, and we think they should begin to live up to that potential.

The Solution Development Prompter described in previous chapters is all about dialogues, based on "conversation architecture." There's no inherent reason why this kind of architecture can't be recreated in the context of the Web. Given adequate investments in programming, a Web site should be able to discover the interests of the Web visitor and, based on those interests, present content in a sequence that simulates a sales call.

We remain optimistic. Think how far these technologies have come in less than 2 decades. Even with today's technologies, we believe, it should be possible to build a Web site capable of developing a visitor's vision, either to qualify a buyer or—depending on the type of offering and expense—to take a sale all the way to closure. With tomorrow's technologies, it should be far easier.

Letters, Faxes, and Emails

These can be effective ways to create demand, either on a companywide basis or within a salesperson's territory. If best practices are going to be shared companywide, Marketing should provide a readily accessible inventory of sales-ready messages that are industry and title specific, so that individuals are not reinventing the wheel. Let us defer this discussion until the next chapter, where we'll focus on prospecting efforts within an individual territory.

Redefining Marketing's Role in Demand Creation

To summarize: Marketing can play a critical role in creating demand for a company's offerings. If Marketing is going to serve as the front end of sales cycles, then its messages across all media should be consistent with the salesperson behavior we espouse: namely, leading with business issues with people who can make decisions and allocated unbudgeted funds.

Marketing should be the keeper of Sales-Ready Messaging, but should not be expected to accomplish this in a vacuum. Sales should provide constructive input, continuing to fine tune material so that it reflects best practices in the field.

Marketing and Sales have to agree on the definition of a lead. We submit that a legitimate lead contains three components:

- Vertical industry
- Title
- Goal

There are only a certain number of people out there who are already looking to change. Chances are, they already have a preferred vendor in mind. Demand generation entails causing people who weren't looking to change to begin a buying cycle. This segment represents many times the potential number of people who are already looking, and offers the advantage of allowing salespeople to be proactive and become Column A, instead of being reactive and competing for a silver medal.

People who are not already looking to change have no budget allocated, so the focus in those organizations should be on people who have the authority to free up unbudgeted funds. And, as always, we strongly recommended leading with business issues and usage, rather than the traditional "spray and pray" approach.

As we have seen, CustomerCentric Selling cannot begin until buyers share either a business goal or a problem that a vendor's offering can help them address. Whether you are designing advertising campaigns, participating in trade shows, or putting on seminars, you should begin with the end in mind: creating qualified leads for the sales organization.

In summary, few companies have a working definition of the interrelationship between Sales and Marketing. Companies implementing CustomerCentric Selling embrace the following description of each function's role:

Marketing, through its programs, is responsible for getting buyers who are not currently looking to change to consider looking. Marketing is also the keeper of the tools needed to take a businessperson from a goal to a vision of a solution.

Salespeople execute the sales process using Sales-Ready Messaging. In doing so, they are responsible for documenting calls so that sales managers can audit and grade the opportunities in the pipeline.

CHAPTER 10

Business Development
The Hardest Part of a Salesperson's Job

ONE OF THE BIGGEST CHALLENGES that salespeople face is building and maintaining sufficient opportunities in their pipeline so they can meet their quotas. When pipelines are inadequate, many salespeople are subjected to intense pressure—whether imposed internally (by their own desire to excel) or externally (by their manager [or spouse]). In many cases, salespeople fail because they are unable to generate interest, and thereby do not initiate buying cycles with buyers. Once in the door, they can do a creditable job; they're just inept at opening the door.

Prospecting is an activity that many organizations do exactly wrong. Many companies ask their brand new salespeople to cut their teeth on the prospecting of new territories. As they progress—assuming they survive—more and more of their work consists of servicing continuing customer accounts. Their prospecting responsibilities, therefore, either decrease or disappear entirely. The salesperson gets the idea (sometimes from his or her sponsoring organization) that prospecting is somehow beneath his or her dignity.

In fact, the vast majority of salespeople would consider the world a better place to live if they *never* had to take responsibility for uncovering new opportunities. Given a choice of 4 hours of cold telephone prospecting or having a root canal, many experienced salespeople would opt for the latter. But this is shortsighted. First, they've already demonstrated that they have some talent at prospecting; otherwise, they would have been long gone. The company needs ongoing utilization of those skills. And second, at least as we see it, a salesperson's overall skills erode if he or she loses the ability to generate interest from strangers. Third, our definition of prospecting is causing buyers (including existing customers) who weren't looking to change, to look.

In this chapter, we'll look at the different ways that salespeople drum up prospects—including telemarketing, referrals, and written communications and suggest techniques for making the prospecting process more customer-centric, and therefore more successful.

The Psychology of Prospecting

Prospecting difficulties come in two flavors: "cannot" and "will not." Each flavor requires a different response.

On an ongoing basis, most sales managers assess whether a pipeline contains sufficient opportunities to allow a salesperson to achieve his or her assigned quota. This analysis is usually done without regard for the mix of new accounts versus add-on business. If a pipeline is thin, sales managers tend to focus on the quantity of prospecting activity, often without helping salespeople improve the quality of their efforts. After a period of time, if a manager determines that one of the salespeople is not generating enough prospects, the knee-jerk reaction is to mandate that a higher percentage of his or her time be spent uncovering new opportunities. And in some cases—namely, cases of "will not"—this is the best way to go: Mandate more activity, and monitor subsequent prospecting behavior closely.

But ordering someone to spend more time on a given task does little good if the individual lacks the requisite skills to accomplish what is expected. And this brings us to the more common problem: "cannot." By and large, salespeople are proud and highly motivated individuals; in fact, in many cases, the desire to excel takes precedence over financial motivation. So lackluster prospecting results are most often due to skill deficiencies. And poor results due to poor skills quickly plant and reinforce the notion that prospecting is drudgery. In other words, "cannot" turns into "will not."

On a recent client engagement, we were hired to assist a vice president (VP) of Sales in reviewing the pipeline of all eighteen of the company's salespeople. We scheduled a 45-minute conference call with each of the salespeople, with the VP sitting in as well. Each salesperson was asked in advance to be prepared to discuss his or her top three opportunities.

During each discussion, we asked—at different times, and in different ways—how the salesperson first learned about each opportunity. Out of fifty-four opportunities in their collective pipelines, a total of four had been proactively prospected. It turned out that in many cases, the salesperson's entire prospecting activities were limited to calling Marketing and asking a pointed question: "Where are the leads from the last trade show?" This opened the eyes of the VP of Sales, who had no idea how little proactive prospecting was being done by his salespeople.

Sales performance is largely driven by human nature. It's very common for salespeople to follow an outstanding quarter with a lackluster one. Why? Because they stopped prospecting as soon as their pipeline looked reasonably healthy. This is human nature: Less attractive activities get put on tomorrow's list. How many times have you made a to-do list, and discovered at day's end that you had done only the tasks you detested the least? So it is with prospecting. Salespeople are extremely creative at finding reasons why they are too busy to prospect.

Everyone who has tried it will agree on one thing: Prospecting can be a humbling experience. Nevertheless, it needs to be done. Closing business is good news: You get the transaction. But there's accompanying bad news: One opportunity has been removed from your funnel, and now needs to be replaced.

In many cases, the first place prospectors turn to is the telephone.

Telemarketing and Stereotypes

We've already touched on the negative stereotype of sales as a profession. Pretty consistently, public opinion polls place salespeople and lawyers on the bottom two rungs of the ladder of honorable careers. At the very bottom of the bottom, we would guess, are telemarketers who interrupt your family at dinner to sell you stuff at home. In fact, some people get so upset about being disturbed by sales calls at home that they buy electronic "zappers" to identify and screen out computer-dialed calls. Most of us try to introduce telemarketers to Mr. Dial Tone as quickly as possible.

Understanding that they have to sink the hook as quickly as possible, telemarketers resort to one or more techniques that they've been taught to get your attention and keep you on the line. For example, they

- Overuse (and frequently mispronounce) your name
- Ask, "How are you today?"
- Begin with, "I'm not trying to sell you anything"
- Ask inane questions, such as, "How would you like to get a higher return on your money?"
- Talk nonstop for the first 90 seconds (if you give them that long)

Since nothing we write will make telemarketers go away—and since you may be on the hook to be an effective telemarketer—let's look at some sample dialogues, and think about what works and what doesn't through the lens of CustomerCentric salesmanship. Imagine you are sitting in your den and the phone rings. You pick up the receiver, and you hear:

This is Tom Robinson with Acme Heating. How are you this evening? (brief pause) Acme takes pride in our outstanding reputation for customer service. We offer a complete line of furnaces and would welcome an opportunity to spend about 30 minutes discussing your requirements. We'll be in your area Wednesday evening. Would 7:00 or 8:00 work better for you?

Not bad enough to set your teeth on edge—probably—but there are several things that prospects might find objectionable in this approach, all of which reduce the likelihood of the seller's getting that appointment. For example:

- The script contains an insincere personal question in the second sentence. They are calling to sell you something—do they really care how you are?
- Next, a biased opinion regarding customer service is offered. Doesn't every company say its service is outstanding?
- The script mentions a specific product (a furnace). What are the chances that you were thinking about a new furnace—in other words, that you were already looking to change? Leading with product makes it likely that the buyer will ask about cost early in the conversation (assuming that there *is* a conversation). It would

be virtually impossible for the seller to provide a meaningful response, given the variables of house size, insulation, oil versus gas, and so on. And as we've already seen in other contexts, without the potential value of an offering being established in advance, virtually any figure will seem high. Of course, the salesperson can simply be evasive about price, but this can be deadly, especially early in the call.

- The script as written exerts pressure by asking, presumptuously, for an appointment at two specific times that are convenient to the seller—and does so without having generated potential interest.

The objective of this script is to get that appointment. We suggest, however, that the script could be far more effective if there were an initial attempt to gain mindshare. Yes, there's a chance that someone is sitting out there shivering, and thinking about how their current heating unit needs to be replaced. But in almost every case, there is little upside in leading with product (the furnace). Let's assume we make an attempt to improve our odds by doing some precall planning and research. By reviewing recent real estate transactions and stopping by Town Hall, we learn that a particular house has been purchased within the past 2 months, and was built in 1937. Here is a different script, which attempts to generate interest in 30 seconds or less:

> *This is Tom Robinson with Acme Heating. We've been working with homeowners in Park View Estates since 1979. A common concern of people buying older homes is the high cost of heating them. I've helped my customers reduce energy costs, and would welcome an opportunity to discuss some approaches with you.*

Note that we've eliminated the personal question. The opinion about customer service has been replaced with a fact that helps the homeowner reach the conclusion that Acme is an established and reputable business. Rather than mentioning a furnace, we attempt to gain mindshare by referring to the "high cost of heating older homes." This keeps the potential field of discussion broad in the prospect's mind; it might have to do with insulation, water heater or burner maintenance, or other topics, all of which fall into the category of "energy costs." The script heads off a premature discussion of price, and ends in a way that makes a yes/no response difficult.

Some Basic Techniques

The script is extremely important, and so is the way you deliver the script. Following are some basic delivery techniques for successful telephone prospecting. These apply to all kinds of phone sales efforts, so keep them in mind as you read later sections of this chapter.

As you probably have already discovered, when you are prospecting, it is important that it not sound as though a script is being read. Therefore, you need to internalize the script. (This is not the same as memorizing; by "internalize," we mean make it your own.) Practice by delivering it into your own voicemail, then playing it back to evaluate your delivery. When actually making the calls, use a long phone cord, or a cell phone, or a headset, or any other device that will allow you to pace and gesture. Your voice and delivery tend to be more natural and animated when you are in motion than when you're sitting at your desk.

Another suggestion is to smile. While we have no research to support the notion that smiling will improve your results, it can't hurt. People can "hear" your smile. You'll feel better. So why not try it?

Generating Incremental Interest

Studies show that on average, telemarketers have less than 20 seconds to generate initial interest. This window can be shorter or longer, depending on how "salesy" the person sounds and how tolerant the person receiving the call is.

In light of that sobering statistic, the initial objective of a telephone script must be to establish curiosity in the mind of the buyer about how to address a need, achieve a goal, or solve a problem. As you'll see, we recommend attempting to create incremental interest with the initial script to gain mindshare and see if you (as the seller) can earn another few minutes to uncover a goal. If you're successful in this effort, you then may want to see if the need can be further developed over the phone. (Most salespeople make a mistake when they try to schedule an appointment at the earliest possible time.)

We'd now like to change the scenario somewhat. Let's imagine that you are a salesperson calling a prospect at his or her office. This means that you're attempting to interrupt the prospect's business day, rather than his or her personal life, which in many cases is easier (but still not easy) to accomplish.

Our definition of prospecting is attempting to cause people who weren't looking to change to consider doing so. As we've seen in earlier chapters, if the expenditure hasn't already been planned, then no budget exists for it. Therefore, your goal is to initiate contacts at levels senior enough to free up funds (create budget). Your chances of success will be improved by using a "rifle" rather than a "shotgun" approach, one that is specific to a particular title, business issue, and industry segment.

We demonstrated this approach in Chapter 8 when we created a menu of issues for a customer relationship management (CRM) offering. In looking at titles, our approach would be to initiate contact with prospects at the CEO or CFO level, because in many cases a VP of Sales or a CIO would lack the ability to get unbudgeted funds.

Let's assume that we've chosen to target CFOs of software companies. The next step is to choose what we believe would be the highest-probability business issue a CFO would be facing. This can be done across the board by making a judgment call on industry trends, but customization after visiting a company's Web site or doing some research can improve success rates.

Having said that, there is a constant risk of "paralysis by analysis" in sales. Some salespeople are so reluctant to make cold calls that they spend all their time researching. (On their to-do lists, researching is a more attractive option than prospecting.) You simply can't afford to wait until you know the birth dates of all board members, have analyzed the past four annual reports, and have calculated the associated "acid ratios." Past a certain point, it's better to just dive in, having made some intelligent assumptions.

In looking at the menu of potential business goals of a CFO, without having specific knowledge about a target company our inclination would be to choose "forecasting accuracy" from the menu. Out of 100 CFOs, how many do you feel are satisfied with the accuracy of the monthly forecast provided by their senior sales executive? The choice of this business issue provides the broadest range of potential acceptance. And while they're not happy with the current forecasting methods, most CFOs have concluded there isn't a better way to do it, and haven't given thought to how to improve forecasting.

With telephone prospecting, we've found you will have a higher success rate if you lead with a business problem, give a root cause, and finish with the corresponding goal. Therefore, the goal of "improved forecasting accuracy" from the menu of goals should be changed to the problem of "inaccurate forecasting." In addition, you need to get the problem to be more specific, by offering a reason (for which you have a usage scenario) that the CFO may be experiencing that difficulty. Because a CRM system offers the ability to capture close rates by salespeople, this represents a high-probability reason for inaccurate forecasting.

Here, then, is the suggested script:

> *This is John Busby with The XYZ Company. I've worked with software companies since 1995. A common concern other finance executives have shared with me is inaccurate revenue forecasts caused by varying close rates of their salespeople. We've helped other companies improve their forecasting accuracy, and would like to discuss some approaches with you.*

Experience suggests that when a person in a business setting answers the phone, you have 30 seconds or less to generate initial interest with your script. (Note that you've gained a little time over a call into the home.) For that reason, we don't suggest asking how the person is (you will be perceived as insincere), or whether or not this is a good time (given an out, buyers will say no).

In keeping with the rifle versus shotgun philosophy, the company or industry should be referenced. Even vendors with horizontal offerings do the majority of their business with mainstream-market buyers who don't want to be first, meaning that they want to know that your company has done business with others within their market segment. We also include the title of the person we are calling on. We suggest avoiding the use of the title "vice president," because in some industries (e.g., banking and financial services) there are multiple levels of vice presidents (such as AVP, EVP, Sr. VP, and Sr. Executive VP), and a senior vice president may be offended if you speak of "working with vice presidents." Instead, use the function (Sales, Marketing, Finance, IT, and so on) followed by the term *executive*. Virtually all people in organizations like to be referred to as executives.

The most important portion of the script is the wording of the business issue. In order for you to read the script in 30 seconds or less, the issue must be concise (twenty words or less). As noted, the best hit rates we've seen have been achieved by leading with a problem, including a reason for the problem that points to one of your usage scenarios. Consider how much less compelling the script would be if it read: " . . . other finance executives have shared with me is the inaccuracy of revenue forecasts." Tweaking a few words in stating the problem and the reason behind it can dramatically affect success rates.

A quick word here on a resource that sales organizations leave largely untapped: their customers. One of the best ways to verify that your menus of goals/problems and prospecting scripts are on target is to ask a corresponding title within your existing customer base for an informal review and edit. (This is a favor that you would ask only of a satisfied customer, of course.) Two—and maybe three—good things can come out of this. First, and most important, you can gain valuable insight into how best to approach the customer's counterparts. Second, you flatter the customer by asking and valuing his or her opinion. And third, if circumstances permit, you might ask if the customer can think of any real-life prospects on whom the menus and scripts could be tested.

Some Common Scenarios

We believe that if the script initiates a conversation with the prospect, it was successful. So let's discuss the responses you are most likely to get, and how to handle them. Keep in mind that you cannot begin to sell until a buyer shares a goal or admits a problem that you can help to address. Here are some potential buyer responses:

1. *The buyer shows no interest.* "I don't have that problem and/or I'm not interested." It could be the person is busy, is in a bad mood, doesn't have his or her attention grabbed by the business issue, doesn't like salespeople, doesn't face that problem, and so on. The most important thing to remember in this situation is not to take the rejection personally. This is easier if you prospect using a script and a plan, rather than winging it. (It's not *you* they don't like; it's the script.)

When you get this response, offer the other menu items for that title. You can make the transition by saying:

Other issues finance executives I've worked with are facing include

- Low margins due to the increasing cost of sales
- Increasing cost of Marketing efforts to generate leads
- Lost cross-selling revenue because IT cannot provide a single view of customers

Would you like to learn how we've helped our customers address any of these issues?

This yes/no question ends in one of two ways. Either the buyer is curious about one or more of these items, in which case you can begin a conversation, or the buyer says he or she is not interested. In the latter case, thank the person for his or her time, get a dial tone, and make your next call. Keep in mind that prospecting can be done at several different levels in the same organization. Even if one or more people you contacted were not interested, if you have menus and scripts for other titles within that organization, you can continue your effort to begin a buying cycle at that account.

2. *The buyer shows immediate interest in discussing an issue from the menu.*

3. *The buyer expresses mild interest and asks you to forward information.* Inexperienced salespeople tend to see this as a positive sign. More experienced salespeople are more cynical: They believe (with good reason) that this is a convenient and reasonably polite way to get salespeople to leave you alone. When the time comes to follow up, the prospect (or more likely, the assistant) will say that he or she has reviewed the material and will get back to you if interested. Our suggestion is, pursue these leads systematically, but don't hold your breath in anticipation of a positive response.

When you get a request to send information, do both the prospect and yourself a favor by indicating that you have an extensive set of offerings, and you would like to get a better idea of the prospect's particular areas of interest so that the material you send will be targeted toward them. Either this will allow a conversation (your desired result), or the prospect will ask that you just send the information. In this circumstance, we believe that you still have prospecting to do, as the buyer has not shared a business objective with you. Instead of sending a full set of four-color brochures, consider sending something along the lines of a prospecting letter, fax, or email that is geared toward getting the buyer to consider looking to change. (We'll discuss these tools subsequently.)

In cases where the buyers express interest but don't explicitly sign on with the goal mentioned in your script, your continuing objective is to get them engaged. This means a continuing conversation—either now or later. "Now" means extending this phone conversation, which means, in turn, that you ask if this is a convenient time. "Later" means either on the phone or in person.

To the extent that you control this choice, you should think carefully about how best to use your time. Many salespeople immediately request a face-to-face meeting, but such meetings can be time intensive. You should consider the title of the person you are talking with, the size of the prospect company, and the amount of time needed to make a face-to-face call. Given the obligatory social niceties involved in meeting someone for the first time, you may well find that you can get more done in a 15-minute phone conversation than in a 30-minute meeting.

If a phone call sometime in the near future is the next step agreed to, make sure that the appointment is booked on both persons' calendars—yours and the prospect's—and that time is blocked out for that purpose. It's rarely good enough to agree to "talk Tuesday afternoon." Tuesday afternoon will come, and something else will replace the phone call as a priority—unless a specific time has been reserved.

Let's assume that the prospect is curious and has time now to continue. Keep in mind that a buying cycle has not yet begun because a goal has not been shared. There's more work to be done. The transitional phrase could be

> *It may be helpful for me to tell you about work I did with another finance executive of a software company who wanted to improve the accuracy of her forecast. This was difficult because close rates varied widely by salesperson. Each month, this executive found that she had to discount the numbers she was getting from Sales, because they were too optimistic. She wanted to capture close rates by salespeople at different parts of the sales cycle on an ongoing basis, so that each month, they could be applied against the gross numbers to create a forecast. We provided that capability. As a result, her forecasting accuracy has improved by 54 percent.*

You'll recognize this as a Success Story, described in previous chapters. The Success Story is used to build credibility for both the salesperson and his or her company. It also attempts to cause someone who was not looking to change to share a goal. Part of that effort is to highlight an area the buyer was unaware of, had not considered, or believed was unachievable.

After sharing the Success Story, it is time to provide the prospect an opportunity to speak. The range of responses ideally has been limited to an area the salesperson would like to focus on, with the ultimate intent of having the buyer share either a business goal or a problem. About 90 seconds into the call, you've earned the right to ask, "Is forecasting accuracy an issue you'd like to discuss?" If the buyer says yes, you will see how to proceed in the next chapter. If the buyer responds with a no, thank the buyer for the time and branch to dial tone.

Thus far in our scenarios, we have given the salesperson the great luxury of being able to talk directly to the targeted title. Unfortunately, that does not happen as often as salespeople would like. Many territory salespeople rely almost exclusively on the telephone when attempting to uncover new opportunities, and while the telephone offers the advantage of minimal time and effort up front, studies suggest that it is not a very effective way of contacting executives.

Therefore, we believe, salespeople have to cover their territories with additional methods, beyond phone calling. These methods include referrals, letters, faxes, emails, recommendations, and seminars on an ongoing basis.

The Power of Referrals

Satisfied customers, as mentioned above, represent a huge potentially untapped asset. People who have made a buying decision have a natural tendency to conclude that they've made a wise choice, which can be further validated if others make the same decision. Consider this: It is rare to get a negative response when you ask people how they like their expensive new car (even if they've had a less than stellar experience with it). Even unhappy customers want to validate their choices, so happy customers tend to be more than willing to help a vendor succeed by finding new accounts.

There are three common reasons why vendors fail to reap the benefit of referrals from their clients:

1. Salespeople fail to ask for referrals.

2. When getting referrals, salespeople fail to ask for a "warm" referral, meaning that their customer will make an initial call or do an introduction. Beyond that, salespeople don't make an attempt to discover from their customers what specific business goals or problems the prospect may be facing.

3. When calling prospects they are referred to, salespeople fail to go much beyond saying: "Joe Smith is one of our happy customers and sug-

gested I contact you." With a referral, as with all other prospects, your objective is to have the prospect share a business goal or problem so you can start selling. One of the best ways to do that is to share a Success Story for the customer that referred you. One of the easiest circumstances in which to make the connection is when the titles of both your customer and the referral are the same. When they are not, be sure you are attempting to relate to business issues the prospect is facing. Go into the meeting with a plan, including a menu of potential goals for the person you are calling on.

Letters/Faxes/Emails

Written correspondence prior to making phone contact can dramatically increase your chances of getting through on the phone and uncovering new opportunities. Here are some guidelines to follow:

1. Shorter is better. Any prospecting letter longer than one page is not going to be read by many prospects.

2. Early in the correspondence, it is critical to get the buyer's attention. This can be accomplished by offering a menu of potential goals or problems.

3. Minimize hype and opinions that start the buyer in the direction of concluding that the message is too "salesy."

4. A prospecting letter is not a place to get the buyer to understand very much about your company. Focus instead on generating curiosity. If you achieve this short-term objective and the buyer becomes interested, he or she will want to know more about your company.

5. Understand that there is a high probability that the correspondence will be screened by the executive's assistant.

6. Aim high (maybe higher than your targeted title), because if the executive is interested, you may be referred to a lower level.

Our experience has been that email is the least effective way to make an initial contact in writing. Simply put, if an executive (or assistant) doesn't recognize the email address of the sender, the chances that the message will be opened and read are small. The title of the email becomes extremely important: It must be scripted very tightly to generate enough interest, perhaps even indicating that some research about the target company has been done, although space is limited.

Prospecting letters also have their limitations. As with direct mail, their biggest challenge is getting opened and read before getting pitched. Many salespeople hand-write addresses on envelopes and use a stamp rather than a postage meter to increase the odds that their prospecting correspondence will get read.

Many salespeople like to use letters prior to calling, because when they get the assistant on the phone and the assistant asks, "Who is this, and what is it regarding?," they have an easy response: "This is Dan Ahrens of XYZ Software, calling to follow up on my letter dated November 18. Is Joe available?"

This sounds like a good tactic, but in fact, of the possible responses, most are not favorable. The options, starting with the only good one:

1. The assistant agrees to put you right through.
2. The assistant doesn't recall your letter.
3. The assistant threw your letter out.
4. The letter has been misplaced.
5. The assistant read the letter and concluded it was not of interest.
6. The assistant brushes you off: "I'm sure he's read it. We'll get back to you if we are interested."

So although letters can be effective, they face multiple barriers: getting opened, read, passed along, saved, and so on. Letter campaigns take time, can incur expense in processing and tracking, and usually involve a delay before follow-ups can be done.

For these and other reasons, faxes offer several advantages. First, consider what has happened to the volume of faxes you receive. With the advent of email, scanning, and attaching documents to emails, the number of faxes being received has dramatically decreased. We see that as an advantage. Faxes aren't in envelopes that may be "round-filed" before being opened. Faxes sent in the morning can be followed up the very same day. Consider the fax shown in Figure 10-1, which seeks to gain mind space for our product (CustomerCentric selling techniques) in the mind of one Ben Zoldan.

Many of our clients find that sending a letter by fax is an effective way to improve the odds of gaining a conversation with the target title. One

To: Ben Zoldan   From: Michele Khoury
Date: xx/xx/xx   Re: Interview on your Web Site

In the interview posted on your Web site, you stated a goal of having XYZ Company double its revenues in the next 3 years. To achieve this objective, do you believe Sales and Tactical Marketing will have to work in concert? If so, here are some areas that may be important to achieving your goal:

1. Marketing campaigns should generate interest at targeted decision-maker levels.
2. When calling at executive levels, salespeople should lead with high-probability business issues, rather than your offerings.
3. When evaluating pipeline, sales managers need a consistent grading system, so they can disqualify low-probability opportunities.
4. On an ongoing basis, sales managers should be able to assess their salespeople on six individual skills to identify deficiencies, and they should be able to help their salespeople improve in these areas.
5. When making calls, salespeople should consistently position offerings specific to title/industry and business goals via Sales-Ready Messaging.

CustomerCentric Selling helps clients define and implement sales processes to address these and other issues. I would like to schedule 15 minutes to discuss your sales environment, and mutually determine if further investigation is warranted.

I'll call this afternoon at 4:30. I look forward to talking with you.

Figure 10-1 Seeking to Gain Mind Space

of the advantages of this approach is that if the executive's assistant sees the fax, he or she gets a clear idea of what you would like to discuss. If the assistant feels some of the items are of interest, the fax provides Sales-Ready Messaging to help him or her explain why a phone conversation may be warranted.

Prospecting plus Qualifying Equals Pipeline

Salespeople generally dislike trying to contact strangers, but prospecting activity on an ongoing basis is essential to meeting or exceeding an assigned quota. For enterprise solutions, the difference between a good and a great year could boil down to causing two additional prospects per month to consider changing. The second key aspect of creating and maintaining a productive pipeline is qualifying and quantifying a buyer's need for your offering—and that is the subject of our next chapter.

Developing Buyer Vision through Sales-Ready Messaging

IN PREVIOUS CHAPTERS, we've emphasized the importance of getting to the point where a buyer has either shared a goal or admitted a problem that the CustomerCentric salesperson's offering can help them address. This is a watershed event, in that it starts a buying cycle. Buying cycles end in one of two ways:

- *A decision is made to buy*—either from you or from another sales organization.
- *Buyers decide not to buy*. The most common reasons buyers don't buy are that they conclude the proposed offering is too risky or complicated, it can't be cost-justified, or their priorities shift. The phenomenon of "no decision" is more common with mainstream-market than with early-market buyers.

The sharing of a goal makes a salesperson's job significantly easier, because the buyer now sees potential value in improving one or more business variables. This can create a sense of urgency, depending on how much potential improvement can be achieved. Sellers are usually trying to push sales cycles ahead. Now, there may be a sense of a cost of delay. While the buyer is deciding what to do—change or not change—the buyer may realize the enterprise is losing money. Once a goal has been shared, the seller is positioned to start developing the buyer's vision by using Sales-Ready Messaging.

Patience and Intelligence

While having a buyer share a goal is a highly positive event, it also can be the catalyst that causes traditional salespeople to misbehave. Picture a traditional salesperson, for example, making a call on a finance executive. The executive says, "Our forecasting accuracy has been awful, and this is an area in which I'd like us to improve." What response will most traditional salespeople make in this situation?

If a traditional salesperson's process does not have patience built into it, he or she most likely will attempt to project his or her vision of a solution onto the buyer, rather than developing a vision that the buyer owns. Many launch right into something to the effect of, "Here's what you need to improve forecasting accuracy!" Then begins the intense "spray and pray" of features, many of which the executive doesn't understand, isn't interested in, and may not even need. Mix in some ownership for the vendor or seller achieving the buyer's goal, and you have a potential lost opportunity.

Sharing a seller's opinion or trying to impose that opinion on a buyer won't work in most cases. Instead, once a goal is shared, the traditional salesperson needs two qualities in order to take a CustomerCentric next step:

- A questioning etiquette that provides artificial patience to avoid giving the seller's opinion of what the buyer needs.
- Artificial intelligence in the form of questions designed to (1) understand the buyer's current environment, (2) understand what parts of the offering are needed, and (3) propose usage scenarios to the buyer.

These two components, integrated in the Solution Development Prompter (SDP), provide a template enabling sellers to deliver Sales-Ready Messaging. These templates help traditional sellers become CustomerCentric by leading the buyer to a vision of a solution that the buyer owns.

Let's say a CFO expresses a desire to improve forecasting accuracy. The CustomerCentric way for sellers to exhibit patience and frame the conversation is to ask, "How do you forecast today?" This allows the buyer to discuss his or her current approach, which in turn allows the following positive things to happen:

- The salesperson gains an understanding of how the CFO currently forecasts.
- The cost of poor forecasting and/or the potential benefit of more accurate forecasting can be established.
- The usage scenarios the buyer is most likely to want and need can be uncovered and offered.
- Usage scenarios the buyer is unlikely to need can be identified and avoided.
- The buyer concludes that the salesperson is competent, by virtue of being able to ask intelligent questions related to forecasting accuracy.
- The buyer concludes that this salesperson is different from the negative stereotype.
- The seller allows the buyer to decide which usage scenarios are needed.
- The buyer can decide if having those usage scenarios would empower him or her to achieve the goal of more accurate forecasting.

While few would disagree that these are all great outcomes, it is sobering to realize that the vast majority of salespeople (90 percent?) will be unable to achieve them without Sales-Ready Messaging, which ultimately positions a company's offerings. Once the components of a conversation (vertical industry/title/goal) have been established, salespeople can benefit by executing Solution Development Prompters. Sales organizations can also benefit because the output of these calls becomes more objective and less dependent on the salesperson's biased opinion.

Good Questions, in the Right Sequence

In the balance of this chapter, we're going to describe, step by step, how a seller would use a Solution Development Prompter to develop the buyer's vision. First, though, it might be helpful to think about the different types of questions that can be asked, and when to use each:

- *Open questions* require "essay" answers, allowing the buyer to take the conversation anywhere. Buyers feel safe, but the downside is that the conversation may not go in the direction the traditional salesperson wants to go. The only open question contained in Customer-Centric Selling is: "What are you (or your organization) hoping to accomplish?" This allows buyers to talk—but if they don't bring up a business objective, the salesperson has the menu of goals from the Targeted Conversations List as a safety net to steer the conversation.
- *Framing questions* offer the best of both worlds, in that the buyer is free to expound, but the salesperson has placed boundaries on the direction the response can take. "How do you forecast today?" is not an open question, because the response will relate to a topic the salesperson wants to discuss: forecasting. Questions beginning with the word *how* help facilitate conversational sales calls. Buyers do not feel "sold" when salespeople ask framing questions.
- *Closed questions* require short, specific answers. Potential answers to a closed question would include yes, no, a number, and so on. Closed questions are best used after framing questions, to drill down on and quantify specific areas. Also, note that the only way a salesperson can convert a usage scenario to a capability is by posing a yes/no question to the buyer and getting an affirmative response.

Once a buyer has shared a goal, we recommend starting with a framing question beginning with the words: "How do you _____ today?" It is a logical, safe question that is virtually guaranteed to get buyers to describe their current process, which is exactly where a CustomerCentric salesperson wants to go.

Once a buyer has responded, it is time to follow up with diagnostic questions, ideally biased toward usage scenarios that your offering provides. In order to accomplish this, as previously noted, we adhere to Stephen Covey's concept of "starting with the end in mind." That is the reason why, in Chapter 8, we developed the potential capabilities using the EQPA (event, question, player, action) formula, in the form of usage scenarios on the right side of the Solution Development Prompter. We then built the diagnostic questions on the left side (see Figure 8-1).

These diagnostic questions are now used to discover which usage scenarios the buyer is likely (and unlikely) to want. The salesperson follows up with the buyer by asking the questions in a sequence that flows within the call, takes detailed notes, and—when finishing the diagnosis—does a summary to make sure both the buyer and the seller are on the same page.

A Good Conversation

Let's walk through a dialogue between a CustomerCentric salesperson and a targeted decision maker at the VP of Finance/CFO level. (Refer back to Figure 8-3.) The decision maker wants to forecast more accurately, and the salesperson is using a Solution Development Prompter developed for selling sales force automation/customer relationship management (SFA/CRM) applications:

Salesperson: *How do you forecast today?*

Buyer: *With great difficulty. Our overly optimistic VP of Sales gives me a monthly forecast that I have to reduce by about 50 percent just to be close. Even then, many of the specific opportunities he forecasts will close do not. Luckily, we get some unexpected business most months, or we would really be in a pickle!*

Salesperson: *How do your forecasting metrics vary by district?*

Buyer: *We have hired sales managers from a number of major companies, and they all seem to have their own way of qualifying and grading opportunities. At this point, I don't believe we have a standard grading system that is enforceable.*

Salesperson: *How many salespeople do you have, and do many rush or feel pressured to do their forecasts?*

Buyer: *We have 200 salespeople, and from what I hear they all despise forecasting.*

Salesperson: *Do you think those who are below quota are overoptimistic in an attempt to show enough in their forecast so it looks as though they are going to get caught up?*

Buyer: *That seems logical to me. It would be best to verify that with some of our sales staff.*

Salesperson: *How do salespeople report progress to their managers on opportunities in the forecast?*

Buyer: *I'm led to believe it is done on an ad hoc basis. Sales managers are asking questions as the forecast is being created.*

Salesperson: *How do your managers determine which opportunities on the forecast are stalled?*

Buyer: *There doesn't seem to be any standard way. Even if managers know an opportunity is stalled, they seem reluctant to remove anything from the pipeline. We recently closed a deal that had been on the forecast for 13 months! When I ask if an opportunity should be removed, my VP of Sales reminds me of the one that took 13 months to close.*

Salesperson: *How do managers assess the current status of opportunities? How do they coach reps to qualify and disqualify prospects?*

Buyer: *If we have a way to assess the status of an opportunity other than calling the salesperson and asking his or her opinion about an account, I am unaware of it. I believe our managers pressure more than they coach—especially at quarter's end.*

Salesperson: *Do forecast probabilities vary by salesperson?*

Buyer: *Based on the experience and year-to-date (YTD) quota position of the salesperson, they vary widely. There are a limited number of reps in whom we have a high degree of confidence as relates to bringing in what they projected.*

Salesperson: *How do sales managers adjust for this, and do you adjust the numbers you get?*

Buyer: *I would hope managers would take close rates of salespeople into account, but it must be on a seat-of-the-pants basis. Managers are under pressure as well, so their YTD position against the district's quota also affects forecasting at this level. As I mentioned earlier, I typically adjust the number I get from my VP of Sales by about half.*

Salesperson: *If one or two large opportunities can make or break a forecast, how do you track those prospects?*

Buyer: *We missed our year-end earning target because two large opportunities that were supposed to close by December 31 didn't. Here it is, almost the end of March, and still neither one has closed. So yes, absolutely, large opportunities can make or break a quarter! But other than every C-level executive in the place calling the VP of Sales twice a day, there is no way for us to track those large opportunities.*

Salesperson: *What would better visibility on these opportunities mean to you?*

Buyer: *As CFO, I can deal with bad news much more effectively if there is some lead time. If a large opportunity drops off the forecast early in a quarter, we can do some belt tightening and hopefully find some other sources of revenue. My job is immeasurably harder with "high-wire act" finishes to our quarters. Any bad news from sales late in the quarter becomes an unpleasant discussion in staff and board meetings.*

Salesperson: *Let me summarize what we have covered so far. You have difficulty forecasting revenue, and it has affected your ability to hit your earnings targets. There is no consistent, companywide standard to use when grading opportunities. Unqualified opportunities find their way into your pipeline. It is difficult for managers to track progress. Close rates vary widely between salespeople, and you have a difficult time keeping updated on make-or-break deals. Ultimately, you have to reduce the forecast you receive by as much as 50 percent. Is that a fair summary?*

Buyer: *Yes, that pretty much describes how things happen today.*

Salesperson: *What approaches have you considered to improve forecasting accuracy?*

Buyer: *Other than changing Vice Presidents of Sales every couple of years, I am not sure what else we have tried or could try. I've had several sales executives in my career tell me that I just didn't understand sales.*

Salesperson: *Based on our discussion so far, may I offer a few suggestions?*

Buyer: *Please do.*

Salesperson: *After making sales calls, would it help if your sales people were prompted to report progress on that call against a standard set of company milestones for each opportunity in their pipeline?*

Buyer: *I have been clamoring for a standard set of milestones we could all use and understand. Prompting the salespeople seems like a good way to collect data after each sales call. I believe it would help.*

Salesperson: *When reviewing a salesperson's pipeline, would it be useful if your sales managers could access a secure central database* *from any location, evaluate the status of opportunities, and email suggestions to reps to improve the chances of winning the business?*

Buyer: *I believe so. We didn't discuss it, but many salespeople work out of remote or home offices.*

Salesperson: *On an ongoing basis, would you like a system that would track historical close rates for each salesperson by milestone, and apply them to your pipeline to help you predict revenue?*

Buyer: *I would like that! I might not have to tweak the numbers by 50 percent or more. It would be refreshing to apply a little science and logic to our forecasting process.*

Seller: *When evaluating the status of large opportunities, would it be beneficial if you or any C-level executive could access a central database via laptop anytime/anywhere, and review progress against milestones without having to talk to your VP of Sales?*

Buyer: *Yes.*

Salesperson: *If you had standard milestones updated after each sales call, an accessible pipeline database for coaching and reviewing progress, the ability to track historical close rates by milestone, and the ability to assess make-or-break opportunities from your laptop, do you think you would be able to achieve your goal of more accurately forecasting revenue?*

Buyer: *Yes, and I'd feel more confident going into board meetings if we had a better handle on forecasting.*

This conversation, of course, is something of an ideal. It mirrors the first role-play we have attendees execute in our CustomerCentric Selling workshops. The role-play coaches, who serve as buyers, are passive and cooperative the first time through so as to allow participants to walk before they run. The subsequent six role-plays become more challenging and realistic.

In the example above, the seller enjoyed the luxury of having a buyer readily share a goal and be willing to engage in a candid and pointed conversation, with the salesperson doing a lot of directing (through questioning). In sales calls, conversations almost never follow a script. But the SDP provides a guideline for (1) diagnosing the buyer's current situation with a bias toward your offering, and (2) developing a custom vision that the buyer owns. Please note that in this example, the buyer agreed to all four major diagnostic questions, and therefore the seller offered all four usage scenarios. In making calls, if a buyer does not agree to a reason the company cannot achieve a goal, the seller would not offer the corresponding usage scenario.

Competing for the Silver Medal?

Now let's now look at a more difficult conversation. This is a phone call, initiated by a lower-level buyer doing due diligence to justify buying from Column A:

Buyer: *Hello. This is Anita Quote with the ABC Company. We have decided to purchase CRM software. We have budget, and we want to make a decision soon. How quickly can you provide a demonstration, pricing, and a proposal?*

Salesperson: *First, can you tell me your role at ABC Company?*

Buyer: *I'm a senior analyst in our IT department.*

Salesperson: *It would be helpful if I could first get a sense of what your organization is hoping to accomplish with your CRM system.*

Buyer: *At this stage, I'm not prepared to get into a detailed discussion. What I really want is pricing information to determine if you should be placed on our short list of CRM vendors.*

Salesperson: *In order to make a recommendation, I need to get a better understanding of your requirements. Some of the other companies I've worked with were attempting to improve in one or more of the following areas:*
- *Reduce the cost of sales*
- *Increase cross selling*
- *Improve forecasting accuracy*
- *Increase sales revenue*

Are any of these objectives driving your company's evaluation of CRM?

Buyer: *Our major objective is improving forecasting accuracy, but as I've said, I don't have time to have a detailed discussion.*

This buyer's attitude is significantly different from that in the previous call on the CFO. This buyer already has an idea of what she wants. It's possible that she's already settled on one of your competitors, and is feigning interest, either to satisfy her company's bid procedures or with the intent of using your price as a lever to negotiate the best deal from Column A.

At the end of the dialogue presented above, you are very likely to get a poor response to the question: "How do you forecast today?" But an alternative is to ask: "As relates to forecasting, what specific CRM capabilities are you looking for?" Or, "How would you use a CRM system to forecast?" These questions encourage the buyer to share what she has settled on so far. They may also elicit an answer that tells you that Column A has not created capabilities to help the buyer fully understand how their offering could be used. Sometimes—based on the buyer's response and use of industry buzzwords—it is possible to determine which sales organization occupies Column A.

After the buyer has responded, your mission is to clarify in your mind (and potentially the buyer's mind) what capabilities are needed. Ideally, you can extend the list of requirements by adding a capability that the competition does not have—or that your traditional salesperson competitor might have failed to discuss, because he or she did not have Sales-Ready Messaging and was forced to wing it.

When dealing with a buyer who does not appear to want to have an open discussion, we suggest asking yes/no questions, going down the right side of the Solution Development Prompter to determine which capabilities the buyer will agree to. The most typical responses:

- "Yes, we want that" tells you that most likely Column A has already made that a requirement.
- "That isn't one of our requirements, but it could be helpful" is the best response, because it indicates that you may have the potential to introduce a different requirement. When you are coming in as Column B, the best way to improve your chances of winning is to bring up requirements Column A either can't meet or hasn't discussed.
- "No, that isn't something we need" can be true, but there are a few other possible interpretations. It could be that the buyer doesn't fully understand the usage scenario, or it could be that you are calling on the champion of Column A, who doesn't want to change the existing specification. In any case, if you feel it is a capability that you

would like to introduce, we'll show a fairly gentle way to make another attempt later in the call.

By asking the EQPA questions, you are earning the right to ask, "How are you currently forecasting?" At this stage in the call—as opposed to right after getting a reluctant buyer to share a goal—you may have established enough credibility (and earned enough space) in the mind of the buyer to get a reasonably detailed answer. Once the buyer has finished his or her answer, you can then ask the diagnostic questions corresponding to the capabilities agreed to. If by asking diagnostic questions you begin to build a case in the buyer's mind for a capability that was initially dismissed, you can do a minisummary and ask the capability questions again.

Vision Building around a Commodity

Solution Development Prompters can be used to facilitate virtually any sales discussion that can be distilled down to a buyer and business issue. We have worked with companies that sell what is perceived as a commodity, and—with some modifications—the vision-building model still works.

Let's say, for example, that you are a regional overnight delivery service, and you have the following differentiators when compared to national carriers:

- You can accept pallets.
- Your weight limits on packages are higher.
- Pickups can be made as late as 8:00 PM.
- Deliveries can be as early as 7:30 AM.
- All shipments are ground-based and within a 300-mile radius.
- You can deliver to a construction site without an address.
- You can offer a 20 percent savings over national carriers.

In this case, nearly every prospect on whom you're calling is already using and familiar with one or more overnight delivery services. Many traditional salespeople would lead with price in this situation, but this is a dangerous approach. Many customers would conclude that they would receive inferior service from a previously unknown carrier who initiates a discussion based on lower price. Another problem with this approach is that it creates a commodity sale mentality. Even if successful in generating interest, the buyer is likely to invite other carriers in to have them compete on price.

In selling situations such as this, it is important to give the buyer a reason to be unhappy with the current service. This can be done by selecting a Success Story highlighting one of your strengths and one of a national carrier's potential weaknesses.

The question that follows a Success Story can't be too obvious. For example: "How do you handle your overnight deliveries today?" is so basic as to be insulting. Since most people feel they understand how to use an overnight delivery service, a more appropriate question would be: "What would it take for you to consider switching overnight delivery companies?"

After getting the buyer's response, you can then ask the usage scenario questions on the right side of the Solution Development Prompter, with each of them being a potential differentiator. The seven differentiators listed above would have to be chosen judiciously, based on the title and industry the salesperson is calling on. A manufacturing company may be interested in shipping pallets, but a law firm or a bank would not be. Do your homework, here: A company billing its clients on a cost plus basis might not find a lower price attractive.

Let's assume that you (again, a representative for the regional overnight delivery service described above) are calling on the office manager of a law firm. After a brief introduction and Success Story about another law firm that elected to use your service, the conversation might go as follows, using the SDP shown in Figure 11-1.

Salesperson: *What would it take for you to consider switching overnight delivery companies?*

Buyer: *We're pretty satisfied with FBN Overnight Delivery's service.*

Salesperson: *Most people are satisfied with FBN, but let me ask: When attorneys are faced with a deadline, would it be helpful if you could arrange on-site pickups as late as 8:00 PM?*

Buyer: *We usually can get things done by 5:00, but 8:00 would be helpful to us.*

Salesperson: *When clients need quick turnaround, would you like to be able to have deliveries to them made as early as 7:30 the next morning?*

Title: Business Manager, Law Firm   **Goal:** Improved customer service for document deliveries
Product/Service: Overnight Delivery Service

> What has your experience with your current carrier been?

> What would it take for you to consider switching your overnight delivery service?

Frame · Diagnose · Confirm

Diagnostic Questions

1. If your attorneys are pressed to meet a deadline, what options do you have with your current service? How often has this become an issue? Has the quality of the firm's work ever been compromised by having to meet a deadline? What problems did that cause?
#,%,$,E?

2. How often do clients want documents prior to 10:30 AM and how do you handle these requests? Have you incurred expediting charges? How many of your clients would find getting documents three hours earlier beneficial?
#,%,$,E?

3. How often have airport logistical issues caused documents to be late? How understanding were clients of these delays? For clients within a 300-mile radius, was it strange to realize flight cancellations caused the delay?
#,%,$,E?

4. For documents being shipped in the tri-state area, do you feel air-based transport to be overkill? Would you agree ground-based transportation would be less costly to your delivery service?
#,%,$,E?

Usage Scenarios

Event: When attorneys are faced with tight deadlines
Question: Would it be helpful if
Player: You
Action: Could arrange on-site pickups as late as 8:00 PM?

Event: When clients need quick turnaround on documents
Question: Would they like
Player: Your firm
Action: To have the ability to make deliveries as early as 7:30 AM?

Event: When shipping critical documents within a 300-mile radius
Question: Would
Player: You
Action: Feel more comfortable having your deliveries be ground-based and thereby avoid potential delays due to airport closings or flight cancellations?

Event: When shipping documents within a 300-mile radius?
Question: Would
Player: You
Action: Like the ability to lower costs by taking advantage of ground-based delivery service?

Figure 11-1   Solution Development Prompter: Selling Overnight Delivery Services to a Law Firm

Buyer: *Some of our clients would want contracts or documents that early.*

Salesperson: *When shipping critical documents within a 300-mile radius, would you feel more comfortable having your deliveries be ground-based, and thereby bypass delays due to airport closings and similar problems?*

Buyer: *We really haven't had many issues related to weather delays in deliveries.*

Salesperson: *When shipping documents within 300 miles, would you like the ability to lower overall costs by using ground-based delivery?*

Buyer: *Our clients have become very cost-conscious, so we would be interested in reduced shipping costs. In fact, now that I think of it, most of our clients are local.*

What's happened here? You've gotten a lukewarm response to the third usage scenario, but the buyer has responded well to the other three. After framing a question—such as, "What has been your experience with FBN's services?"—to bring the conversation to the left side of the SDP, you would do the diagnosis for reasons 1, 2, and 4 to obtain details and quantification on how not having the corresponding capabilities is affecting the business manager and the law firm. After summarizing the diagnosis, you would then summarize the buyer vision and seek the buyer's agreement:

Salesperson: *To summarize, if you could have the abilities to arrange pickups as late as 8:00 PM, arrange deliveries as early as 7:30 AM, and reduce the cost of next-day deliveries, then would you consider trying our service?*

Buyer: *Certainly I would be interested. First I want to take a further look at your company. If things check out, I would be willing to give you a try.*

There is no right or wrong way to navigate an SDP, provided a seller can end with a question to verify the buyer vision. Given a choice, we prefer doing the diagnosis (left side) first, but the primary consideration is being in alignment with the buyer. If a buyer already knows what he or she wants, begin with the usage scenario questions.

The purpose of the Solution Development Prompter is to arm sellers with artificial patience and artificial intelligence to determine which usage scenarios the buyer is likely to need, simply by asking questions. These usage scenarios become capabilities when the buyer agrees they would be useful. The final step is to see if by using all the capabilities, the buyer would be empowered to achieve the desired goal. This is accomplished by asking, "If you had (summarize the capabilities), then could you achieve (buyer goal)?"

Once a buyer vision has been created, you should see if the buyer will share any additional goals, so you can create further visions and develop associated value. After developing shared buyer goals, the next step is to begin qualifying the buyer—a critical requirement in successful selling that we'll cover in the next chapter.

CHAPTER 12

Qualifying Buyers

Many organizations have great difficulty forecasting top-line revenues. We believe that this reflects an underlying problem: Pipelines are full of unqualified buyers. Most organizations have no standard way of accurately assessing which prospects are likely to buy.

Our strong sense—as will become clear below—is that the sales manager should disqualify buyers, based on the best available correspondence between the salesperson and the prospect. The alternative is to abdicate this responsibility to individual salespeople, which almost inevitably leads to unqualified buyers being in the pipeline, resulting in inflated top-line revenue estimates. So how do the sales manager and the salesperson work together to qualify buyers, build pipeline, and develop more accurate forecasts?

A prerequisite is to agree on a standard set of terms describing the Key Players involved in making buying decisions. This facilitates qualifying multiple Key Players who play different roles in a given opportunity. A prospect with all roles filled is a better bet at forecasting time.

We define Key Players as being those individuals whom a seller must access in order to sell, fund, and implement the offering. As you would expect, the number of Key Players is proportional to the size and complexity of what is being sold. Here are our definitions of the Key Players:

- *Coaches* want the seller to win the business, and are willing to provide information and do inside selling. They have only limited authority within the organization, but they can serve as the eyes and ears for a salesperson as an opportunity develops.
- *Champions* provide access to Key Players, as requested by the salesperson, and can be found at any level within the prospect organization. Generally speaking, the higher within the organization your Champion, the better your chances of success and the shorter the sales cycle. The ideal situation is to have your Champion also be the decision maker (see below). In such cases, the buyer will often volunteer access to other Key Players even before the salesperson asks for that access, and this access will be to people *below* him or her in the organization—a good thing. While bottom-up access is necessary at times, the first choice is top-down.
- *Decision makers* can make the vendor selection and cause unbudgeted funds to be spent, which (as explained in earlier chapters) is critical if a seller initiates a buying cycle in an organization that wasn't looking to change, and therefore had no budget for change. In addition, a decision maker can commit internal resources to evaluate a salesperson's offerings. In the case of purchases by committees, there can be multiple decision makers.
- *Financial approvers* are the people who must sign off on expenditures. Their role can range from being passive (rubber stamp) to being an active and involved player in the decision process. Gaining financial approval is easier when this person understands the value of addressing the goals the organization wants to achieve.
- *Users* and *managers of users* are people involved in using the offering. For implementations affecting a wide group of people within an organization, supportive and enthusiastic users can be critical to a seller's success. Users can help sales campaigns by providing a groundswell of support. (Conversely, their reluctance or skepticism can scuttle an otherwise viable opportunity.) Users don't usually have business goals. Their concerns are more personal: They want to decide if the offering will improve their stock in their company and simplify or complicate their lives. It's rarely possible for a seller to interface with all potential users, but getting (at least) some opinion leaders on board—including, for example, managers of users—can be a critical step in making the sale.
- *Implementers* are the people responsible for migrating from the current method to the new offering. Often their major concern is not a

corporate objective. They will be measured on their ability to integrate the new offering on schedule and under budget. They prefer doing business with vendors that offer professional services and ongoing support.

- *Adversaries* are individuals who either don't want to change, want to control change internally, or want to do business with a competitor. They can include, for example, Champions for a competitor, individuals whose power is derived from the current method of doing things, IT staff members who want to develop the desired capability internally, and so on.

In our experience, salespeople tend to avoid their Adversaries, which is generally a mistake. A salesperson's objective should be to convert, neutralize, or eliminate Adversaries. Of course, this needs to be done carefully. For example, a one-on-one meeting can be confrontational, and can further polarize opposing positions. Instead, we suggest including people who are on your side when you meet with Adversaries—preferably, a proponent who outranks your Adversary.

These definitions of members of the buying committee become the basis for discussing and developing strategies for specific opportunities. Look at Figures 12-1, 12-2, and 12-3. In these charts, we've laid out three different sized opportunities and identified the Key Players and their associated titles and goals. (Note that there are occasions where a Key Player plays more than one role.) Also note the emphasis on goals: the starting point of all CustomerCentric Selling.

This may look like a lot of extra work. But given a simple organizational chart software package and a little practice, it should prove relatively easy. And in our experience, understanding, preparing, and updating simple charts like this helps both the salesperson and the sales manager, as they work together to qualify opportunities.

Qualifying a Champion

One key element in the qualification process is to identify and reinforce a Champion. When the salesperson is calling high, the Champion will often be self-nominating. He or she will often volunteer access to Key Players. More often, of course, he or she has to be asked through the kinds of CustomerCentric Selling correspondence with buyers. After a call on a potential Champion, the salesperson should be required to answer the debriefing questions in Figure 12-4.

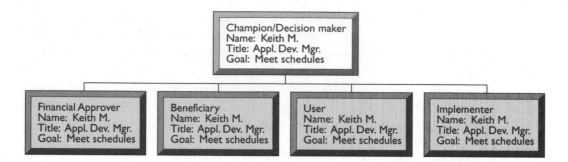

Figure 12-1 Opportunity Organization Chart: Middleware Opportunity—$35,000

Once the answers to the debriefing questions have been edited and approved, the seller now composes a Champion Letter. The Champion Letter, fax, or email serves four important roles:

- It provides a sanity check for salespeople to verify that they have articulated the buyer's goal, current situation, and vision.
- After sellers demonstrate mastery of this process, sales managers can allow the Champion Letter to be sent without being edited. In such cases, it allows the manager to audit a salesperson's achievement of milestones to see if a prospect is worthy to be in the pipeline. Any process must have an audit trail, and, assuming that salespeople create visions using Solution Development Prompters, all of the

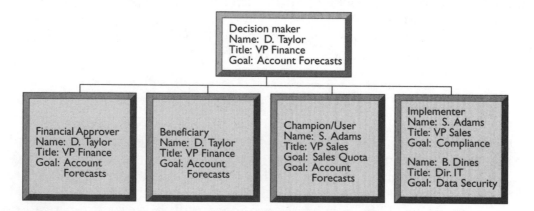

Figure 12-2 Opportunity Organization Chart: Sales Process Automation—$250,000

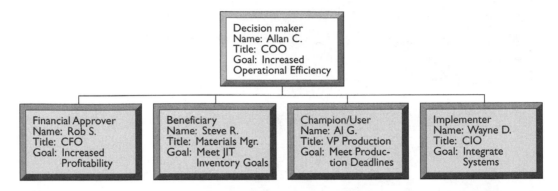

Figure 12-3 Opportunity Organization Chart: ERP Deployment—$2 Million

debriefing questions contained in the Champion Letter must be answered.

- It serves as a reminder to the buyer of the conversation with the salesperson. Unlike vendor brochures, this letter minimizes the chance of the buyer becoming confused if he or she is evaluating offerings from other companies.
- It facilitates internal selling by providing prospect-ready messaging (the words for your Champion to use to explain or defend his or her interest). For this reason, many salespeople prefer to email the Champion Letter on the day of the call, and follow up via snail mail. Our preference is email, which can be forwarded easily to Key Players.

We include a sample Champion Letter in Figure 12-5. We believe that the sales manager should be involved in writing, or at least editing, Champion Letters until he or she is confident that the salesperson can accom-

Opportunity source?
Name, title, and company?
Buyer's goal(s)?
Current situation?
Whom else do *we* want involved?
Buyer's vision(s)?
Personal/dollar value to person/organization?
Roles of buyer?
Next step(s)?

Figure 12-4 Sales Call Debrief Questions

To: Wendy Komac@xyzsoftware.com
From: DBranfman@spa.com
Subj: Follow up to our conversation

Dear Wendy,

Thank you for your interest in SPA.com. The purpose of this letter is to summarize my understanding of our discussion. You told me your primary goal is improving revenue projections with a more accurate sales forecast.

Today's forecasting metrics vary by office, many unqualified or stalled opportunities are in the pipeline, close rates vary widely by salesperson, and earnings have been impacted when major opportunities don't close when forecasted. You said missing earnings for another quarter could affect valuation by as much as 20%. You believe you could improve forecasting accuracy if you had the following capabilities:

- After every sales call, your salespeople would be prompted to report progress against standard companywide milestones
- When reviewing pipelines, your sales managers could evaluate progress and email suggestions regardless of their location
- On an ongoing basis, the system could track the close rates of every salesperson and apply them to predict revenue
- When a quarter hinges on a make or break opportunity, you and other senior executives want the ability to inspect progress against company milestones before finalizing your projections

You indicated that you are interested in further investigating SPA.com. Based on my experience, I suggest our next logical steps are

1. Confirm you are in agreement with my summary of our discussion.
2. Arrange telephone or in-person interviews with your VP Sales, Sales Operations Manager, and CIO, who would all be involved in the implementation of Sales Force Automation.
3. Summarize our findings to the group and determine if a further evaluation is appropriate.

I will call you on Tuesday, January 7 at 9:00 AM to review this letter and discuss our next steps. If that time is not convenient for you, please let me know an alternative. I look forward to working with you and your organization.

Sincerely,

Dave Branfman
Senior Account Executive
SPA.com

Qualification Milestones

1. Goal(s)
2. Current situation
3. Vision(s)
4. Value
5. Access to Key Players

Figure 12-5 Sell Cycle Control Champion Letter (Email): Qualifying the Buyer plish this without help. Having a half dozen good models in the drawer should build that confidence in both parties.

Take a minute to read the first three paragraphs of our sample letter. Here's where the goals, current situation, vision, and value for the Champion are summarized. (The insert in the upper right-hand corner is not included in a real Champion Letter.) Please note that all answers to the debriefing questions come from executing the CustomerCentric Selling process. Traditional salespeople need both a map (milestones) and explicit directions (a defined sales process plus Sales-Ready Messaging).

In previous chapters, we've hammered away at the importance of consistency in messaging. What many organizations fail to realize is that a great deal of selling occurs while the salesperson is not present at the prospect organization. How? After a successful sales call, many buyers attempt to share their excitement with other people within the organization. In fact, the better the call, the more likely this is to happen.

But how confident are you that your message will get across accurately? Consider how long it takes a salesperson to become proficient at relating the offerings in a way that makes sense to the many different buyers he or she calls on. Most likely, this is an intensive, full-time effort over several months. How well prepared is a buyer who spent 45 minutes with a salesperson to recreate the excitement the buyer felt about a vision of using the offering to finally achieve a goal or solve a problem?

Take an example from everyday life. You attend a professional meeting, and the after-dinner attraction is an inspirational speaker (who most likely has practiced and delivered this same talk many, many times over the previous months or years). You are carried away by the speaker and the subject, and—on returning home—you attempt to convey your excitement to your spouse. Hard to do, right? Most likely, it's one of those "you had to be there" situations, and you may find that your enthusiasm is now muted. Maybe that speaker wasn't that good, after all. . . .

So messaging is important in your correspondence from the very first encounter with a potential Champion. Give the Champion the scripts he or she needs in order to serve as your surrogate.

Now look at the fourth paragraph of our sample letter, which begins, "You indicated that you are interested. . . ." One of the trickier and more important building blocks of the Champion Letter comes toward the end, where the salesperson attempts to shape the further investigation of the opportunity. This is where the salesperson attempts to get the Champion to agree to provide the salesperson with access to Key Players. Which Key Players? The titles will vary, depending on the complexity of the offering, how many people will be affected during the implementation, the size of the proposed expenditure, and the size of the target organization. Another variable may be the state of the economy. During difficult financial conditions, even add-on business with existing customers may require more sign-offs, and at higher levels, than previous orders. A rule of thumb is to review your Targeted Conversations List.

For these reasons, the sales manager should be involved in these decisions, at least until the salesperson has demonstrated the ability to make these kinds of determinations. The sales manager should not hesitate to get reinvolved in these decisions if circumstances change, either on the seller's end or on the buyer's end.

This approach—requesting access to Key Players in the Champion Letter—relieves the seller of the burden of having to request access during a call. At the same time, though, it ensures that this critical step is actually taken. Some traditional salespeople are primarily concerned about getting and keeping opportunities in their pipelines, and are therefore hesitant to ask tough qualification questions. This isn't acceptable: An opportunity isn't real until access to the entire buying committee has been granted and documented, which leads us to the next step.

Following Up on the Champion Letter

Once the Champion Letter has been sent, the salesperson needs to follow up on that communication in order to get the buyer's agreement to the following points:

- The letter accurately summarizes the conversation(s).
- The buyer is willing and able to provide access to the requested titles.
- After interviewing all Key Players, there will be a chance to gain consensus that further evaluation is warranted.

Once the salesperson has verified these points and can produce the Champion Letter, the sales manager can now grade this prospect as a C. As we'll emphasize again later, sales management should perform grading of pipeline—and forecasting in general. It should *not* be the responsibility of salespeople, who historically are optimistic and are motivated by their desire to have their manager believe that everything is O.K. within their pipelines, regardless of the actual condition of those pipelines.

There will be times when the follow-up call to verify the contents of the Champion Letter will not go according to plan. (If it always did, there would be less reason to write Champion Letters.) Buyer "push back" or disagreement must be resolved if the prospect is to be considered viable.

The buyer may question or dispute the contents of the letter, in which case a discussion is necessary to clarify issues. If the discussion succeeds, the Champion Letter should be modified to reflect whatever changes are necessary. The seller qualifies a Champion after obtaining the buyer's acceptance of the revised letter.

Sometimes the salesperson's request for access to Key Players may be challenged or denied. In the following paragraphs, we present the most common reasons why access is denied—at least initially—and suggest ways to handle them.

1. *The buyers indicate that they will sell it internally.* This reluctance may be an indicator that you are Column B (vying for a silver medal), especially if the buyer is the one who initiated the contact. The prospect may have been instructed to get pricing, but not grant access to others. Or, alternatively, buyers may simply want to maintain control and get all the credit for introducing the concept to others. In our experience, any one of these conditions dramatically reduces your chances of success in both selling and forecasting.

We suggest making it clear that your Champion is welcome to accompany you on meetings with Key Players whenever he or she feels it is appropriate. This may help to address the issue of the person's wanting to maintain control and exposure. We have also found it effective to make the (accurate) point that you and the prospect have spent only a brief period discussing your offerings, and that it is unfair to place the burden of selling the offering internally on his or her shoulders.

2. *The buyers say that Key Players' involvement is unnecessary.* In these cases, the salesperson can and should point to potential implementation issues if everyone is not on board from the outset. Another option is to indicate that unless Key Players are aware of an evaluation, both the prospect and the salesperson may wind up spinning their wheels by undertaking an unsanctioned initiative.

3. *The buyer is skeptical, and indicates that it is too early to involve other people.* Depending on the complexity of your offering, this may be a valid concern. Up to this point, you (most likely) have had only a conversation or two with the potential Champion about your offerings. Perhaps this is the juncture to offer a proof session or demonstration with a fairly straightforward quid pro quo: "If the proof satisfies you, then will you get me access to the specified Key Players?"

When attempting to get access to Key Players, the salesperson should be politely persistent. This is important. It simply can't be sidestepped. Failure to have conversations with these people leaves the salesperson and company vulnerable to long sales cycles, no decision, silver medal competitions, and other bad things.

If access is not forthcoming, it is important to figure out what's really going on: Is the Champion unable to provide access, or unwilling? If a prospect is unable to obtain access to decision makers, the salesperson needs to ask who could provide that access. If a prospect persists in being unwilling to grant access, the sales manager should be involved in making the decision as to whether or not to keep competing for the sale.

Qualifying Key Players

Once a Champion agrees to provide access to Key Players, phone conversations or face-to-face sales calls should be scheduled. Ideally, the Champion and the seller together should strategize the sequence of these calls. Often a Champion can prepare a Key Player for a call, and—in some cases—the Champion may want to accompany the seller on certain calls. These meetings tend to yield more favorable outcomes if your Champion has copied Key Players on your correspondence. When a Champion identifies a potential Adversary, we suggest calling on that person last and asking the Champion to participate.

The good news is that calls on Key Players may be less challenging than initial calls on potential Champions, because a few hurdles have already been passed. Key Players may have a sense that incompetent or insincere salespeople would not have been granted access. In fact, the chances of successful Key Player calls are often influenced by the power your Champion wields within the organization.

The objective in decision maker and Key Players calls is to briefly introduce yourself and your organization, summarize the previous calls made within the account, give the buyer an opportunity to share his or her goals, diagnose each, create visions, and establish value. For these reasons, preparation is vitally important. Great preparation will keep you out of a number of traps. For example, there are some stereotypical "salesy" behaviors that can lead buyers to draw unfavorable conclusions about a salesperson they are meeting for the first time. Part of your job, therefore, is to demonstrate to the buyer that you don't conform to the stereotype of traditional salespeople.

Again, great preparation helps. We suggest that you arrive prepared with a "call introduction," a summary of the meetings within the account to date (goals, current situation, visions), and a menu of potential goals, Success Stories, and corresponding Solution Development Prompters for each potential goal of the title that is being called on.

Salespeople must develop the call introduction in their own words, but it should be concise and fact-based (rather than opinion-based). Here is an example of a call introduction—typically delivered after introductions have been made and a certain level of rapport has been established.

> Today I'd like to briefly introduce XYZ Company, summarize meetings I've had with other members of your organization, discuss your objectives, and mutually determine if there are areas where our offering would have value for you.
>
> XYZ Company enables organizations to use our offerings to reduce engineering design cycles, thereby shortening time to market. We were founded in 1995, and last year achieved $95 million in revenue. Some of our clients include Boeing, Hewlett-Packard, and IBM.
>
> I was introduced to your company by Larry Firth, your VP of Production. He would like to reduce scrap (goal) by having the number of late engineering changes reduced. I also met with Kevin Hale, your VP of Engineering, who indicated that he wants to reduce engineering design cycles and reduce recalls due to product defects (goals). That gets you up to date with the meetings I've had so far. Perhaps you can tell me, in your role as CFO, what are you hoping to accomplish?

At this point, as in the conclusion of the telephone-prospecting script, your objective is to have the buyer share at least one specific business goal for which you have a prompter. (To get a sense of how to handle the possible responses, review the previous chapter.) In calling on a Key Player, however, keep in mind that another situation may arise. Sometimes senior executives merely want to meet the salesperson and understand the conversations that have gone on to date. Since they are able to connect the dots on their own, they may not necessarily need to share a goal during the meeting.

In the example cited above, once the CFO understands that his staff believes they can reduce scrap, shorten engineering design cycles, and minimize recalls, that may be sufficient for the salesperson to win the CFO's support for the project. It's almost always worth asking, "What are you hoping to accomplish?" But if the question doesn't elicit a goal, don't push it. A sensible next step is to tell a Success Story and/or offer a menu of goals for the CFO. If there still is no positive response, the salesperson should engineer a polite exit. This entails thanking the CFO for the opportunity to apprise him or her of progress to date, informing the CFO that a meeting will be held after all Key Players have been interviewed to gain consensus to proceed with the evaluation of the offering, and inviting the CFO to participate in that meeting.

As early as possible in the buying cycle, as implied in the above scenario, the salesperson should conduct meetings with all Key Players. This accomplishes several objectives:

- Everyone understands the potential benefit to him- or herself and the organization.
- Getting everyone involved can often result in larger payback and therefore justify potentially larger transactions.
- Having multiple points of contact in the organization means that you may not have to start all over if one person gets fired, is promoted, leaves the company, or dies.
- If there is a strong Adversary, he or she will be identified fairly early. If the Adversary is powerful and can't be neutralized, the salesperson (in concert with the sales manager) may decide to withdraw rather than go the distance and lose, bringing only a silver medal back to the office.
- Again, this is a reality check. It is highly unlikely that a prospect will grant these interviews to anyone who doesn't represent Column A.

Like the Champion call, these calls on Key Players should be documented. Whenever a new goal is shared, the equivalent of a Champion Letter should be generated, although the request for access to Key Players should be eliminated.

Qualifying RFPs

We touched on the subject of RFPs (Requests for Proposal) in Chapter 5. Sellers also receive RFQs (Requests for Quotation) and RFIs (Requests for Information).We'll refer to them collectively here as RFPs.

RFPs represent a particular challenge when it comes to qualifying buyers. As also noted, they tend to come in two flavors:

- Those that you "wired" because you were Column A
- Those that someone else occupying Column A wired, and for which you are being asked to serve as a silver medalist

Yes, there will an occasional "stray bullet" where the sender of the RFP doesn't know the requirements, and therefore has not established a favored vendor. We find these to be rare, and they most often turn out to be fishing expeditions—either for companies to discover what is available out in the market, or for their IT department to receive free education in order to generate specifications for in-house projects. We have found that many of these situations turn into long sales cycles, with a high probability of no decision being made.

By their nature, RFPs slow down the buying process. They are more common among mainstream-market buyers. Companies use several justifications to defend the time and effort involved in issuing RFPs:

- Companies find out what offerings are available.
- Vendors talk about one another, allowing a more informed choice.
- Companies meet due-diligence requirements.
- Companies get free advice/consulting.
- Companies can make an assessment of vendor submissiveness.
- Vendors bid against one another.
- Companies give the appearance of being fair to all vendors.

As an aside, many organizations talk long and loud about their cost of sales. Amazingly, though, few calculate what it actually costs to generate and monitor RFPs with multiple vendors. Consider an organization that issues an RFP to six vendors, with the intent of stirring up a price war, for a $75,000 transaction that has the potential to allow them to save $5000 per month. Conservatively speaking, the time to generate, publish, distribute, and provide adequate time for vendors to respond to the RFP will add 90 days to the process. Let's also assume a cost in labor-hours of $3000 for the resources required to interact with six vendors (again, that's conservative). Without regard for the time and effort needed to actually write the RFP, which may involve expensive talent, here is an estimate of the imbedded costs:

$$(\text{3-month delay}) \times (\$5000/\text{month potential savings}) = \$15,000$$
$$\underline{(\text{6 vendors}) \times (\$3000 \text{ cost}/\text{vendor}) \qquad\qquad = \$18,000}$$

Total cost of RFP process $\qquad\qquad\qquad\qquad = \$33,000$

Based on these figures, the RFP must enable the issuing company to negotiate a $42,000 ($75,000–$33,000) price with the gold medalist just to break even.

Having looked at this from the side of issuing organizations, let's consider a vendor's perspective. Over the past 12 months, how many RFPs has your company responded to where you were reactive rather than proactive (meaning, you were surprised when you received the document)? Now estimate your win rate on those "opportunities." If that figure is acceptable, feel free to skip the next few paragraphs.

We worked with a client that had an entire department whose sole responsibility was responding to RFPs. The average response took 80 labor-hours—and the company's 145 responses to unsolicited RFPs over the previous 12 months had resulted in precisely three wins. Perhaps your win rate on unsolicited RFPs is better than 2 percent. (We hope so.) But it's probably not satisfactory. The hard fact is that if you play by rules that have been prewired by your competitor, more often than not you will be receiving a silver medal. On analysis, most companies discover that responding to RFPs wired by other vendors is an unprofitable practice.

So let us propose a qualifying alternative.

When issuing an RFP, organizations want something from vendors: namely, a column (either A or—more likely—something east of A) on the spreadsheet. We suggest that you offer a column in exchange for access to a Key Player. If the organization issuing the RFP won't give you access, this is a clear signal that the relationship will end unhappily for you.

The message, whether an opportunity is discovered proactively or reactively, is to scrub the input into your pipeline. Sales managers (unless they choose to make an exception) should require documented access to Key Players before authorizing the resources needed to compete. Would you prefer gold or silver?

In the next chapter, we look at the challenge of managing a sequence of events across the life span of a sale—the selling organization's equivalent of project management.

Negotiating and Managing a Sequence of Events

IN THIS CHAPTER, we'll look at the challenge of transforming the sell cycle from a realm of mystery—which is how some buyers and sellers view it—into a rational and orderly process.

But first, to introduce the subject, let's imagine that a salesperson has worked on a major opportunity for 4 months. Let's imagine further that a CustomerCentric Selling sales consultant is hired to analyze each opportunity in the pipeline, and the consultant asks the salesperson to estimate when this particular opportunity will close. For the purposes of this example, let's assume the CustomerCentric Selling sales consultant knows the decision maker on this transaction, and can ask him or her to provide a date when the sale can be made. What is the likelihood that the buyer's date will be later than the seller's date?

A few observations:

- Most closing is driven by the agenda of the sales organization, with little or no regard for the buyer. Many organizations that are under pressure to meet monthly, quarterly, or annual targets resort to "blitzes" to bring in business, based on those internal pressures.
- The vast majority of closing occurs before the salesperson has earned the right to ask for the business. When salespeople attempt to close

orders before buyers are ready, they run the risk of being perceived as a traditional pushy salesperson—or, worse, of scaring the buyer off entirely.

- If a salesperson closes before a buyer is ready, discounting is the most common method of giving the buyer a reason to sign early. In these premature efforts to close, a great deal of negotiating is done with non-decision makers. This can be demeaning for buyers who can't commit. In some instances, the discount offered to non-decision makers becomes the starting point for the real negotiations.

In our workshops, we sometimes ask participants, "How can you know when a transaction is closable?" There is almost always a prolonged silence, as people realize that this question is not readily answerable with their current approach.

In fact, many organizations (buyers and sellers) view sell cycles as random series of events that sometimes result in orders. Salespeople push buyers to go through sales cycles without gaining consensus or commitment. Many salespeople do not ask for, and therefore fail to get, access to the people within the prospect organization who will be required to sell, fund, and implement the recommended solution. How many "opportunities" in your current pipeline have at least one documented buyer goal?

Just as a competent chess player thinks several moves ahead, salespeople should do the same as they attempt to facilitate the buying process. Despite the fact that every sale appears to be unique, based on the size of the transaction and the size of the prospect organization, there are many common steps in the buying process that have a high probability of recurring.

By agreeing to and adhering to a clear Sequence of Events, the salesperson provides documentation that allows sales management to continue auditing and grading opportunities. Like the qualifying efforts described in the previous chapter, this removes overoptimistic opinions from the forecast, and minimizes the phenomenon of salespeople "selling" their managers on how good their pipeline is. When they make their forecasts, sales managers should have the benefit of a piece of paper that shows a planned Sequence of Events for each potential sale, and what progress has been made in that sequence.

By documenting sales efforts and gaining commitment to sequences of events, sales managers can play a vital role in deciding what deserves to be in each pipeline. As soon as an opportunity does not look winnable, the sales manager should brainstorm with the salesperson as to how to change the landscape of the decision. If the two of them together are unable to figure out a way to do this, they should withdraw from the opportunity. The alternative is hanging in there with a high probability of being one of several silver medalists.

When documented by means of a clearly stated Sequence of Events, the process of controlling a sales cycle begins to resemble project management. The decision process embedded in a sales cycle has a defined beginning and end, and—as noted above—the selling organization has the ability to assess progress and probabilities of success throughout.

There's also an ancillary benefit: When the seller handles sales cycles in a highly professional manner, buyers are likely to conclude that the selling organization's implementation will be professional, as well. This perception can allow buyers to feel more comfortable with a given company, and especially with a relatively untested company selling complex offerings. We believe salespeople and the companies they represent can make the *way* they sell a competitive advantage and a differentiator.

Getting the Commitment

The first step, of course, is getting the commitment from the buying organization to move forward with the evaluation of the offering.

As noted in the previous chapter, we believe that prior to committing to a buying cycle, salespeople should meet with all Key Players to understand their issues, determine if their offering represents a fit for the buyer's environment, establish potential value, and gain consensus that a formal evaluation makes sense. Key Players should understand what's in it for them. They should then come to some consensus and agreement on (1) the steps needed to reach a decision and (2) the timeframe for the overall evaluation.

Now it's time to move the process forward. To do so, the salesperson has to orchestrate getting all the key people together. This is the meeting that, in the previous chapter, you invited the chief financial officer to attend. The seller has to summarize progress to date and verify that the buyers feel there is enough potential benefit that further investigation is warranted. Finally—and most important—the seller has to obtain a commitment to proceed.

At some point in this process, the seller may attempt to push toward a commitment by pointing out a fact that should be obvious, but often isn't: By taking the time to evaluate this particular offering, the buyer is making a serious commitment of time, resources, and effort. Yes, the seller has a lot at stake, but the buyer, too, has money on the table, and that pile of chips is only growing. (Of course, the seller can be prepared to point out the cost to the buyer of *not* moving, as well.)

Looking for a commitment benefits the selling organization in several ways. First, it continues the qualification process. (If this opportunity is going to fizzle, let's find out sooner, rather than later.) Second, the selling organization wants to shape the sales cycle as much as possible. Simply put, would you rather sign a lease prepared by your landlord, or one prepared by you?

Looking for a commitment doesn't always succeed. A salesperson selling enterprise software recently told us about his attempts to obtain agreement on a $100,000 opportunity that he was working on. The VP of Engineering and the CIO were in favor of committing the resources necessary to work with the vendor. The VP of Manufacturing, though, had a track record of having difficulty with implementing technology, and was known to be a potential Adversary. Sure enough, during the meeting designed to gain consensus, the whole deal came unraveled, as the VP of Manufacturing argued passionately, and ultimately succeeded in convincing everyone, that it was "not the right time" to consider new software.

So is our recommendation—scheduling a meeting to extract a commitment from the organization—a bad idea? We don't think so, because we believe that in sales, bad news early is actually good news. Would you rather learn that the "opportunity" is a pipe(line?) dream in month 1, or in month 6, after you have expended a great deal of time and resources, and have been carrying it on your forecast as having a high probability of closing?

Keeping Committees on Track

After obtaining consensus from the committee that the value of the potential solution warrants further investigation, there is a great chance to begin qualifying the opportunity. The first thing the salesperson should ask the committee is what they would *like* to see in order to evaluate the offering. This will usually elicit requests for demonstrations, site surveys, proposals, and so on. These are things that will take a sales organization a great deal of time and effort. Conservative mainstream-market buyers are also apt to ask for things a salesperson does not want (or lacks the authority) to commit to. Examples would be a money back guarantee, a lengthy free trial with no exposure, and the like. While early in a company's history salespeople may have to make concessions, as the offering matures and an installed base has been established, these requests become unreasonable. How does a salesperson respond?

One option is to take them head on, potentially responding, "We would never be willing to do that for you." In light of the fact that you've just gotten consensus to continue with considering your offerings, this represents an inopportune time to take such a hard stance. Keep in mind that you have a decision maker or makers with their subordinates in a meeting. It is likely that the senior executive wants to flex his or her muscles on a salesperson. An alternative is to merely acknowledge you've heard the request without agreeing or disagreeing.

Once the prospect has had an opportunity to respond to what the management would like to see in order to evaluate your offerings, the salesperson now has a chance to share an example of a Sequence of Events template showing typical steps previous buyers have taken on the way to making a decision on the offerings. Hopefully, this can serve as an outline for a final agreement on the steps and an approximate timeframe for the buyer's arriving at a decision. A sample is shown in Figure 13-1.

The salesperson can end the meeting by disarming any misconceptions in the event the committee has asked for things that he or she cannot commit to by thanking everyone for their time and indicating he or she will take the list back to the office and propose what he or she feels is the best way to proceed. If it is clear there is a single decision maker, the suggestion would be to commit to sending a draft copy to that person for review. After that step, any necessary changes could be made prior to copying the other members of the buying committee.

After negotiating the internal resources the company is willing to commit, the salesperson can send a cover letter and draft copy of the Sequence of Events. A phone call or meeting to follow up should be scheduled with the decision maker, to ensure that the person has had a chance to review the document. The salesperson will then ask what, if any, changes are necessary. At this stage, any unreasonable requests (i.e., a money back guarantee) would be notable by their absence in the draft of the Sequence of Events. This means one of two things will happen. One possibility is that the buyer will not raise that point, in which case you can proceed. The other would be for the decision maker to challenge the fact that the money back guarantee was not offered.

The salesperson could then ask the reason for wanting a guarantee. It is likely that the buyer will explain that it is to mitigate risks associated with the decision. At this stage, the salesperson (if this is not one of your

Date	Checkpoint	Event	Billable	Responsibility
May 28	✓	Prove capabilities to committee members	$20,000	SPA.com
June 11	✓	Survey current system		SPA.com
June 11		Develop implementation plan with IT		Both
June 11	✓	Share survey results and provide estimated cost		SPA.com
June 18	✓	Facilitate cost versus benefit analysis		Both
June 18		Define success metrics		Both
June 18		Provide contracts for legal review		SPA.com
July 4	✓	Gain legal approval of contracts		Both
July 11		Make corporate visit		Both
July 18	✓	Deliver proposal		SPA.com
July 25		Begin implementation		Both

Figure 13-1 XYZ Software Sequence of Events

very first customers) could respond that because fifty-three other companies have already implemented this application, the company would not be in a position to offer a guarantee, but the prospect can visit one of the company's customers who has already successfully implemented. If the buyer insists on a guarantee, the salesperson may have to determine if this is a showstopper, in which case the buying cycle may come to a grinding halt. While this is not the desired result, most would agree that it is better to find out now rather than at the end of the sales cycle. Bad news early is good news.

When the salesperson calls to follow up, it is a bad sign for a decision maker to agree to the Sequence of Events without requesting changes. This would be a sign that either the document hadn't been reviewed or the prospect was taking the commitment lightly. The correct response is to change dates or challenge some items. Your objective is to be able to remove the word *DRAFT* from the document, but it is most effective if the buyer makes changes because then he or she takes some ownership in the buying cycle. Some of our clients purposely leave some dates blank so the buyer is forced to make changes.

Gaining Visibility and Control of Sales Cycles

In any event, if and when the Sequence of Events has been successfully negotiated with the decision maker, we suggest that at that point all committee members should be copied with the Sequence of Events. Both buyer and seller now have an agreed-on approach to making a buying decision. Buyers find it comforting (and unusual) to be working with a salesperson who has already thought to ask about and negotiate the steps leading to a buying decision. At this point, the seller has gotten agreement from the committee for the approximate duration of the sales cycle.

As for controlling the buying cycle, both the buyer and seller share veto power at each checkpoint. That is to say, each of these steps represents an opportunity for either party to withdraw from the evaluation.

Why Would Either Party Withdraw?

Consider for a moment the potential reasons a buying committee would elect to withdraw from a negotiated evaluation: a change in priorities, an acquisition, a reorganization, insufficient payback on the proposed project, references don't check out, investigation shows the offering not to be a good fit, and so on.

Now brace yourself as we begin to list reasons for a vendor to elect to withdraw from an ongoing Sequence of Events. Some traditional salespeople cannot begin to fathom any circumstances that would make them effectively remove an opportunity from their pipeline. Here are some potential reasons for a vendor to withdraw: Customer expectations may be unreasonable, the offering may not be a good fit, the transaction may not be profitable, a review may show that the prospect is not creditworthy, and so on.

While all these reasons are valid, the best reason to withdraw is that you realize the opportunity is not winnable. The manager who wants the sales staff to compete to win, not to keep busy, usually must make this decision. As soon as you believe you are not Column A and you cannot change the requirements list, it's time to find a different opportunity to work on. Traditional salespeople, wanting to hang in until the end (and keep their pipelines inflated), sometimes have to be forcibly removed from the "prospect."

Most typically, the Sequence of Events will serve as a road map, but will tend to be a living document. That is to say, about once a month it may need to be republished to reflect any alterations that need to be made either to the events or to the timing of events. Once this process is in place, sales managers enjoy several potential benefits:

1. They can coach salespeople through the process step by step.
2. Planning for allocation of resources can be done.
3. Each checkpoint the buyer agrees to further validates the buyer's commitment and increases the likelihood of a successful completion.
4. Sales managers have the ability to assess (disqualify) opportunities if they do not appear to be winnable.
5. It is unlikely that buyers looking for Column B, C, or D would commit to a Sequence of Events with a silver medalist.
6. It is far easier to forecast close dates because buyers have agreed to tentative dates for delivery of a proposal and a decision. This helps take vendors away from the tendency to close based on their agendas.

Negotiating the sales cycle also addresses a problem that virtually all salespeople face: not knowing when an opportunity is closable. Our belief is that the right time to close is when a Sequence of Events has been completed to the buyers' satisfaction and the seller's satisfaction. Our clients learn that each step in the Sequence of Events is a miniature close and that asking for or getting the order is a logical conclusion.

While we are on the subject of buying cycles, one of the most frightening situations occurs when a mainstream-market buyer is being asked to commit to a large expenditure (let's say $500,000) for an application that has never been implemented before. Many Key Players consider the potential impact on their careers if the anticipated results aren't achieved. The Sequence of Events can be used to mitigate risk by providing a "pay as we progress" approach. By this we mean that the $500,000 expenditure can be broken into smaller pieces (feasibility study, preliminary design, prototype, and so on) that are billable events. After each, both the buyer and seller assess where they stand and make a determination as to whether to proceed.

Reframing the Concept of Selling

Earlier in the book, we articulated our desire to reframe the concept of selling as helping a buyer achieve a goal, solve a problem, or satisfy a need. This definition applies to the buyer-seller relationship. At a higher level, we believe that the Sequence of Events approach empowers our clients to extend this philosophy to a company-to-company perspective. Negotiating the steps in the buying cycle enables all committee members (the prospect organization) and all members of the selling organization to be on board with the stated objective of determining if the offerings can satisfy the overall needs of the prospect. As soon as this doesn't appear to be possible, either party can opt out of expending further resources.

Mainstream-Market Buyers

In previous chapters, we described the phenomenon of mainstream-market buyers. Sales cycles with these buyers most often move at a slower pace than those involving early-market buyers. These mainstream-market decisions are almost invariably made by committees consisting of several people, with the majority of them having the ability to scuttle the project by saying no, but lacking the authority to say yes. Mainstream-market buyers are often governed by one or both of the following principles:

1. They are looking, but they lack a strong commitment to buy. Salespeople in these situations may begin throwing resources at the opportunity, hoping that the right thing will happen. In these cases, they run the risk of providing free education. These can be relatively easy situations for mainstream-market buyers to be involved in because the vendors do virtually all of the work as the buyer is getting exposure to new approaches. Unless compelling reasons to act can be uncovered by the salesperson, the result may well be no decision. The most common reasons for this result are

- The salesperson never negotiated a Sequence of Events with all Key Players.
- Business goals or problems were never identified.
- The buyer did not fully understand what he or she was buying or how it would be used.
- There was no compelling benefit versus cost.
- The buying committee was concerned about the staff's ability to implement the recommendation.

2. If, for some reason, a mainstream-market buyer gets serious about making a decision, it is a virtual guarantee that the buyer will shop the transaction around by talking with other companies offering similar products. In some cases, if there are no comparable offerings in the market, the buying decision will come to a screeching halt. Mainstream-market buyers want to compare offerings from at least two or three different companies. Doing so may verify in their minds that it is too early to risk going ahead with the project. They are likely to postpone a decision unless or until the offering gets to a point where multiple companies are in that space and the offering shows the potential to become the de facto standard.

Assuming that there are alternatives, mainstream-market buyers will feel compelled to invite at least three companies to assess their needs and make a recommendation. We refer to this process as "running a beauty contest." While it is an advantage to have been the vendor that caused the sales cycle to begin (Column A), many unfavorable things can begin to take place. Despite the fact that a start-up company has a superior offering, mainstream-market buyers are apt to evaluate more established companies. Even if the seller has inferior offerings, doing business with a known corporate entity potentially lowers exposure to risk and second guessing if the project fails to meet expectations. Within the technology sector, for years IBM was seldom thought to have the latest or least expensive offerings. IBM did, however, represent the safest choice. Many transactions were won by appearing to be the safer alternative. At times, inviting two or three different companies to present their offerings will confuse mainstream-market buyers, which always have "no decision" lurking in the background if things get overwhelming.

Negotiation
The Final Hurdle

T HE NEGOTIATIONS COVERED IN THIS CHAPTER center on the conversations that (1) follow the evaluation process and (2) precede the formal customer agreement to move forward. Many of the ideas contained in this chapter, however, have their roots in the concept of quid pro quo, which CustomerCentric sellers use throughout the sales cycle.

Unfortunately, when it comes to negotiating, there are no magic bullets. The salesperson has to be prepared and has to stick to the game plan. A misstep can cause significant damage. If salespeople fail to establish value and earn the respect of Key Players as peers, for example, the buyer has the upper hand when the time comes to negotiate. If the seller has been subordinate throughout the sales cycle, giving whatever the buyer requests and getting nothing in return, who do you think has the upper hand when the subject of price arises?

Sticking with the disciplines outlined in this book is not always easy, and the stress of negotiating can cause a seller to revert to traditional behavior. But this can be doubly damaging. If during the sales cycle a seller has taken the approach of helping the buyer achieve a goal, solve a problem, or satisfy a need, and then suddenly shifts to persuading, convincing, and "hard closing," the buyer is likely to feel manipulated and begin to lump the seller into the pervasive negative stereotype.

Traditional Buyers and Sellers

Let's consider the positions, expectations, and relationship of buyers and sellers in a traditional negotiation, beginning with the position of both parties at the start of negotiations.

Home teams, as most sports fans know, have a decided advantage. Negotiations are usually carried out at prospects' locations, so these encounters are "away games" for sellers. The seller is therefore at a disadvantage from the outset. Most of the circumstances surrounding the negotiation favor the buyer. The buyer sits in his or her leather chair, for example, which tends to be slightly higher than the cloth chair the salesperson occupies. The buyer is the host, providing all creature comforts; the seller can only accept or decline those comforts.

Buyers are perfectly willing to conclude a potential closing meeting without consummating the transaction. In fact, sometimes they prefer it that way. People buying cars in the traditional fashion understand that sometimes the best way to determine if they have gotten the best offer is to leave the showroom. (Note that car salespeople work on their home turf, which changes some of the dynamics.) If the car salesperson sees the buyer walking out the door, he or she may also see the sale slipping away—and hurriedly start negotiating downward.

Given this phenomenon, many buyers prefer to negotiate over the course of multiple meetings. The starting point for each meeting after the first is the last (lowered) price from the previous meeting. Experienced buyers are fully aware of the quarterly pressures that selling organizations face, and may time the real closing meeting to coincide with that cycle.

Buyers have the luxury of knowing that regardless of how adversarial or personal a negotiation may get, forgiveness is only a phone call away—if, that is, they award the gold medal to the seller they've been battling with. Buyers don't usually have a great deal personally at stake. Sellers, by contrast, have commissions, pride, and career paths on the line—stakes that are heightened in the case of large transactions toward the end of a quarter. The buyer can be patient, comfortable in the fact that it makes little difference to him or her whether the contract is awarded on December 28 or January 10. The buyer can sit back and see how badly the seller wants this deal to happen now.

Experienced buyers know what they want to pay and have a proactive plan for getting to or below that figure. Sellers—wanting to get the deal, and assuming that the negotiated price will be less than the initial asking price—tend to ad lib responses to the buyer's implicit strategies and explicit comments. Smart buyers have at least three vendors competing, know their vendor of choice, and rarely show their hand. Buyers try to keep all vendors paranoid, and convinced that price will drive the ultimate decision. Sellers can seldom be certain that they are Column A, which is exactly what the buyer wants.

As emphasized in previous chapters, the essence of CustomerCentric Selling is shaping conversations between buyers and sellers. Not surprisingly, we view negotiations in exactly the same way. Of course, conversations about business issues (framed by title/vertical industry/goal) are very different from negotiation conversations. But the good news is that this latter kind of conversation is easier to predict and script. You have a buyer attempting to get the best possible deal and a seller trying to close the transaction and (in theory) get the highest possible price.

So let's look at negotiation as a conversation the seller has earned the right to have, because he or she has executed all the necessary steps in the sales cycle and has otherwise behaved in a consistently professional manner. While you can seldom be sure you are the gold medalist, CustomerCentric sellers can take heart in knowing that the buyer has already said yes in making commitments at each checkpoint in the Sequence of Events.

The Six Most Expensive Words

Buyers expect discounts. Sellers expect to discount to get the business. Buyers squeeze sellers on price. Sellers expect to get squeezed. It is a generally accepted barbaric ritual of buying.

So it never should come as a surprise when, early in the negotiations, the buyer asks the seller for the "best possible price," or words to that effect. One of the most common, least appropriate, and most expensive responses a salesperson can make to such a request is, "Where do we need to be?" These six words give the buyer the following impressions:

- The seller is not controlling the discussion.
- The seller has already acknowledged that discounting is necessary and appropriate.
- The seller has wide latitude and authority to discount.
- Negotiation is not the seller's strength, given the weak opening salvo.

Lawyers cross-examining hostile witnesses are taught never to ask a question to which they don't know the answer. The same holds true for salespeople starting negotiations. Whether a buyer's answer to those six words is reasonable or not, the question allows them to put a stake in the ground that the seller is forced to address. Smart buyers will cite a figure well below what they are willing to pay.

Here are some common errors made by salespeople (often with the support and direction of senior management of the companies they represent) during the negotiation process. Some will be familiar from previous chapters; others are new.

- In the absence of an agreed-on Sequence of Events, the attempted closing is timed to serve the salesperson's agenda, rather than the buyer's. The most common way to get buyers to sign earlier than they want is by enticing them with discounts.
- Salespeople attempt to close non-decision makers. This can be demeaning to a "buyer" who in fact is merely a messenger. Beyond that, whatever discount is offered becomes the starting point for further negotiations, if and when the decision maker gets involved.
- Salespeople selling noncommodity offerings mistakenly believe they can negotiate their way into Column A by treating price as the only variable. Ideally, negotiating should take place *after* the buyer makes the decision to buy from a particular salesperson.
- Many salespeople have difficulty tolerating silence while negotiating. Smart buyers remain quiet for a few seconds after asking the salesperson the price, or after being asked to buy. In the closing process, many sellers experience a marked loss in their ability to listen, understand, and respond (a phenomenon we call *vapor lock*).
- Many salespeople get (unnecessarily) defensive. Defending or explaining the price during negotiation is generally counterproductive. At this stage, the buyer is merely doing his or her job. He or she simply wants the best deal, and really isn't interested in whether or not the pricing leaves your company sufficient profit.
- Salespeople compromise their power by saying things like, "That's the best I can do for you." This statement alone can make it impossible to close that day. Smart buyers ask who within the organization can do better—and pointedly instruct the seller to bring that person to the next meeting.

- Sellers who are behind quota should not negotiate large transactions without the involvement of their manager. The good cop (seller)/ bad cop (manager) game can be played to the seller's advantage.

We were teaching a workshop recently, and one of the attendees—let's call him Bill—seemed distracted for the first day and a half. At one of the breaks, we asked him if everything was all right. He told us that the buyer's decision on a major transaction was being made that Friday. He had quoted $960,000, but his Coach had let him know that the organization had budgeted $850,000—a price that Bill was ready to meet. The CIO was the decision maker, and had requested a new quote. Bill's manager happened to be a role-play Coach at the workshop, so at lunch, we took the opportunity to brainstorm about how Bill and his manager should proceed.

During the workshop, Bill had come to understand that he was Column A, having initiated the opportunity with a cold call. He was concerned, though, because Column B had been called in, and was the acknowledged industry leader in that market space. Based on our discussion, Bill and his manager agreed on a course of action, which Bill then set in motion before the lunch break was over. First, he called the CIO and said that he was not going to provide a revised quotation. He also asked for a meeting with his manager and the CIO on Friday afternoon at 4:00 PM, and this request was granted.

This was good news. Our sense was that if they were not going to get the business, it was unlikely that the CIO would give them an appointment late in the afternoon on the day the decision was supposed to be made. After making the phone call, Bill looked as though the weight of the world had been lifted from his shoulders on his return to the workshop. He and his manager had agreed on the proper course of action and were now pursuing it—something that they evidently had not done much of in the past.

The workshop ended Thursday, and we asked Bill to get back in touch with us and let us know how the situation played out. On Monday, Bill called and told us that he had closed the order on Friday for $960,000. He admitted again that he had been ready, and even anxious, to drop $110,000 from the price, and probably would have gone even lower if it had looked like he had to. The result was a windfall of $110,000 that went straight to the bottom line of Bill's company.

While "always" and "never" seldom apply to sales, this situation (and others like it) leads us to conclude that sellers should always negotiate as though they are Column A. Why do we break our own rule in this way? In the situation just described, what if Bill was Column B and had rebid $850,000? That number would have been used to negotiate a better price from Column A, the preferred vendor. When he refused to rebid, one of two things was going to happen: Column A would get the business anyway, or the buyer would come back to Bill because he was the vendor of choice. Therefore, when you are asked for a best and final price, we suggest asking the buyer if (1) you are the vendor of choice and (2) price is the only remaining obstacle to doing business. If the answers are not yes and yes, we suggest that you ask the buyer to get back to you if and when you become the vendor of choice, at which point the negotiation can take place.

Traditional selling behavior dictates that if you are losing, you should discount as much as possible. You will either get the business yourself—by discounting yourself into becoming Column A—or force your competitor into significantly dropping the price. We disagree with both aspects of this tactic. Desperation discounting late in the buying cycle seldom secures the business. And since all vendors drink from a common well of pricing, irresponsible low-ball prices are bad for all vendors.

There is another reason not to offer "fire sale" discounting if you are losing late in the buying cycle. Assume Column B offers ridiculous pricing, but still loses to LMN Company. The following month, the roles are reversed. As Column B this time, the salesperson from LMN Company gets the bad news from the prospect that Column A has been chosen. What is the LMN representative likely to say? How about something like,

> *I appreciated the opportunity to compete for your business and gave it my best shot. While I don't agree with your decision, I understand that you are doing what you believe is best for your company. And hey—just so you know—last month we were awarded a bid competing against Column A at MNO, Inc., but not before they offered an unbelievably low price. If you want to do business with Column A, you may want to contact Joe Jones at MNO to get details on the pricing that he was offered. In any event, I wish you well. Please contact me if I can be of service in the future.*

In other words, the aggressive discount offered in a losing situation now comes back to haunt the vendor who has moved from Column B to Column A. Assume that one way or another, the word will get out as to how your company is selling. If it does get out, will you be happy? Will you be well positioned for your next negotiations? What happens to the perceived value of all the vendors' capabilities in your target markets?

The Power of Posturing

Sometimes the best negotiating stance is not to negotiate—as long as you're in a strong position, and you strike a pose that is informed and reasonable. We call this *posturing* (without the negative connotation normally associated with that word).

Let's say a Coach asks the seller's best and final price. Wisely, the seller—call him Ben—asks if his company has been selected, and if price is the only remaining open item. The Coach says yes. Now Ben asks, "Doesn't Sherry have final signing authority?" The buyer agrees and sets up a meeting for Ben and Sherry. Not surprisingly, Sherry begins the meeting by squeezing Ben on price:

> **Sherry:** *Ben, thanks for coming in today. Our organizations have spent a great deal of time on this project, and we believe that you have earned our business. I compliment you on understanding our business issues and defining exactly what we need to do to improve our results. My staff is comfortable with your recommendation. Having said that, one of the reasons we are even considering your offer is that our margins have taken a beating, and we believe your offering can help. But in this climate, $250,000 is a significant expenditure, and I would like you to sharpen your pencil so we can see if we want to get started.*

Sherry has been through negotiations numerous times. Given the size of the expenditure, she already has an idea of what type of discounting should be possible. The vendor decision has been made, and now it is a matter of getting the best possible deal. Ben knows the pricing was presented as a step in the Sequence of Events 3 months ago, and in fact was a delineated checkpoint. By not challenging it back then, the buyer implicitly agreed they could afford it. Now that it is time to buy, though, they want to pay less.

Rather than responding with the deadly six words, Ben surprises Sherry:

> **Ben:** *I don't understand, Sherry. We presented pricing 3 months ago. If it was an issue, why wasn't it raised then?*

Sherry is somewhat taken aback by Ben's assertive (but accurate) response. Quickly gathering her wits, she counters:

Sherry: *Well, I felt the pricing was high when you presented it, but I was sure you left some room to negotiate.*

Ben: *The pricing is based on our volume purchase discount. Is there anything you want to take out?*

Sherry: *We need all the proposed capabilities. Frankly, I need you to take out about 10 percent of the cost.*

Ben: *As I recall it, your cost-benefit analysis shows a payback in 5 months. Doesn't it make sense to get started now?*

Sherry: *Well, yes. We want to get started, and that is why we scheduled this meeting. The cost-benefit analysis will look even better if you lower your price.*

Note that in this dialogue, Ben was pressured for a better price no less than three times. Each time, he postured, using questions that politely said no to each of Sherry's requests. Each "no" was unemotional and was virtually impossible for her to challenge or disagree with. The buyer has already made the decision to buy, but has the emotional hurdle of needing to believe she is getting the best possible deal. By saying no three times, Ben is actually helping Sherry make her decision.

Without getting too formulaic about it, posturing often consists of preparing three questions that politely decline the request for a better deal. These should be planned in advance and customized to each situation. Ending these polite no's with a question puts the ball back in the buyer's court. Our experience indicates that it is impossible to drop price while listening. Here are some examples of polite no questions:

- *Put it on the buyer's shoulders:* "Is there anything you would like to take out?"
- *Feign surprise:* "You've known the cost for 2 months. Why is this coming up now?"
- *Remind the buyer of the value:* "By your numbers, the savings are $36,000/month. Shouldn't we get started?"
- *Reference buyer goals:* "We've spent a lot of time together in the past 4 months because you want to improve forecasting accuracy by 30 percent. Has anything changed?"

- *Reference usage:* "Didn't you say that after calling on customers, you want your salespeople prompted to update pipeline milestones, so managers can help with qualification and you can improve the accuracy of your forecast?"

Some buyers will agree to go forward after one, or two, or three of these polite "no's." If so, the seller receives an order for the full amount merely by posturing—that is, without negotiating. In the example so far, Ben has not yet reached the point where negotiation is appropriate. Posturing provides artificial patience during a stressful time and maximizes the possibility of a more profitable transaction.

Negotiating

In some cases, of course, buyers will continue to press for a better deal, and getting the order will require more than posturing—it will require real negotiation. In real negotiation, there are two key components: *get* and *give*. Note the nontraditional sequence of these two words, which is deliberate: get, then give.

Throughout the buying cycle, as noted in previous chapters, the seller should be trying to establish an atmosphere of quid pro quo. This is sometimes hard to sustain, since the buyer has been conditioned to wield disproportionate power with traditional vendors and sellers. But when the seller is offering a way for the buyer to achieve a goal or solve a problem, he or she doesn't deserve to get run roughshod over. Prior to giving, therefore, the seller should first ask for something from the buyer. Why?

Because

- If the seller offers a concession, the buyer will take it and still want a lower price.
- The psychology is to convince the buyer that he or she is getting the best possible deal. If the buyer first has to make a concession, the seller's concession will appear to have more value.
- If the buyer will not agree to a concession, the seller should leave without offering what he or she was willing to give, and without burning the bridge.
- Getting the buyer's commitment first allows a conditional "give." This empowers the seller either to get an order or to leave without

setting a lower number that will become the basis for subsequent negotiating meetings.

There are many different things a seller can ask for. Our suggestion is that it be something that is of value to the seller that causes the buyer to "put some skin" into the negotiation. Examples could be

- A deposit up front, with the balance due in 30 days
- A larger transaction (accelerating the order of future requirements)
- A longer lease term or maintenance commitment
- A press release documenting results
- An introduction to another division or department

It should be noted that the seller cannot ask the buyer to commit to providing the "get" that is requested. The question is whether it would be possible for the buyer to do what is being asked. For example:

Seller: *For me to consider a concession, I need something from you.*

Buyer: *What do you have in mind?*

Seller: *Would it be possible to extend the maintenance contract from 1 year to 2, and for you to serve as a reference for four prospects over the next 12 months?*

Buyer: *I don't see a problem with extending the maintenance agreement. And, assuming our implementation is successful, I could serve as a reference for you.*

Seller: *If you extend the maintenance agreement and agree to be a reference, I'm willing to include our forecasting module, which has a value of $10,000, at no additional cost. Would you like to move forward?*

Buyer: *Is that the best you can do?*

Seller: *It is. Can we move forward?*

Buyer: *Make the changes to the agreement, and let's go ahead.*

In short, our approach to negotiating makes use of things the seller learned during the buying cycle and attempts to foster a spirit of quid pro quo in order to get to the actual closing under acceptable terms.

The Conditional "Give" and Close

After the buyer agrees that the "get" is possible, the seller then conditionally offers the "give" and asks for the business: "If you are willing to (summarize what the buyer said was possible), then I would be willing to (offer your "give"). Can we move forward?"

After asking this question, the seller must wait for the buyer to speak. Only one of two things can happen at this point: The seller will either get an order or have to walk. If the buyer does not close, we suggest leaving, because at this stage, any sweeteners put the seller back on the slippery slope of traditional negotiating. The seller should also take the concession off the table, out of play. We suggest ending the meeting in the following manner: "That's what I was prepared to offer. While it doesn't appear we can proceed today, this transaction makes sense for both of us. Why don't we give our positions some further thought? I'll call you Wednesday and see if we can try to reach agreement."

The seller's willingness to exit may persuade the buyer to move ahead. Whether it does or not, the intent is to avoid having the failed closing become adversarial, and to leave the two parties trying to move ahead with something that is a win-win. If the negotiating meeting is rescheduled, the seller needs to come prepared with a different set of gets and gives and see if the two parties can come to terms.

When sellers discount, they are giving away bottom-line dollars. If a salesperson averages a 15 percent discount, for example, he or she must close about six transactions to net the dollar equivalent of five undiscounted sales. By any measure, this is costly. If a seller is prepared, he or she can minimize these costs by coming out of the negotiation with a better price.

Apples and Oranges

One standard negotiating technique used by traditional buyers is comparing the price of a lesser offering to the seller's price. If the seller responds to this tactic by posturing, he or she somewhat weakens the position, because the discrepancy between the two offerings has not been addressed.

A more effective countermeasure is to be prepared to cite one of your major differentiators—that is, a capability that you provide that the lesser offering does not. As an example, assume that a sales force automation package from your competitor, the ABC Company, costs 30 percent less—a big difference—but, unlike your product, does not dynamically track close rates by individual salesperson at each stage of the sell cycle. The discussion might go as follows:

> **Buyer:** *We like your system, but ABC's offering is 30 percent less than yours. What can you do for me on price?*

> **Seller:** *You could choose to go with ABC, but have you considered that by having to use standard close rates for each step of the pipeline, a salesperson with a low close rate could inflate the gross forecast by entering two or three large opportunities? Can you see how that could cause you to miss your target?*

> **Buyer:** *We would run that risk by using standard close rates.*

> **Seller:** *One of the things we discussed was that when the forecast is being generated, our system can apply historical close rates for each rep at each milestone, so the final forecast will be adjusted. One of your major issues is forecasting accuracy. Are you more comfortable with applying customized close rates by rep?*

> **Buyer:** *I would have a higher level of confidence.*

> **Seller:** *So comparing our offering and ABC's really isn't an apples-to-apples comparison, is it?*

> **Buyer:** *Not exactly, but I would still like to see you sharpen your pencil.*

At this point, after neutralizing the unfair comparison, the seller can now begin posturing with the prepared polite "no" questions.

Summary

Few salespeople admit that they are anything but outstanding negotiators—even if their approach is to discount until a buyer says yes. But if a sales cycle has been executed properly, the close should be a logical conclusion, rather than a fire sale or an arm-wrestling contest. Preparation is critical, and the seller should be prepared in advance to execute the following steps, as needed:

- Verify that you are the vendor of choice, and that price is the only obstacle to doing business.
- Make sure that you are negotiating with a decision maker.
- Head off apples and oranges comparisons by having a differentiator and a situational question to highlight the buyer's need for it.
- Posture by using prepared polite "no" questions to respond (as many as three times) to requests for better pricing.
- Ask the buyer if the "get" you want is possible.
- Offer your conditional "give," and be prepared to walk if the order does not close at that point—leaving the door open, of course, for further rounds, but only after taking your concession off the table.

CHAPTER 15

Proactively Managing Sales Pipelines and Funnels

Many college students are procrastinators. The days before papers come due and exams arrive are stressful indeed as they scramble to catch up. And while this is far from optimal, in terms of a learning experience, most procrastinators somehow manage to squeak by and complete their courses successfully.

Farmers can't work this way. The farm owner has to plan for the coming growing season. On a predetermined schedule, adjusted as necessary to reflect the prevailing weather conditions, the farmer has to turn over the soil, plant, fertilize, weed, and harvest. There is no way to stall, or to compress the steps needed to bring a crop to harvest.

Unfortunately, most salespeople act more like college students than like farmers. They approach their year-end quota in much the same way procrastinating students approach semesters: confident that they can cram as needed if they fall behind their year-to-date (YTD) target. Is there a more optimistic person in the world than a salesperson sitting at 37 percent of quota going into the last quarter? (We have yet to meet such a person.) Most lagging salespeople convince themselves that somehow, the elusive numbers will be hit by the end of the year. The surge of hope stays alive until the last week or two, when they finally admit to themselves that this year is a lost cause, and that it's time to "sandbag" orders so that they can hit the ground running the following year.

Salespeople simulate electricity: They follow the path of least resistance. Procrastination is an easy trap to fall into. And procrastination with respect to YTD quota position is reinforced by a salesperson's desire to have as many opportunities in the funnel as possible. Yes, if you add up all the items listed, the resulting figure may approach the gross domestic product of a small Central American country. But a closer look reveals that many of the "opportunities" listed in most pipelines have little chance of closing. This underscores the need for managers to grade funnels with an eye toward (1) setting appropriate activity levels and (2) disqualifying low-probability items.

As noted in a previous chapter, we distinguish between pipeline and funnel management. Pipeline milestones are graded and used by sales management for the purpose of forecasting, while sales funnel milestones are graded and used by sales management to assess the quantity of selling activity and the quality of selling skills at the individual salesperson level.

Left to their own devices, many salespeople compete to stay busy. In our view, the role of sales managers is to help them compete to win. But the prospect of putting a salesperson on an improvement plan—or, worse, firing an underperformer and recruiting and training a replacement—is enough to make a sales manager procrastinate like a college student.

The goal of managing pipeline is predicting what will close—forecasting—but these predictions are driven as much by personal agendas as by reality. A salesperson who is below quota has a specific agenda when forecasting: get my manager to believe that there is sufficient activity so that I can keep my job.

One major challenge in forecasting is that companies lack consistent qualification elements. Managers with experience at different companies bring along their own approach to grading opportunities. Even when companies attempt to impose standard milestones, an "80 percent probability" actually varies from salesperson to salesperson, and from district to district. The problem is that these milestones rely on a subjective judgment: Has the opportunity progressed to that level, or not? Well, tell a traditional salesperson who is behind quota that by the end of next week, she must have five opportunities at a certain milestone. By the end of next week, she will have six (thus allowing a margin for error, if one is successfully challenged by the manager). You can set your watch by it, but would you want to forecast these opportunities?

Predicting the date that an opportunity will close is a challenge for even the best salespeople. It's simply not their call. Forecasting can be as meaningless as pushing a few dates back by 30 days and tweaking a few numbers (especially when there is little or nothing that has been added in a given month). And these summaries tend to blow away in the first wind, in any case. If a salesperson forecasts a transaction to close in September, then forecasts it in October, and it finally happens in November, the accuracy is 33 percent—but what's remembered is that the salesperson got the business.

Salespeople despise forecasting because, in most cases, they are being asked to lie in writing. They know all too well that the exercise of forecasting is likely to bear little or no resemblance to reality. In fact, the major value of forecasting is that it has the potential to give salespeople with inadequate pipelines a wake-up call 12 times a year—that is, a message from on high that there are inadequate opportunities in their pipeline, and that they must increase their business-development activities.

So let's look at ways to get to better forecasting, in part by removing salespeople from the process.

Milestones: Getting the Terms Straight

In order to break away from the insanity referred to euphemistically as forecasting, a number of complementary components are necessary:

1. Sales-Ready Messaging, designed to position offerings specific to title, vertical industry, and goal, which provides less subjective input into the pipeline
2. Auditable correspondence between the seller and the buyer
3. Sequences of Events containing estimated close dates, as negotiated with the buyer
4. Companywide milestones, with defined ways to achieve and document them
5. Sales managers (not salespeople) who are willing and able to audit milestones, grade pipeline, disqualify low-probability opportunities, and predict what will close
6. Senior executive commitment to ride through potential "push back" from salespeople and sales managers who prefer less visibility and accountability

Items 1 through 3 have been described in previous chapters. So let's start with CustomerCentric Selling *milestones*, which most of our clients modify as needed and adopt as companywide standards. First, refer to Figure 15-1.

- *Inactive* means that an account fits a company's target market and is assigned to a salesperson, but there is no current activity. A salesperson's business-development efforts should focus on getting a buying cycle to start by getting a targeted Key Player within the account to share a goal, which would advance it to the next milestone.
- *Active* indicates that contact has been made and some form of interest on the part of the customer or prospect has been expressed.
- *Goal Shared* is the initiation of a sales cycle in CustomerCentric Selling; it indicates that a targeted Key Player has shared a desire to achieve at least one goal that is on the menu of business issues the seller can help them address.
- *Champion* status can be granted only by the sales manager. It happens only after all the qualification elements have been achieved: the letter, fax, or email has been sent; the buyer has agreed to the content; and the buyer is willing to provide access to Key Players. The sales manager must have reviewed the customer document and graded it as a C, usually after a brief discussion with the salesperson.

  The opportunity remains a C while all Key Players are being interviewed, either in person or on the phone. All calls should be documented with each buyer, and there should be agreement that the content reflects the conversation that the seller had with them. After all Key Players have been qualified, there is an attempt to qualify the opportunity. Some of our clients like to not only track the number of months an opportunity is at this level, but also get a sense for how many Key Players must be interviewed and how many have been called on. A greater number of Key Players most likely means that an opportunity will remain a C for a longer period of time.
- *Evaluating* status is determined by the sales manager, but only after the salesperson has gained consensus from Key Players that further investigation of the salesperson's offering is called for, and a Sequence of Events has been accepted by the buying committee. At the end of that month, the salesperson provides a copy of the cover letter and Sequence of Events, and the sales manager can change the status to E (and update the Sales Force Automation/Customer Relationship Management (SFA/CRM) system) if it is deemed a qualified opportunity.

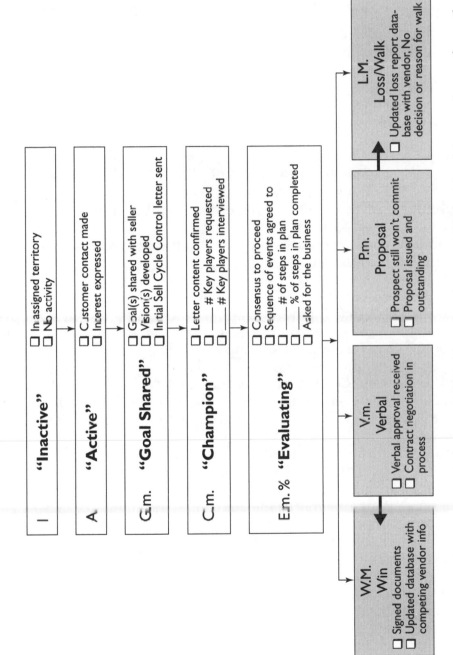

Figure 15-1 Grading Opportunities: Funnel Milestones (m = no. of months; M = total no. of months; % = % complete)

Opportunities remain at this stage until one of three things happens:

1. The buyer withdraws (and the opportunity becomes a loss).
2. The seller withdraws (and the opportunity becomes a walk).
3. The seller asks for the business after the Sequence of Events has been completed.

Once the seller has asked for the business, the opportunity goes into one of four grades:

W (Win)	An order with all necessary documents signed.
L (Loss)	The buyer informs you that he or she will not be moving forward with you.
V (Verbal)	The buyer has given you a verbal commitment to go forward.
P (Proposal)	A proposal is provided to the prospect with a decision due.

A few notes about the chart. Many of our clients choose to assign probabilities to the G, C, and E grades. Until you accumulate your own historical data with your forecasting system, we suggest assigning initial probabilities of 25 percent for the Champion (C) level and 50 percent once the manager assigns the Evaluating (E) level to an opportunity. (Organizations with SFA or CRM systems may ultimately collect percentages for individual salespeople, enabling them to fine-tune forecasting accuracy.) For an E prospect, each checkpoint agreed to increase the chances of getting an order.

Capturing the number of months (m) that a line item in the pipeline has been at a particular stage allows the sales manager to identify opportunities that are not progressing. For E status, adding a percentage to reflect the percentage of steps in the Sequence of Events that have been completed can also provide a meaningful point of reference for the manager. For the grades of W and L, it may similarly be useful to track the total number of months (M) that an opportunity was in the pipeline before you won or lost. After losses, data indicating whether the winner was a named competitor or there was no decision (meaning no gold medal was awarded) should be entered.

By implementing the system shown in Figure 15-2, managers can detect early-warning signs that a given opportunity is stalled or in trouble. For each pipeline milestone shown, you'll see two examples: one that is

Grade	Example	Explanation
Grade G Goal	G.1/150,000 G.3/100,000	Buyer shared goal, less than 30 days old, $150,000 potential More than 30 days old, still no Champion
Grade C Champion	C.1/300,000 C.3/100,000	Champion, less than 30 days old, still interviewing Key Players More than 30 days old, too small for large no. of Key Players—stuck?
Grade E Sequence of Events	E.5.50%/300,000 E.1.25%/600,000	4 months old, 50% complete, low $—stuck? 1st month of plan, 25% complete, large account
Grade L Walk/Lose	L.2/300,000 L.1/600,000	Disqualified after less than 2 months—bad news early is good! Went the distance (11 months!) and lost
Grade P Proposal	P.1/100,000 P.4/600,000	Had to deliver proposal, less than 30 days old Responded to RFP over 3 months ago—need to take back
Grade V Verbal	V.1/400,000 V.2/200,000	Verbal less than 30 days old—still should be good Verbal over 30 days old—problem!
Grade W Win	W.5/400,000 W.8/200,000	Win—4-month sell cycle Win—7 months to close $200,000 order—did we make any money?

Figure 15-2 Funnel Management Examples

on track, with normal parameters for a viable opportunity; and another that is beyond normal conditions. While there may be extenuating circumstances, the latter situation should prompt the manager to have a conversation with the salesperson. If necessary, both can agree on a course of corrective action to get the opportunity back on track. Alternatively, it may be appropriate for the manager to disqualify this line item from the pipeline, rather than allow the seller to toil with a low probability of getting the business. (Remember: Bad news early is good news.)

Even without an SFA/CRM system, sales managers can now forecast by asking each salesperson to fax or email the latest copy of the Sequence of Events for each opportunity. By reviewing these documents, the sales manager can assess each opportunity with a reasonable degree of objectivity and consistency (in an apples-to-apples sense).

In order to home in on forecasting accuracy, we suggest that sales managers maintain three pipeline categories for each salesperson:

1. Add-on business with existing customers, having the highest probability of closing
2. New account business in which you were proactive and started as Column A
3. New account business where you were reactive and started as Column B, C, and so on

Forecasting is now a monthly review of pipeline, with sales managers choosing which opportunities are likely to close and the Sequences of Events providing lots of visibility and realistic close dates.

This monthly review also affords an opportunity to be proactive with salespeople who might be procrastinators. "Train wrecks" within a funnel do not happen overnight. Let's see how a manager can be proactive in anticipating a shortfall in a given funnel. A few variables are necessary to provide sales managers with visibility one sales cycle ahead, as shown in this example.

1. A salesperson's annual quota: $1.5 million
2. The average length of a sales cycle: 4 months
3. The probability that an E will close: 50 percent
4. Any shortfall in the salesperson's YTD quota attainment: 0

One way to reduce procrastination is to break down a quota to a monthly number—in this case, $125,000/month. Multiplying this by an average sales cycle tells you that in 4 months, a salesperson will be expected to close $500,000. If, however, the salesperson closes 50 percent of the Sequences of Events that were put in place, the funnel target would be twice that figure, or $1 million. This means that at any given time, when you take a snapshot of a salesperson's funnel, you would like to see at least $1 million at E status, as graded by the sales manager. If you were halfway through the year and the salesperson was $100,000 behind the YTD number, the target would be the standard of $1 million plus ($100,000/50 percent), or $1.2 million.

This may seem like a mouthful, so let's look at the activity balancing example below, where the per month quota is $125,000, the average sell cycle is 4 months, and there is a 50 percent probability of closing a Grade E prospect.

$$\frac{(\$125,000)\ (4\ months)}{50\%} = \$1\ million\ target\ for\ "E"\ pipeline$$

$1 million + (YTD shortfall $\times$ 2) = target for the next 4 months

By doing this calculation on a monthly basis, sales managers can help salespeople stay ahead of the curve. While managers should review changes to, and volume of, A, G, and C entries, E opportunities provide the best sense of how things will look one sales cycle ahead. If the E funnel is below target, business development activity must be increased. The conversation could sound like this:

> *Jane, you have been running on your numbers through April, but this month you only have $800,000 in E business. Over the next month, I want you to make sure that you increase your business-development activities. My suggestion would be to make a minimum of 10 new contacts per week. I'd also like to see you migrate two opportunities from C to E, and I will work with you on doing that. Hopefully, next month you'll have sufficient new opportunities in your funnel so that we'll both feel better about where you'll be YTD in September. We can then revisit how much of your time should be spent on business development.*

This approach, in other words, emphasizes proactive rather than forensic sales management. If a salesperson competes for 8 months and loses, it is no longer solely his or her responsibility. Each month (or more frequently), the sales manager should have made a qualify/disqualify decision at all checkpoints in the Sequences of Events that were approved. The Sequences of Events also allow a sales manager to get further upstream on opportunities, to coach new or struggling salespeople all along the way, and to have control and ownership of the forecast he or she provides.

When these kinds of analyses are performed on a monthly basis, course corrections can be made to maximize the probability that salespeople will achieve their numbers—and thereby minimize turnover, either voluntary or involuntary. Involuntary turnover, as suggested above, is difficult for all parties involved. From the company standpoint, there is a significant expense inherent in recruiting and training a replacement, lost continuity within the territory, ramp-up time for new hires, and management time spent on the territory during the interim period. By the time many managers (and salespeople) realize they are in trouble, it is often too late to save that year. An analysis on a monthly basis, therefore, is well worth the time it takes to perform.

In a previous chapter, we distinguished between "will not" and "cannot" attitudes in a salesperson. "Will not" is, in most cases, a management issue. "Cannot" is a skill issue, and will serve as the basis of the next chapter.

Assessing and Developing Salespeople

O<small>N AT LEAST AN ANNUAL BASIS</small>, most Human Resources (HR) departments require sales managers to formally assess their staff. And despite the fact that the sales manager should have reviewed twelve (or more?) forecasts from each salesperson over the course of those 12 months, it can be a tough job to sit down and formally analyze what has transpired in a year.

Consider the following outstanding, average, and difficult performance reviews, which are composites from our experience working with salespeople over the years.

Salesperson A, Mary, consistently achieves 200-plus percent of quota. The manager invites Mary into his office, and begins

Mary, it is difficult to put into words what a pleasure it is to have you on my team. Thanks for your contributions over the past year. I've filled out your evaluation, so take a minute to review it and ask any questions you may have. (Mary spends 2 minutes reading the glowing evaluation and has no questions.) Well, then, this will go into your personnel file. I'm pleased to give you the maximum 5 percent raise on your base salary. Let me know if there is anything I can do to help you going forward. At this stage, my inclination is to just get out of your way and let you sell. Congratulations on a tremendous year!

Salesperson B, whom we'll call Joe, struggles to make his numbers. Two of the last three years he has made quota (as he did last year) by a few percentage points. He achieved 92 percent of quota 2 years ago. He enters the office and hears:

> *Joe, let's review your performance evaluation. Take a few minutes to look at it, and then we can talk. (Joe sees several areas where he is considered average. There are a few areas showing his skills to be above average, balanced by areas needing improvement. It is a fair assessment that accurately points out his strengths and weaknesses.) Joe, I hope you agree with my assessment and comments. Overall, I'm glad to have you on the team, but I wish you could increase activity within your pipeline. If you were to increase prospecting activity, I think you could . . . (The discussion drones on for about 30 minutes, including comments about skill sets that must be "shored up," interspersed with compliments about strengths. The meeting grinds to a conclusion as Joe signs the evaluation.) Joe, I hope this session was worthwhile. I want you to strive to increase activity and make your numbers by the end of October. Won't it be nice for us to be able to enjoy the holiday season at the end of this year? I've put in for a 2 percent raise in your base. Let's make this the year that you knock the fences down.*

Keith, Salesperson C, finished the past year below 50 percent of quota, and is sitting at about 50 percent of quota year-to-date halfway through the year. This review promises to be difficult:

> *Keith, why don't you come in and take a seat. (The manager rests his chin on both hands, effectively covering much of his face, and starts to talk.) Keith, Keith, Keith, this has been a rough couple of years for both of us. Do you see things getting any better? (Keith mumbles a vague, uninspiring answer.) Well, based on your performance over the past 18 months, we have two choices. One is for HR to get involved. We would put you on a performance improvement plan and give you a 90-day period to get year-to-date against your quota. It would necessitate weekly meetings and mounds of paperwork. If after 90 days you still weren't tracking to your numbers, I'd have to terminate you. Do you think that you can close that much business in the next 3 months? (Again, Keith's answer fails to inspire confidence.)*
> *Look, Keith, I know you have a family, and candidly, I'd hate to have to terminate you. Off the record, we could look at things another*

*way. If you feel you can't make your numbers, the next 90 days could
be put to a different use. I won't be taking attendance, so you'd have
time to explore other options. Most people find it is easier to find a job
while they have one. Why don't you sleep on it, and let me know how
you'd like to proceed. In the meantime, don't tell anyone we had this
conversation. Maybe a fresh start at another company is just the thing
you need to get your career on track. Let me know what you decide.*

Sound familiar? Anyone who has managed salespeople has faced these
situations. (And maybe you've even been Mary, Joe, or Keith at some
point in your career.) Mary is a customer-centric seller who neither wants
nor needs to be managed, and will consistently produce. Joe is typical of
traditional salespeople, who constitute the majority of sales forces. Every
year, making quota is an adventure, and one that typically goes right to
the end of the year. Keith's situation is a nightmare for everyone. He may
be unskilled, unlucky, or lazy. Most likely he'll be working for another
company within the next few months, regardless of whether he opts for
the performance improvement plan or immediately begins a job search.

The reviews presented above are typical of those received by salespeople who have not been supported by Sales-Ready Messaging and a
sales process. The traditional sales manager knows what he or she is doing, in terms of traditional methods of motivating the sales force; he or
she also seems to have a pretty good sense of the salespeople. But it's
certainly fair to ask: Is this the first time that Joe has heard that he needs
to improve? How long has Keith been bumping along on the bottom without intervention from above? Can either Mary or her manager articulate
what makes her a customer-centric superstar?

In this chapter, we want to introduce a sales management process to
assess and develop salespeople.

Golf Is Easier

The title Sales Manager is misleading. We believe a manager's primary
responsibility is to develop people. The reality is that most traditional
sales managers—including the one in our example above—are adminis-
trators attempting to drive numbers. They tell their direct reports what
to do and in what quantity, but are unable to teach them how to do it.
Sales managers have many different modes; they may try to motivate, in-
timidate, nurture, mentor, and so on. They finally admit defeat when their
mode switches to counseling people out of the business.

But more often than not, the issue is not one of motivation. Most underperforming salespeople sincerely want to do better, but lack the necessary skills. All the encouragement, incentive programs, and intimidation in the world can't teach a salesperson to sell. If Keith is intelligent and motivated—which, after all, was part of the hiring model—then having him do more of what he's already doing is unlikely to get him to improve his performance.

As noted in an earlier chapter, most sales managers got their jobs because they were naturally talented salespeople. They don't necessarily understand how or why they were successful, yet they are now charged with passing their intuitive selling skills onto their direct reports. The path many sales managers in this situation take to get salespeople up to speed is osmosis: "Watch how I sell, and learn (because I can't describe it)." Often intense during the first month or so after a new hire signs on, this kind of "training" tends to fall off precipitously shortly thereafter. The sales manager has other things to do—there's another new hire that needs the benefit of osmosis.

On balance, skill-transfer results using osmosis are disappointing. Osmosis is a poor substitute for sales process. And without process, selling resembles an art more than a science.

Assessing and coaching skills without understanding the basic mechanics of selling is next to impossible. When professional athletes experience slumps, there are standard ways of identifying and correcting the problem. A professional golfer, for example, has several ways to identify swing flaws and correct them. First, there are generally accepted mechanics associated with a golf swing (head down, left arm straight, and so on). The golfer in question may view videotapes of a sound golf swing (either his or her own, or that of another player). Many have a "swing coach" who works with them. Even the process of identifying the problem—a problem on which the golfer and the coach can agree—gives rise to a surge of hope: This problem can be fixed! And this, in turn, gives the needed motivation to spend all that time on the driving range and playing practice rounds.

Is there a sales equivalent to the golf story? The answer is, "There *should* be, but it's hard to find." Consider a salesperson whose performance was previously at acceptable levels, but has been in the doldrums for the past year and a half. Some harsh realities:

1. There are few generally accepted and useful rules of selling. There are general notions: listen, don't lead with product, selling begins when

buyers say no, always be closing, and so forth. Some of these we (the authors) subscribe to, and others we take issue with; but at the end of the day, our motivation in creating CustomerCentric Selling was that there was nothing close to a useful road map of how to sell, especially when compared to an activity such as hitting a golf ball.

2. Selling habits have been developed through an unstructured series of individual trial-and-error experiences. Instead of good "muscle memory," the salesperson has bad muscle memory, and self-diagnosis becomes extremely difficult. This makes it virtually impossible for someone to coach a salesperson out of a slump. As previously mentioned, Neil Rackham discovered that as sellers become more familiar with their offerings, they begin to lose patience and empathy in asking questions and listening to their buyers. This behavior is virtually impossible to self-diagnose.

3. There is no "practice range" for salespeople. If a golfer hits several bad shots on the driving range, ego aside, there are no negative consequences. In fact, it may help in isolating flaws. But salespeople have no "range" on which to experiment. They are under pressure to produce numbers (more so when they are in a slump), and they do not have the luxury of trying new approaches without potential consequences. A poor call reduces the number of prospects in the finite territory by one—and, in practical terms, for the duration of the salesperson's current employment.

4. As relates to development and improvement, salespeople live on remote islands. One of the biggest challenges comes when the salesperson disagrees with his or her manager about a given course of action. There is no surge of hope like that experienced by the golfer and the coach. Slumping salespeople must work their way out of it alone. The sales manager is likely to make the problem worse if he or she applies pressure by demanding increased levels of activity (i.e., quantity) without influencing the quality of activity. Most people's performance degrades under pressure.

Assessment: What Doesn't Work

Sales management without sales process is largely a forensic (after-the-fact) exercise. Managers perform silver medal autopsies after losses and

222 CUSTOMERCENTRIC SELLING

during annual HR reviews. They wind up not helping either Joe or Keith, and—most likely—firing Keith or persuading him to move on.

But imagine if managers could be proactive instead of reactive. Proactive steps—corrective surgery—could reduce the need for autopsies. Why does it take a loss (or nagging from HR) for managers to act? We believe it is because most sales managers are merely driving numbers. Lacking the ability to assess and develop their people, they assess and develop their people's numbers, instead. But this is exactly backward. If sales managers could develop their people, the numbers would take care of themselves.

First, let's look at flaws in the assessment process. Let's assume the annual evaluation requires sales managers to rank salespeople as one of the following overall categories (we've added our editorial counterpoint in italics):

1. Exceptional salesperson who consistently exceeds quota and provides leadership to the office. Displays outstanding knowledge of offerings, possesses strong administrative skills, exhibits strong account control, and shows ability to disqualify poor opportunities from his or her funnel. Requires minimal guidance, and is a candidate for promotion into sales management.
   Sales management would be a breeze if these people could be cloned.
2. Steady performer who meets or exceeds quota the majority of the time. Has a tendency to work identified opportunities and grow ongoing accounts. Sometimes gets entangled in low-probability opportunities. A more aggressive business development plan and more structured approach could bring performance up to the next level.
   Sales managers are happy to have people like this on the team. They need occasional coaching, but by and large they can be trusted with small to medium opportunities.
3. Struggles to keep activity levels to a point where the pipeline reaches targeted levels. Requires extensive coaching, and requires managers to make joint calls whenever feasible. Needs extensive support on all opportunities and coaching on a weekly basis.
   This had better be a new hire on the way to becoming a 2. If he or she doesn't show progress within the next year, though, there will be a tough decision to make.
4. Has difficulty generating meaningful activity in territory. Marginal understanding of both offerings and industries called

on. Micromanagement is necessary, both in reviewing activity from the previous week and in planning activity for the following week.

Unless dramatic improvement is realized in the short term, it appears that either a hiring error has been made or the salesperson's skill or motivation has eroded. Unless things change, a performance improvement plan or termination looms on the horizon.

Selling is one of the strangest professions. Performance is measured exactly—sometimes to within hundredths of a percentage point. Companies calculate commissions to the penny. Many companies require managers to assign a single grade to reflect their assessment of a salesperson's perceived skill set that can influence his or her career path. But in reality, is this precision? Can a single grade reflect the skill set and abilities of a salesperson? We believe the answer is no.

Taken collectively, the skill set and personal characteristics required to consistently exceed quota are staggering. We know renowned doctors, lawyers, and professors who would starve as salespeople: They just don't have what it takes. For a complex offering, we believe a salesperson needs a minimum IQ of 120, strong verbal and written skills, the courage and confidence to accept a position where only a portion of his or her compensation is guaranteed, and so on. So can a sales manager effectively rate someone like this on a scale of 1 to 4? Not likely.

Performance Does Not Always Mean Skill Mastery

Let's assume that Ron was the third salesperson hired by a start-up company that is now publicly traded and has revenues of $150 million. Ron was involved in the initial large sale to an early-market buyer 8 years ago. This sale validated the company's offering, and he received extensive support in that sales effort from the founder and other senior executives. For the past several years, Ron has averaged 225 percent of quota, largely by handling the growing requirements of three major customers. Ron's last cold prospecting call was made several years ago, when the thin condition of his pipeline drove him to make a call.

Ron has achieved legendary status, and preferential treatment, within the company. People wonder why he has never gone into management. The answer is simple: Ron has realized that his personal strengths and his quality-of-life goals all indicate that sales is the best position for him.

Ron's manager treads lightly and consistently grades him as a 1. Failing to do so would probably prompt a call by Ron to the CEO complaining about his manager and the review, and necessitate changing the grade on the evaluation in Human Resources' file.

According to his annual reviews, Ron is a 1 in the areas of need development, account management, negotiating, qualification and control, and so on. Peeling back the onion, however, it turns out that he is *not* a 1 in the skill of business development and prospecting—in fact, he is a 4. At this stage, it is impossible to tell if the problem lies in skill (cannot) or attitude (will not). In any event, Ron's manager is not doing him a favor by ignoring this glaring deficiency. Ron is, in effect, coasting. Smart salespeople know intuitively that they are worth what they can earn in their *next* sales position. If for some reason things go south with this company, Ron may face the challenge of finding and accepting a territory with a company where he does not enjoy sacred cow status and most likely will not be given the largest installed accounts to develop.

Seven Selling Skills

As shown in the previous chapter, sales managers can be proactive in analyzing pipelines so that activity levels can be increased. This approach helps the manager influence the quantity of activity. We'd now like to show a technique for upgrading the quality of activity. To do so, we've distilled selling into seven skills:

- New business development
- Solution development
- Opportunity qualification and control
- Proof management
- Access to Key Players
- Negotiation and closing
- Monitoring success metrics

These skills tend to come into play at different times in the buying cycle, as shown on the left side of Figure 16-1. On the right side are the deliverables that a sales manager can monitor to assess the skills of each salesperson. A discussion of proof management and monitoring success

Figure 16-1 Funnel Management: Skills and Deliverables

metrics is beyond the scope of this book and will be covered in the forth-coming *CustomerCentric Selling Field Guide*.

The shapes of funnels vary greatly by salesperson. The funnel of someone exhibiting high activity but low skill mastery in the area of business development could look like a martini glass, with many conversations (As) needed to generate Gs. As opportunities enter and progress through a salesperson's funnel over the space of a few months, if there are blockages where deals tend to stall, this points to a probable skill deficiency. We'd like to show how to assess funnel data so that skills can be assessed and—wherever necessary—the sales manager can come up with specific plans containing activities needed to shore up weaknesses.

Let's now assume that over a period of 2 or 3 months, there are blockages in a salesperson's funnel—which, again, point to likely skill deficiencies. Look at Figure 16-2.

An insufficient number of As entering the funnel points toward a problem with business development. In response, the manager could set a minimum number of first contacts per week or month, but that would

Funnel Blockage

Potential Reasons

From "T" to "A"
(Prospecting)

- Lack of new opportunities to call
- Inadequate use of compelling scripts/tools
- Difficulty aligning with buyer
- Inability to get buyer to share goals or admit problems

From "A" to "G" or "C"
(Solution Development)

- Calling too low to engage Champion level buyer
- Issues on tools are too low level
- Poor goal identification and solution development skills
- Poor understanding of how to negotiate access to Key Players

From "C" to "E"
(Qualification)

- Issues on tools are too low level
- Poor goal identification and solution development skills
- Poor understanding of how to set up or obtain Decision Maker agreement to sequence of events

From "E" to "P"
(Sales Process Control)

- Negotiates sequence of events with non-Decision Makers
- Difficulty mapping Opportunity Organizational Chart
- Cost versus benefit not quantifiable/not based on buyer's numbers
- Implementation issues not addressed

From "P" to "V"
(Negotiation)

- Lost control at the end of the sales cycle (no predecision review scheduled)
- Unprepared for negotiation (no worksheet with polite no's and quid pro quo)
- Unprepared to address buyer risk issues

From "V" to "W"
(Closing)

- Out of alignment (closing too soon)
- Logistical issues

Figure 16-2 Analyzing Funnel Blockages

not address the quality of the effort. A proactive CustomerCentric sales manager would do the following:

1. Ask to see the letters, faxes, and emails that the salesperson is using to generate interest. It could be they are not worded properly, or are geared toward the wrong vertical industry or title. The manager could help write the documents and design a more effective strategy.

2. Ask the seller to spend some time with a peer who has realized great success in business development. It may be appropriate for the person who is struggling to listen to one of his or her peers making calls, or following up on leads, to see that person's approach.

3. The sales manager could role-play being a buyer taking a prospecting call from the seller.

Blockages in getting prospects from A to C would point toward a lack of skill in getting buyers to share goals. The manager could spend time reviewing the following areas:

1. Review the menu of goals for each Key Player that the seller is using.
2. Help the seller generate and use the Success Stories that take a buyer from a latent need to sharing a goal.
3. Role-play with the seller to walk him or her through approaches to getting goals shared or problems admitted.

If opportunities stall at G status, there are two areas that are likely to need addressing. The first is that the seller lacks the ability to take a buyer from goal to vision, meaning he or she is either not using the correct Solution Development Prompter (SDP), or is having difficulty executing it. Again, the manager could review the material being used and could role-play with the seller. The manager could also make joint calls with the seller and demonstrate how to use the SDP.

Another reason for stalling at G status can be that the seller has difficulty getting prospects to agree to Champion them and get them to the Key Players who need to be accessed. This difficulty can occur because the buyer's vision is not compelling (letters should be edited), there is not sufficient value in the mind of the buyer, or the seller is not able to defend or explain the need to meet with the Key Players requested. In such cases, the suggested approach would be to make joint calls—either face to face or via conference call. It is also possible that potential Champions are being offered proof without the seller's using a quid pro quo approach to getting access.

If a seller has opportunities that stall after qualifying a Champion, there are several potential areas of difficulty:

1. If most of his or her Champions are at relatively low levels, there may be difficulty relating to more senior executives. This skill can be developed via role-playing and making those executive calls jointly.

2. The seller may be having difficulty in gaining consensus and negotiating a Sequence of Events with the buying committee. The manager should have the seller take him or her to visit accounts where all Key Players have been met, but where no Sequence of Events has yet been finalized.

3. The seller may be attempting to qualify people at relatively low levels within organizations as Champions. As stated earlier, a salesperson's quality of life will be better if he or she can get decision maker level Champions. In such cases, access to Key Players is most often volunteered, rather than the salesperson's having to ask or negotiate for it.

Once an opportunity reaches E status, the seller and manager should have at least a 50 percent chance of having the sell cycle result in an order. In our opinion, the single most important variable in determining win rates is which seller initiated the opportunity (again, caused someone who wasn't looking to change, to look). Having an agreed-on plan in place affords the manager visibility into whether or not the opportunity is moving forward. By evaluating the status at each checkpoint, managers take some ownership of and responsibility for determining that the transaction is winnable. As soon as it appears that things are not proceeding as planned, the manager and seller should strategize as to how to get things back on track. And as always, in some instances, it will be necessary to withdraw. This should (will have to?) be the manager's call.

Leveraging Manager Experience

The manager has to make a judgment call as to whether the pace of progress is satisfactory. This is a complex decision that takes into account whether the seller is dealing with early- or mainstream-market buyers, the size of the organization, the size of the opportunity, and the overall impact or risk to the prospect in moving forward. Here are some warning signs to look for:

1. The buyer starts to push dates back.
2. Access to Key Players becomes more difficult.
3. Line items in the agreed-to Sequence of Events are challenged.
4. Buyer requirements change, potentially influenced by competitors.
5. A Key Player leaves or is reassigned.

When managers are trying to decide at a given checkpoint whether to continue to compete, there is one key bellwether question to consider: "Are we the vendor of choice for at least one of the Key Players—and if not, what can we do to get there?" If the ultimate answer is, "We can't get there," it may well be time to withdraw from the opportunity, rather than throwing time, effort, and resources into what is likely to be a losing cause, resulting in yet another silver medal.

Senior executives of sales organizations may want to monitor average discounting levels by district and salesperson to identify potential skill deficiencies in negotiating. A caution, though: If a potential problem is identified, it may not be the salesperson's. We worked with an organization that had a district manager in Boston who was a terrible negotiator. When he was brought in to help the seller on large transactions, the discounts offered wound up being far greater than those in other offices. (In fact, he had earned the nickname "Moon over Massachusetts" because of his propensity to discount.) For a period of time, his manager had to review and role-play the polite "no's" and get/gives prior to going to the negotiating meeting. There were a few instances where he had to walk prior to getting the business. Within 3 months, though, his discounting fell into the acceptable range.

Another statistic to track is the level of discounting based on the date of the order. Buyers expect the end of the month or quarter to give them better leverage in getting concessions. Whenever possible, an attempt should be made to schedule the Sequence of Events so that the decision date doesn't coincide with a quarter end.

Once a seller has asked for the business, the opportunity goes from an E to one of four milestones. Look at Figure 16-3.

W.M.   The seller got the order. The capital M reflects the total number of months it took to win. An analysis of the length

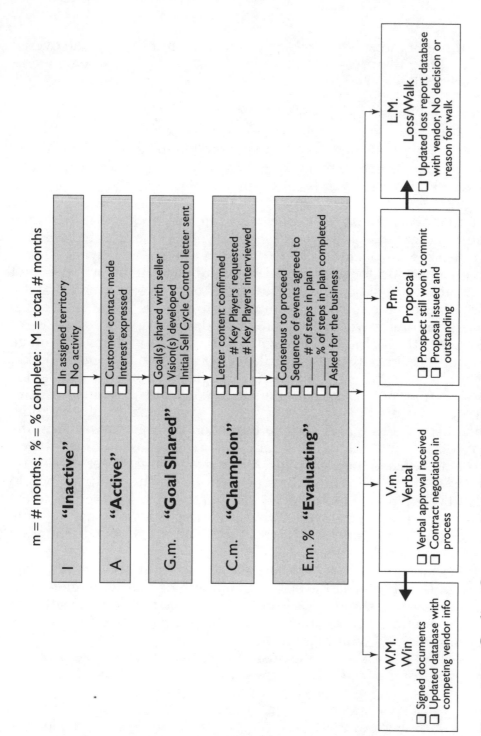

m = # months; % = % complete; M = total # months

I "**Inactive**"
☐ In assigned territory
☐ No activity

A "**Active**"
☐ Customer contact made
☐ Interest expressed

G.m. "**Goal Shared**"
☐ Goal(s) shared with seller
☐ Vision(s) developed
☐ Initial Sell Cycle Control letter sent

C.m. "**Champion**"
☐ Letter content confirmed
☐ # Key Players requested
☐ # Key Players interviewed

E.m. % "**Evaluating**"
☐ Consensus to proceed
☐ Sequence of events agreed to
☐ __ # of steps in plan
☐ __ % of steps in plan completed
☐ Asked for the business

W.M. Win
☐ Signed documents
☐ Updated database with competing vendor info

V.m. Verbal
☐ Verbal approval received
☐ Contract negotiation in process

P.m. Proposal
☐ Prospect still won't commit
☐ Proposal issued and outstanding

L.M. Loss/Walk
☐ Updated loss report database with vendor, No decision or reason for walk

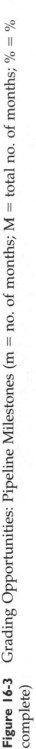

Figure 16-3 Grading Opportunities: Pipeline Milestones (m = no. of months; M = total no. of months; % = % complete)

of winning sell cycles can be helpful in isolating best practices. (The most important single variable often turns out to be how high the entry level within the prospect was.)

L.M.   The seller loses, either to no decision or to a named vendor. Tracking and analyzing the total months of losses may isolate common events that lead to losses, so that hopefully they can be avoided in future sales cycles.

V.m.   The buyer has provided a verbal commitment, but for some reason the contract or purchase order cannot be issued. In such cases, we suggest asking the buyer to sign a nonbinding letter of intent, so that when other vendors call, they can say they have already committed and the decision has been made.

P.m.   The proposal had to be issued prior to the decision's being made.

In our experience, time does not improve the likelihood of winning verbal commitments or getting proposals accepted. Once either is more than 30 days old, managers have cause for concern. When evaluating pipelines, we often see proposals out there for more than 60 days that are still assigned probabilities of 80-plus percent. Every month that a proposal doesn't close means that the chances of ultimately getting the order are decreasing.

In our experience, once a proposal is 45 days old, either it is heading toward no decision or the buyer has made a decision to go with another vendor and has elected not to give the seller the bad news. Even if you have had access to decision makers up to this point, after the proposal is in their hands, they usually don't want to talk with you. Either they haven't made a decision or they've made an unfavorable decision.

In other words, you relinquish a great deal of control once your proposal is delivered. Suddenly, the buyer has everything he or she needs, and access gets more difficult. Rather than wait and hope, consider taking some positive action if the proposal is out longer than you think is healthy for your chances of winning (30 to 45 days?). We suggest a take-back letter or a phone call withdrawing the proposal. If you opt for a letter, don't overnight it. The proposal has been out for over a month, and there is no sense in spending $11.95 to get the letter delivered the next day. Registered mail will have the same impact and will cost significantly less. Figure 16-4 is a sample letter.

April 28, 2003
Allan Campbell
XYZ Company

Dear Allan,

In reviewing my files, it has come to my attention that no action has been taken on the proposal we submitted to you on December 18, 2002. In rereading it, I understand why you may not have taken action. The proposal reflects a lack of understanding on my part of your primary business objectives. If you are willing, I'd like an opportunity to better understand if the usage of our CRM software can enable you to achieve your business objectives. The purpose of this letter is to make you aware of the fact that we are formally withdrawing our offer. Please call me if you have any questions.

Sincerely,

George Agnew
Sales Representative
CRM, Inc.

Figure 16-4   Sample Letter for Withdrawing a Proposal

While some salespeople are terrified at the thought of withdrawing a proposal, the two most likely results are:

1. *The buyer does not call back.* At this stage, it is time to officially remove the opportunity from your forecast. Ultimately, it is better to get rid of deadwood in your funnel and pipeline, have a realistic view of what the next few months look like, and arrive at an appropriate business development plan.

2. *The buyer calls you back and asks why you have withdrawn the proposal.* This is an opportunity to determine whether the buyer is not going to buy, wants to buy, or would be interested in making changes to the proposal and trying to see if a favorable decision can be reached. If given a

second chance, the seller now can focus on helping the buyer understand how to use your offering to achieve goals or solve problems.

A participant in one of our workshops approached us at the 10:00 AM break on the first day of the session. He said that he had five quotes outstanding for over 60 days. Each was for $15,000 to $25,000. We suggested that he call each of the accounts and tell them he was withdrawing the proposals. Although he was skeptical of the wisdom of this move, he went ahead and did so. By the end of the workshop, three of the opportunities had closed. In two of the cases, the buyer indicated sheepishly that they just hadn't gotten around to issuing the purchase order.

Tomorrow Is the First Day of the Rest of Your Sales Career

In our workshops, we encourage salespeople and managers to be honest with themselves, and to assess and regrade every opportunity in their funnels and pipelines. When salespeople grade their opportunities against the new milestones, many discover that silver medal opportunities get purged from their forecast—and fast.

Frequently, after our workshops, our clients hire us to participate in these kinds of regrading sessions. These are usually done via conference call between the first-level manager, the salesperson, and the CustomerCentric Selling consultant. A 45-minute session for each salesperson is scheduled for the first 3 months after the workshop. During each call with the salesperson, the top three opportunities are reviewed. In the first month, the CustomerCentric Selling consultant does most of the talking. (Especially during the first month, it is far easier for a CustomerCentric Selling consultant to disqualify opportunities, because he or she doesn't have any vested interest.) The second session is more of a sharing between our consultant and the sales manager. The client sales manager conducts the third session, with our consultant serving mainly as a safety net.

Most often, the overall value of the pipeline is reduced by 50 to 80 percent. That doesn't mean that 20 to 50 percent of opportunities are removed outright. Instead, it becomes clear that the opportunities are at either A or G levels. When we look at the value of the pipeline, we only look at E opportunities, which have been qualified to the point of having some visibility as to the potential close date. The mission of the seller is to get as many opportunities as possible to a level where the manager can grade them either a C or—ideally—an E. When existing opportunities are qualified to E status, some of the selling activities have already been done. The Sequence of Events is shorter, as the remaining activities amount to filling in the gaps, in contrast to starting with a new prospect.

To summarize: In assessing and developing salespeople, we advocate defining and sticking to a process. The CustomerCentric Selling process introduced in this book is an effective approach. It begins with the consistent positioning of offerings (through the use of Solution Development Prompters), and continues all the way through the development of salespeople—which, in the case of the salesperson, is the sales manager's job. Many of the same techniques that make a pipeline visible and predictable also contribute to improving the performance of the sales force—but only if the sales manager understands and accepts that responsibility.

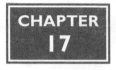

Driving Revenue via Channels

OVER THE PAST SEVERAL YEARS, many organizations have chosen to supplement their direct sales forces with—or even rely exclusively on—sales channels to drive top-line revenue. These indirect organizations include value-added resellers (VARs), distributors, and partners, to which we'll refer collectively as "channels."

These salespeople are not employees of the companies whose offerings they represent and sell. Microsoft is one of the most notable successes in driving a high percentage of their nonretail business through channels. Their channels have not only provided sales presence, but have also allowed Microsoft to minimize the hiring of technical support people to assist in implementations. This approach has been vastly different from that of many other technology companies, which have added support staff as direct employees.

Getting the Right Coverage

For companies that are attempting to use both direct and indirect salespeople, one of the challenges is to define which market segments should be assigned to each, in order to maximize coverage and minimize conflict. We worked with a client selling software ranging from under $10,000 to more than $500,000 who utilized both a direct and an indirect sales approach. We helped them define the desired coverage by working through the chart in Figure 17-1.

The criteria used to determine responsibility were account size on the *y* axis (with the Fortune 1000 being a threshold) and opportunity size on the *x* axis, with $50,000 or higher being designated as a major opportunity and below $10,000 being handled over the phone exclusively. Everyone was comfortable with his or her strategy, and we agreed that it was well thought out.

After we had collectively defined the desired coverage, the next logical question to ask was, "What does the actual coverage look like, today, in the field?" The room was quiet for a few moments. Finally, the most senior executive in the conference room volunteered his opinion—subsequently endorsed by everyone else—that the most extensive coverage was in the quadrant of non-Fortune 1000 accounts under $50,000 (see Figure 17-2).

Further discussion brought out the fact that most of the company's salespeople (both direct and indirect) were engineers who were most

Figure 17-1 Desired Coverage

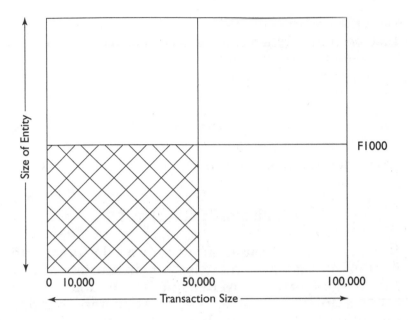

Figure 17-2 Actual Coverage

comfortable calling on engineers—for the most part, non-decision makers. Interestingly enough, their direct salespeople were receiving an override on sales made by the channel. In some cases, in fact, direct salespeople were achieving quota while closing little or nothing themselves.

Gradually, it emerged that the firm's underlying problems lay in two areas. The first was that their direct salespeople did not know how to position their offerings for nontechnical business people. Sales-Ready Messaging and a sales process were used to address this issue.

The second problem was inconsistency and conflict between the desired coverage and the compensation plan. While management can make their wishes known, the best way to influence a salesperson's behavior is to reinforce it with a commission structure. Part of the reason for the decision to implement an indirect channel was to decrease the cost of sales. But in their current situation, the company was actually paying duplicate commissions to both direct and indirect salespeople on most transactions.

In implementing our recommendations, direct salespeople were weaned from their overrides on sales by the channel over 6 months. After that time, the commission plan structure drove them to pursue only Fortune 1000 accounts. When some direct salespeople were unwilling or unable to execute these enterprise sales efforts, they were encouraged to join VARs so that they could continue selling within their comfort zones for small to mid-size opportunities. The channel was given a different compensation structure, receiving 100 percent commission for sales to non-Fortune 1000 accounts that did not require sales support from the manufacturer. They could request support on sales of over $50,000, but in these cases they received only 80 percent of their sales commission.

Who's in Charge?

It is essential that the compensation plan for a sales organization reflect management objectives. Even in the best of circumstances, however, the control that vendors can exert over channels is tenuous when compared with that over a direct sales force. They must attempt to influence without having authority. Control of channels is difficult due to many factors, including:

1. The majority of VARs represent the offerings of multiple companies.

2. Some companies may compete with their channel on certain opportunities by trying to take the business direct.

3. The VARs' interests come first. Relationships work best when the manufacturer's offerings align with the VARs' business strategy and expertise. If the VARs' core business is consulting services, they will focus the majority of their sales efforts in this area. For such companies, representing products may be viewed as a way of generating consulting opportunities. Another VAR may want to generate a higher volume of product sales and have little or no appetite for consulting.

4. VARs representing multiple companies often focus on whatever vendor's offerings are easiest to sell at any given time (i.e., the "hot" product).

5. The methods used to sell are left almost completely up to the VARs, meaning that manufacturers are ceding the customer experience to individual salespeople who don't work directly for them.

6. Some VARs have relationships with a relatively fixed group of customers, and may not exert much effort actively pursuing new accounts.

Poor design or execution of channel strategies are common, which—given the circumstances listed above—shouldn't be surprising. Companies establishing indirect channels may fail to realize that in addition to handing over their offerings, they are inadvertently getting into the same business as CustomerCentric Selling—that is, providing sales training for their business partners. Most of them are not up to this challenge, with whatever training they provide treating their offerings as nouns.

Applying Customer-Centric Principles to Channels

In the same way that many direct salespeople lead with offerings, many *channel managers*—that is, the people in the organization who are responsible for recruiting and supporting channels—are guilty of taking the same approach. We believe, though, that the principles of CustomerCentric Selling can be applied to channels, and we'd like to discuss how the methodology could be used to empower business partners to see how they can increase top-line revenue. We believe that recruiting of VARs can be distilled to business goals, and therefore to conversations.

Calling at high levels is critical when recruiting business partners. The decision to add to or modify the list of companies a reseller represents can cost significant resources and money. The majority of VARs are relatively small organizations. Whenever possible, calling on the owner of the business minimizes red tape, allows early qualification, and shortens the sales cycle. To gain mindshare and be in alignment with the buyer, the initial effort is to convince the business owner that he or she can improve bottom-line results by representing your company and offerings. This is critical when attempting to recruit VARs representing multiple companies. Here is a sample Targeted Conversation menu for the owner of a VAR selling software and services:

- Improve margins
- Make good technology bets
- Improve return on investment of relationships with vendors
- Match offerings with their core competencies and customer base
- Optimize the mix of services and offerings

In an initial call, an attempt should be made to cause a business owner who isn't looking to change (the list of companies the business represents) to consider adding your company to the list. (By now, we assume that you recognize much of this language and approach.) We suggest approaching VARs feeling it is necessary to displace an existing vendor on a VAR's list—presumably the one that is making the smallest bottom-line contribution. VAR owners have a finite capacity as relates to the number of manufacturers they can represent. From the VAR's perspective, optimization of these companies will lead to the best bottom-line result. So your job is to demonstrate that your company belongs in that optimized picture.

Examples of characteristics the owner of a VAR could find attractive about a company and its offerings include:

1. A "hot" market space (e.g., e-commerce in 1998 or customer relationship management in 1999)
2. A unique offering that few, if any, other vendors have
3. An offering that is complementary to existing offerings used by their client base
4. An offering that is a good candidate for add-on business with their customer set
5. A product with a high degree of accompanying services (SAP, PeopleSoft, and so on) if their focus is on professional services
6. Attractive margins or commission structure

A channel manager recruiting business partners should attempt to determine which characteristics represent their strengths, and create a menu of potential goals and Success Stories that will most effectively position the company. By doing a diagnosis first, ideally the business owner can be brought to a vision about the benefits of establishing a relationship.

Once you have gotten the attention of an owner who believes he or she can improve business results by joining forces with you, the next step is to provide an idea of how the owner will be successful. Especially for offerings with a mild to high degree of complexity, support of the channels is important. Once again, consider making a list of what you have available to offer partners. Here is a partial list:

1. Brand recognition
2. Advertising campaigns and promotions
3. Local sales staff available for making joint calls

4. Education and training for both your partners and their customers
5. Sales support
6. Lead generation
7. Web site or intranet to address frequently asked questions (FAQs)
8. Marketing programs and support (local and national)
9. Local technical support
10. 24/7 hotline
11. Quick turnaround of orders placed
12. Willingness to offer exclusive territories

In the same way that salespeople tend to spew opinions, many channel managers tell potential partners how great the support is going to be. But many VARs are "burn victims"; they remember that while past relationships sounded attractive while they were being sold, they ultimately turned out to be a series of broken promises and misset expectations. Getting your proposed support down to the level of usage scenarios will be helpful in making sure both parties are on the same page.

Once the buyers believe that they can improve their business results and understand what support will be available, the last area to discuss is the usage of the actual offerings. This will require resources from both parties. As usual, many such recruiting attempts begin with a product "spray and pray." Yes, products ultimately have to come to the fore—but only after you've gained mindshare regarding the value of doing business, and have helped define the support that the partner will need (and that you can provide).

Fixing Broken Channels

In the early stages of a company's existence, recruiting efforts often concentrate more on the quantity than on the quality of channel partners. Eventually, though, quality has to come to the front of the line. Analyses of the contribution of each channel partner tend to show that a 90/10 rule applies. In other words, 90 percent of the revenue is generated by 10 percent of your business partners.

To encourage great VARs and (potentially) motivate poor performers, it is a common practice to establish three or more levels of partners, as defined by revenue thresholds. The designations platinum, gold, and silver have become standard within the technology arena. The higher the designation, the better the treatment, which may include rebates, cooperative marketing funds, higher discounting level, more favorable payment terms, earliest access to new offerings, and so on. Many vendors using indirect channels realize that they could improve their bottom lines if they were able to focus on top-producing partners. Attempting to pare the list can be a delicate situation, though, especially if an underperforming partner was one of the early companies to agree to become a VAR.

Assuming success in recruiting a channel that will provide you with the desired representation in the market, you still face the following challenges when working through indirect representation:

1. Gaining mindshare about what percentage of resources to allocate to your offerings
2. Making your offerings easier to sell than other suppliers'
3. Achieving consistent positioning of your offerings within the marketplace
4. Qualifying opportunities before allocating resources
5. Forecasting top-line revenue despite being once removed from the salespeople

Once again, we believe that these and other issues can be addressed by integrating a sales process with Sales-Ready Messaging.

Both direct and indirect salespeople display a tendency to follow the path of least resistance. If a vendor can make the offerings easier to sell, with all other things being equal, it stands to reason that resellers will focus a disproportionate amount of effort on that product. Earlier, we discussed the challenge that a salesperson joining a company faces in positioning the offerings of his or her employer. For a VAR representing ten or more companies, the challenge is staggering. It would be virtually impossible for a salesperson to fully understand and develop positioning for more than a handful of offerings. In addition, of course, direct salespeople aren't the only ones who are reluctant or unable—for example—to call on decision makers.

For all of these reasons, and more, we advocate finding ways to give the indirect sales force some (or all) of the same training that the direct sales force receives. The reasons should be clear by now: Once a reseller understands how to execute a Solution Development Prompter (SDP), he or she develops the ability to have conversations with targeted titles within specific vertical segments. We believe that companies providing

CustomerCentric Selling training and customized Solution Development Prompters realize the following advantages:

1. They make their offerings easier to sell, thereby gaining mindshare.

2. More consistent positioning is achieved, and the manufacturer can influence the customer experience.

3. Product training becomes product usage training via SDPs and takes considerably less time, effort, and expense. By building Sales-Ready Messaging around new announcements, the channel is able to hit the ground running and consistently position those offerings. The prerequisite would be having VAR salespeople master the CustomerCentric Selling vision development process.

4. After a VAR has been trained, there is now a consistent vocabulary and a set of debriefing questions that enable the channel manager to help decide which opportunities are qualified, and therefore worthy of sales support and resources.

5. If there is a sufficient level of trust that the VAR is providing funnel visibility, the channel manager has a way to more accurately forecast revenue.

6. If everyone is on the same page, it is easier to segment territories and to intelligently resolve the inevitable channel conflicts, either between VARs or between the VARs and the company they are representing.

7. Training can be used as a "carrot" for VARs that are producing sufficient revenue—a way to enhance their performance while being subsidized by the manufacturer's cooperative funds. For underachieving partners, it can be used as a "stick"—in that to continue the relationship, they must invest in the training, perhaps on their own nickel.

8. Custom Sales-Ready Messaging for VAR new hires as well as for newly announced offerings can enable VARs to make effective calls with a shorter learning curve.

We believe that organizations successfully implementing CustomerCentric Selling can turn the way their salespeople and their VARs' salespeople sell into a competitive advantage. Extending that concept, we believe that CustomerCentric Selling can provide companies using indirect channels an advantage that extends far beyond their offerings, margins, advertising campaigns, and so on.

Many companies have chosen to drive revenue through channels without fully understanding how to integrate product training and the sales process. From a senior executive perspective, the allure of lower cost of sales, fewer direct employees, expanded coverage, and so on has often proved hard to resist. But positioning offerings, as we discussed earlier, is well beyond the scope of a traditional salesperson, whether direct or indirect. A compensation plan reflecting a manufacturer's objectives, Sales-Ready Messaging, and a repeatable sales process greatly enhances the probability of successfully leveraging channels.

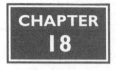

From the Classroom to the Boardroom

Many concepts discussed in books and classrooms appear viable until they are proven not to work in business situations. An engineering student spends weeks learning to make stress-strain calculations to simulate real-world conditions. Many disillusioned graduates learn in the field that this approach is seldom used because the results don't reflect reality. On the job, you make an educated guess during the design phase, build a test unit, subject it to stress and strain, and reinforce components that fail. Having said that, we would like to suggest a road map for implementing the CustomerCentric Selling sales process.

The difference between education and training is practice. In our workshops, true skill transfer takes place during role playing. When closing our workshops, we make a point of acknowledging that the attendees and coaches expended significant effort, but that all we had accomplished was training. Senior executives hire us because they want to implement a sales process. Training is an event during which skills are imparted. The expression "use it or lose it" could have been created to describe the crossroads traditional sellers face on completing one of our workshops. Changing selling habits that have been ingrained for 5, 10, 15, or more years is a daunting challenge.

When successfully implemented, the sales process becomes part of the culture of the adopting company and ultimately shapes the customers' experience. Implementation of the process requires extensive effort on the part of Sales and Marketing, but also requires involvement and support by senior executives, ideally up to the chief executive officer, to realize its full potential. Marketing programs, brochures, Web sites, and product development, to name a few areas, should change to align with the new concepts and approaches that CustomerCentric Selling introduces. The potential reward for companies successfully implementing a sales process is enormous, but we'd be setting unrealistic expectations if we told you it was easy. We have both had occasions where we turned down business because a lack of management support virtually assured that it would have been "drive-by" training.

Key to Implementation

First-level managers are the linchpins in implementing CustomerCentric Selling. Traditional salespeople are reluctant to change. Many lack the self-motivation to try something new. Others are afraid. Those who try and don't encounter immediate success are sorely tempted to return to their old, familiar ways. Most salespeople need the support of their manager to make the migration from being either traditional or customer-centric sellers to becoming CustomerCentric sellers. Two questions to consider if you're on the fence:

1. Would you prefer this approach if you were on the other side of the desk as a buyer?
2. What would your win rate be when competing with a seller capable of executing CustomerCentric Selling?

Sales managers must learn and support the process. Their actions speak louder than their words. Verbalized support for the process rings hollow if they do not utilize the methodology while making calls with their salespeople. Failing to do so sends the wrong message to their direct reports. Salespeople are like your children in that they are hard to fool. A manager's behavior, much more than his or her words, shapes the behavior of the salespeople.

Suggested Approach

In order to gain acceptance and support by managers, the sales process (unlike engineering calculations) has to match your real-world selling environment. Here are some suggestions as to how to further evaluate CustomerCentric Selling:

1. Send a team of three people to a public CustomerCentric Selling Workshop. This affords the following advantages:
   - Verification that the methodology represents a fit for your organization.
   - A foundation from which to discuss necessary modifications to the process and curriculum.
   - Attendees at public workshops can serve as role-play coaches if the company elects to have internal workshop(s).
   - The scope of effort in creating Sales-Ready Messaging can be determined.

2. Define the different types of sales that the process must handle, as described in Chapter 5. If the steps defined for a given sale don't reflect reality, your salespeople will resist implementing the process. We strongly suggest integrating the standard milestones described in Chapter 15 with your customized ones.

3. Create Targeted Conversations Lists for your offerings and vertical markets. Once the titles have been determined, create a list of potential business goals for each. This will determine the scope of the effort to support your sales staff in making calls on Key Players.

4. Create a library of Sales-Ready Messaging to "load the lips" of your salespeople. This should include Sales Development Prompters, Success Stories, phone scripts, and so on. Failure to do so means paying only lip service to the sales process. Sellers making Key Player calls without Sales-Ready Messaging have no choice but to wing it. The outcomes of these calls become the opinions of salespeople (see Chapter 2). In these situations, all bets are off as to qualification, and therefore the quality of the funnel and ultimately the pipeline.

5. If possible, have sales managers attend a workshop first as students. These are the people most critical to the success of the sales process. This allows them two exposures to the methodology: once as a student and once as a role-play coach if you elect to have an internal custom workshop. In terms of commitment, seeing their managers in the back of the room sends a strong message to other attendees.

6. Train your salespeople and others who shape the customer experience. Most of our clients choose to train support or product people who make calls with salespeople as well. Because these people have the busi-

ness and product usage knowledge and no sales background (baggage?), many of them take to our process like ducks to water. For those within your organization who are not making customer calls, but who need to understand the concepts, custom programs can be designed.

7. After the workshop, honestly regrade the existing funnels. Brace yourself for a rude awakening. The value of each salesperson's funnel is likely to be reduced by between 50 and 80 percent. It takes a strong stomach, but the sooner the manager and the seller get the funnel to reflect reality, the sooner they know what has to be done to build it to levels that will sustain quota achievement. As the chief executive officer, chief financial officer, or vice president of Sales, take the same attitude as a library that offers an amnesty program: Return your books (even if you took out *Gone With the Wind* in 1986), and there will be no fines. We just want the books back. That is to say: Without recrimination, this is a new day. Let's get the stale proposals, deadwood, and deadbeats out of your funnels and our pipeline. Instead of senior management discounting an unrealistic pipeline, we want the seller and the manager to do quality control much further upstream in the process.

Sales managers are responsible for allowing opportunities to enter a salesperson's funnel and for grading those opportunities if they advance. Managers now share responsibility for those losses that take several months because during the execution of the Sequence of Events, they agreed to proceed at various checkpoints.

8. For the first 90 days, managers should work with their salespeople to get as many opportunities that remain in the funnel requalified to E status (Chapter 15). Once the salesperson has gained access to all Key Players and gotten consensus to execute a Sequence of Events, the visibility and probability of success dramatically increase. Many of these postworkshop evaluation plans are significantly shorter than ones done for new prospects, as many of the steps may already have been at least partially completed.

9. Reviewing opportunities with salespeople should become net. The debriefing questions in Chapter 12 become the basis for discussion. Generally speaking, the more lengthy the answers to the questions, the more tenuous your position on that opportunity. If the debriefing questions cannot be answered, the salesperson, with or without the manager's help, must make further calls on the buyer. Also, begin to track how the seller learned about the opportunity (proactively or reactively), as we believe

that is the single most important variable in determining win rate. Our experience indicates that 75 to 80 percent of the gold medals awarded go to the salesperson that initiated the opportunity as Column A.

10. Consider having your management team attend a Customer-Centric Selling Management Workshop. This 2-day session focuses on funnel and pipeline management and on assessment and development of salespeople. It amounts to a hands-on workshop for the topics covered in Chapters 15 and 16. We recommend scheduling this session 60 to 120 days after sellers have attended workshops, so that managers have some real-world experience with the new methodology.

11. Any sales process should cover 90+ percent of situations. The intent of our sales process is that *managers* make decisions on exceptions. There will be RFPs for which you understand that you are a silver medalist, but to which you elect to respond. It should be a manager's decision, and please be realistic about the probability assigned, as it most likely will not track with RFPs that you were able to wire.

12. Review compensation plans to verify that they support your objectives. Companies with long sales cycles should consider an alternative to the recoverable/nonrecoverable draw quagmire. After 60 days in the territory, why not have new hires earn bonuses by hitting predetermined milestone thresholds? Achievement of milestones must be verified by sales managers by auditing prospect and customer correspondence.

Some CustomerCentric Selling clients keep their experienced sales reps hungry by having a percentage of their base salary paid on meeting targets for the E funnel on an ongoing basis.

13. When new offerings are in development, create Key Player menus of goals as a sanity check to minimize the chances of introducing a product in search of a market. Sometimes early-market buyers don't or can't bail you out, resulting in product write-offs, not take-offs. When introducing a new offering, make the creation of Sales-Ready Messaging part of the development costs. You may be able to reallocate funds from your product training budget.

14. Once or twice a year, review your most significant wins and losses, along with your competitive position. Sales process and Sales-Ready Messaging represent a journey more than a destination. Please be aware that what worked 10 months ago may have to be tweaked. In sales, the landscape is in almost constant flux.

15. Consider hiring CustomerCentric Selling consultants to help with the design and implementation of the sales process. Having been there and done that in several other organizations, they can provide an industry best practices view as well as an objective outside opinion.

Making Your Sales Process a Competitive Advantage

During our careers, we have witnessed the maturing of technology as it relates to almost all business applications. The advances in accounting, manufacturing, engineering, and supply-chain applications are astounding. Just as we may know more about the moon than about the deepest parts of oceans on earth, Sales (perhaps the most essential business application) has resisted fully successful implementation of technology because it has not been codified in a repeatable process. We believe CustomerCentric Selling can enable you to remove that barrier.

Companies spend untold amounts of money honing their offerings to the point where they have what they perceive to be advantages over others in their market space, only to be sometimes disappointed with their results. Taking IBM's mainframe business as an example, in recent years their offerings were seldom the fastest, the latest technology, or the cheapest. They did, however, do a tremendous job at accessing executive levels of their customers, often one or two levels higher than their competition, and winning on Key Player business issues.

We hope that after reading this book, you have acquired a new outlook on Sales and the belief that best practices can be applied to shaping your customer's experience. When asked the most common reason that salespeople lose, we say without hesitation: They get outsold. While implementation of a sales process is difficult, the potential rewards of making the way your organization sells a competitive advantage are virtually unlimited. CustomerCentric Selling can provide the way to achieve this advantage.

We wish you good luck and good selling.

Index

About the Authors

Michael Bosworth and John Holland are cofounders of CustomerCentric Systems, L.L.C. **Bosworth,** author of the influential book *Solution Selling*, has helped tens of thousands of salespeople and executives define, automate, and implement the organizational sales process. He has been a featured lecturer at the Stanford Graduate School of Business and the Stanford Program on Market Strategy for Technology-Based Companies. **Holland** has achieved extraordinary success as a sales executive with IBM's General Systems Division, district manager with Storage Technology Corporation, and regional business unit manager of Sand Technology. He has worked with and trained hundreds of sales organizations in the United States, Europe, Australia, and Canada. The authors can be reached at www.customercentricsystems.com.